T0353257

SOLIDARITY

About the author

DAVID FEATHERSTONE is a senior lecturer in human geography at the University of Glasgow. He has key research interests in space, politics and resistance in both the past and the present. He is the author of *Resistance, Space and Political Identities: The Making of Counter-Global Networks* and co-editor of *Spatial Politics: Essays for Doreen Massey.*

SOLIDARITY

**Hidden Histories and Geographies
of Internationalism**

DAVID FEATHERSTONE

Zed Books

<small>LONDON | NEW YORK</small>

Solidarity: Hidden Histories and Geographies of Internationalism
was first published in 2012 by
Zed Books Ltd, 7 Cynthia Street, London N1 9JF, UK
and Room 400, 175 Fifth Avenue, New York, NY 10010, USA

www.zedbooks.co.uk

Copyright © David Featherstone 2012

The right of David Featherstone to be identified as the
author of this work has been asserted by him in accordance
with the Copyright, Designs and Patents Act, 1988

Designed and typeset in ITC Bodoni Twelve
by illuminati, Grosmont
Index by John Barker
Cover designed by Rogue Four Design

All rights reserved. No part of this publication may be
reproduced, stored in a retrieval system or transmitted in any
form or by any means, electronic, mechanical, photocopying or
otherwise, without the prior permission of Zed Books Ltd.

A catalogue record for this book is available from the British Library
Library of Congress Cataloging in Publication Data available

ISBN 978 1 84813 596 3 hb
ISBN 978 1 84813 595 6 pb

FOR MO

Contents

Acknowledgements

This book was first prompted by a conversation with Ellen Hallsworth, then commissioning editor for Zed Books. I owe her thanks for such an enthusiastic response to my idea for a book project on solidarity. At Zed, Ken Barlow has been of immense help in seeing this book through to publication. He helped me to focus my initial rather sprawling ideas for the project, and I am grateful for his rigorous engagement with the text. I am indebted to an anonymous reader for a thorough, insightful and constructive critical reading of a draft of the manuscript. Many thanks are due to Robin Gable and Lucy Morton of illuminati for their forensic copy-editing and typesetting of the text.

Richard Phillips has offered much support and engagement for this project and much encouragement in discussions over egg and chips. He has tolerated my frequent arrival in London with good humour and offered generous and very helpful comments on a draft of the manuscript. Andy Davies's engagement with the project and comments on an earlier draft have helped to sharpen the book in many ways. The debt owed here to intellectual engagement and conversation with Doreen Massey is, as ever, immense. I would like to thank Adam McNaughtan for kindly allowing me to reproduce lyrics from his song 'Blood upon the Grass'. Thanks are also due to Getty Images for permission to reproduce the image in Chapter 4 and Mike Shand and the Climate Collective for the image in Chapter 8.

I would like to thank the many helpful archivists at the National Archives, the British Library, the Glamorgan Archives, the South Wales Miners' Library, the Schomburg Center for Research in Black Culture, the Tamiment Library and the Robert F. Wagner Labor Archives at New York University Library, the International Institute of Social History, Hull History Centre, and the Modern Records Centre, University of Warwick. The assistance of Carole McCallum, the Scottish Trade Union Congress archivist at Glasgow Caledonian University, was indispensable for Chapter 5.

Work of this kind is dependent on a steady supply of lefty books. Sorting through the piles of books in Caledonian Books in Glasgow and Judd Books in London has been invaluable, their utility in inverse relation to their fiscal damage. Dave Cope at Left On the Shelf has been very helpful and has provided useful information on the history of left publishing.

I retain a dogged commitment to doing research which is not funded by major grants, something which is decidedly out of joint with the neoliberal culture of the contemporary university. Nonetheless I gratefully acknowledge receipt of a small grant from the Carnegie Trust for the Universities of Scotland for 'The Contested Politics of Climate Change' and a small grant from the British Academy on 'Black Internationalism and the Spatial Politics of Anti-Fascism'.

The material here has benefited significantly from comments, criticisms and engagements from various seminar and conference audiences. I would like in particular to acknowledge comments from audiences at the Alternative Spaces conference in Copenhagen, a session on 'Black Geographies and the Politics of Place' at the Association of American Geographers conference in Washington DC, the Salty Geographies conference, the International Critical Geography conferences in Mumbai and Frankfurt, seminars at the geography departments of Royal Holloway and the

London School of Economics, and the invigorating questioning of the Socialist Theory Seminar at the University of Glasgow.

Workshops on 'Gramsci's Geographies' and on 'Ethnographies of Activism' have helped my thinking on many of the issues that are central to this book. Thanks to Alex Loftus, Mike Ekers, Stefan Kipfer and Gillian Hart for putting together the Gramsci workshop and forthcoming book, and to Sharad Chari and Henrike Donner for their work in stimulating some fine intellectual debates through their two workshops on the ethnographies of activism.

I owe a profound debt to many fellow travellers who have shared intellectual interests and passions that are central to this book. Mustafa Dikeç, Colin McFarlane and Tariq Jazeel all generously shared ideas and thoughts, and offered very useful critical engagements on earlier iterations of the ideas worked out here. Christian Høgsbjerg, Dan Whittall, Caroline Bressey and Bill Schwarz shared enthusisasm and material around pan-Africanism and C.L.R. James. Thanks are also due to Uma Kothari, Nicole Ulrich, Laura Liu, James Sidaway, Aaron Pollack and Wun Chan, and to Paula Hamilton and Jeremy Anderson of the International Transport Workers' Federation. Discussions with Paul Chatterton, Kerry Burton, Pete North, Kelvin Mason and Jane Trowell of Platform shaped the ideas about climate change activism in important ways. Conversations with Lakshmi Subramanian during her time as a visiting fellow in Glasgow were illuminating.

Glasgow geography has been an invigorating environment in which to write and work. I would particularly like to acknowledge the intellectual energy and engagement of Will Hasty, Cheryl McGeachan, David Beel, Johnnie Crossan, Anna Laing, Laura-Jane Nolan, Neil Gray and Paul Griffin. The human geography research group has offered a comradely engagement with and both tolerance and support for this book. I would like to thank Paul Routledge, Andy Cumbers, Danny 'Moccha' Mackinon, Kendra Strauss, Kate Driscoll Derrickson, Hester Parr, Ant Ince, Hayden Lorimer, Chris Philo, Jo Sharp and John Briggs. Bob McMaster and the rest of the lunch crew have endured the spectacle of watching me eat soup with good humour. Ana Langer and Cian O'Driscoll have helped the project along in various ways.

Thanks are due to Kenny and Trish Caird and John McCreadie of the now much lamented Morrison's session for their shared commitment to political song and for extending such a warm welcome to me. Harriet Fletcher, Will Mortada and Jo Cottrell have supported this project in various helpful ways.

The responsibility for the arguments presented here and for any substantive errors is of course my own.

Two friends have gone on during the writing of this book. Duncan Fuller, whose untimely death was a huge loss, was always ready with a solidaristic gesture and is much missed. I am sure that Bob Woods would have raised many quizzical eyebrows at this book but the absence of his support and wry sense of humour is felt nonetheless.

My parents Mike and Tess Featherstone have been hugely supportive of this project, including giving me space to write in the depths of a Breconshire winter in late 2010. Many thanks are also due to Anne and Martin Featherstone. I would like to thank all the Humes for their much valued support.

My daughters Aoibhe and Marni have been great fun to hang out with! Aoibhe's imminent arrival did much to focus the mind while I was writing the book. The first few months of her life have been a time of immense joy. She has enriched the revision of the manuscript in immeasurable ways, not least in giving me plenty of opportunity for thought and reflection in hitherto unexplored parts of the night and early morning. She has taken unrestrained glee in scattering papers and stealing my glasses. Her sense of curiosity and wonder at the world has been inspirational.

Marni has as always been a healthy source of scepticism about my endeavours and enthusiasms. She has exhibited fearlessness in the face of the 'Dave Sty'. That I have not completely disappeared under a mountain of books, papers and tea bags is largely thanks to her. There might not be enough hard rock references here to satisfy her, but I promise to explore the political messages hidden in the œuvre of AC/DC in a future project!

Mo Hume's example and commitment to feminist internationalism have been a vital source of inspiration for this book. It has been my good fortune to benefit from her love, humour, engagement and insight while writing. She has been a constant source of support and encouragement despite the demands placed on us by my writing this book at a time when there have been far more momentous things going on in our lives. Her initial reaction was that neither feminism nor Central America were given their due prominence in my plan for the book. I hope to have at least partly assuaged her concerns. This book is for her.

Races and nations were things like skunks,
whose smells poisoned the air of life.

Claude McKay, *Home to Harlem*

Thinking solidarity politically

If you had passed through the manufacturing districts of Lancashire and Cheshire, in North West England, in the early 1860s you might have heard or read an appeal issued by Frederick Douglass. The American fugitive slave and abolitionist Douglass was a well-known figure in England. He had toured Britain and Ireland extensively in the 1840s during his campaigns for slave emancipation. In 'The Slave's Appeal to Great Britain' Douglass sought to mobilise support for the cause of the North in the American Civil War. He declared that 'the North is fighting on the side of liberty and civilisation, and the South on the side of slavery and barbarism' (Douglass, 1862: 304).

Douglass appealed directly to workers in the cotton factories of the North West. This was significant. The Civil War in America had led to a 'cotton famine' in Lancashire with devastating consequences. This was a direct product of the cotton blockade of the Southern states by forces loyal to the Union. Between November 1861 and November 1862 full-time employment in the Lancashire cotton industry fell by over 300,000.[1] Douglass's appeal asserted that 'humanity could not permit the needs of the British mills to determine the future of millions in slavery'. 'Must the world stand still', he asked, 'humanity make no progress and slavery remain forever, lest your cotton mills should stop and your poor cry for bread?' (Douglass, 1862). Further, Douglass contended that the conflict in the United States had a key lesson for Britain: 'you should base your industry and prosperity on the natural foundations of justice and liberty' (Douglass, 1862).

Douglass's appeal had effects. It was circulated and reprinted. This drew on Douglass's extensive contacts among abolitionist and working-class organizers. Alexander Innes wrote to Douglass assuring him that his 'Appeal' was being read in working-class circles and was having a 'profound effect' in Lancashire, as well as in other parts of the British Isles (Foner, 1981: 104 n23). This 'profound effect' was significant working-class support for the US North. This helped to block the plans of then British prime minister Lord Palmerston to intervene militarily in the Civil War on behalf of the South (Foster, 2000).

Despite the hardships associated with the 'cotton famine' there was strong backing among northern working-class movements for the Union. A mass meeting held in Manchester on 31 December 1862 passed a resolution stating:

> That this meeting, recognising the common brotherhood of mankind and the sacred and inalienable right of every human being to personal freedom and equal protection, records its detestation of negro slavery in America, and of the attempts of the rebellious Southern slaveholders to organise on the great American continent a nation having slavery as its basis. (cited by Foner, 1981: 40)

The meeting at the Free Trade Hall was co-organized by two working men from Manchester: the one-time Chartist[2] agitator Edward Hooson and J.E. Edwards. Edwards was moved to act by the support given by the *Manchester Guardian* to the Confederates. Working-class movements in London mobilized similar support for the North.

Other meetings in Lancashire demonstrated their solidarity. A meeting of the 'distressed operatives of Blackburn' declared that 'they earnestly pray that the civil war now, unhappily, raging amongst you – and which your memorialists deeply lament – may come to a speedy termination in favour of freedom, regardless of race or colour' (Distressed Operatives, 1863: n.pag.). These solidarities were reciprocated. The Union sent shiploads of aid to the distressed workers of Lancashire. The *George Griswold* reached Liverpool in February 1863, with provisions valued at £27,000 and cash donations of £1,333. Workers at the docks 'refused payment for their services' and 'the railways offered free transport' (Foner, 1981: 50-51).

These actions impressed Karl Marx, who as a political exile in London took a keen interest in the Civil War.[3] Marx celebrated the 'pressure from without' that the English working class exerted on the pro-South policy of Palmerston (Marx and Engels n.d., 140-41). This pressure was constructed by working-class movements despite their exclusion from political representation. Marx asserted the significance of this political stance given the 'misery that the stoppage of the factories and the shortening of the labor time, motivated by the blockade of the slave states, has produced among the workers in the northern manufacturing districts'. He hailed the 'obstinacy with which the working class keeps silent, or breaks its silence only to raise its voice against intervention and for the United States'.

These solidarities contributed to the founding of the International Working Men's Association (IMWA) in 1864, one of the first attempts to organize a politicized, working-class internationalism. Marx was one of the key instigators of the International. Marx's 'inaugural address' makes clear the importance of the inspiration of the solidarities forged during the cotton famine for this political formation. 'It was not the wisdom of the ruling classes', he contended, but 'the heroic resistance to their criminal folly by the working classes of England, that saved the west of Europe from plunging headlong into an infamous crusade for the propagation of slavery on the other side of the Atlantic' (Marx, 1974: 81). Such solidarities opened up possibilities for the labour movement in the United States. In *Capital* he contended that 'every independent workers' movement' in the United States 'was paralysed as long as slavery disfigured part of the republic.

Labour in a white skin cannot emancipate itself where it is branded in a black skin' (Marx, 1973: 414).

The International's address to Abraham Lincoln, on his re-election in 1864, likewise drew attention to these working-class solidarities. The address averred that if 'resistance to the Slave Power was the reserved watchword of your first election, the triumphant war-cry of your re-election is 'Death to Slavery'. It noted of the 'men of labour' that 'they bore patiently the hardships imposed upon them by the cotton crisis, opposed enthusiastically the pro-slavery intervention – importunities of their betters – and, from most parts of Europe, contributed their quota of blood to the good cause' (First International, 1864: 52). A proposal for a Member of Parliament to be part of the deputation that presented the address 'was strongly opposed by many members who said working men should rely on themselves and not seek for extraneous aid'.[4]

Marx's engagements with these solidarities are significant. They demonstrate that the emergence of politicized working-class internationalism was driven not only by key theorists or political figures. It was animated by connections forged through political struggle. These connections and solidarities were, as Marx emphasizes, not produced by dispassionate elites; they were forged through the actions of dispossessed workers who had much to gain in the short term by breaking the cotton blockade. They were constructed, then, by what Marx termed 'pressure from without'.

This is a book about the creation of solidarities from below. It argues that they are a powerful force for reshaping the world in more equal terms. They have been central to attempts to make the world anew. The makings of such solidarities have, however, frequently been marginalized and actively silenced. This book sets out to assert their importance. It seeks to tell stories about forms of agency and political activity constructed through mobilizing practices of solidarity. These stories seek to animate accounts of the political left in both the past and the present.

Thinking solidarity

Solidarity is a central practice of the political left. It is indispensable to the activity of radical social and political movements. It has, however, rarely been the subject of sustained theorization, reflection or investigation. Here I define solidarity as a relation forged through political struggle which seeks to challenge forms of oppression. To develop a sustained engagement with the formation, force and importance of solidarity involves engaging with a set of key theoretical challenges. Some of these challenges can be gleaned through an engagement with the solidarities forged with the US 'North' in the context of the Cotton Famine.

First, these actions locate solidarity as a transformative relation. Solidarity has often been understood as being about likeness. This approach obscures the importance of solidarities in constructing relations between places, activists, diverse social groups. This can involve the cementation of existing identities and power relations. It can, however, as frequently be about the active creation of new ways of relating. It is through being attentive to such relations that the dynamism and inventiveness of solidarities can emerge.

Second, there is the importance of solidarity as a practice that can be forged 'from below' or through 'pressure from without'. Such solidarities can be powerfully shaped by working-class groups and movements. This asserts the importance of marginal groups in shaping practices of solidarity. It is a direct challenge to assumptions that subaltern groups, those subject to diverse forms of oppression, lack the capacity or interest to construct solidarities. As the case of Lancashire cotton workers suggests, the forging of solidarities under such oppressive conditions was still achieved. This created political agency which Marx contended stopped the British government intervening in support of the South.

Third, there is the refusal of political activity to stay neatly contained within the nation-state. The solidarities forged through the cotton boycott were shaped by diverse ongoing connections.

They were enabled by the tours of Douglass and connections made with labour movement and religious abolitionists. They were shaped through diverse exchanges, contacts and linkages. These also cut across and challenged the powerful racial divisions that were central to the US Civil War, but that also shaped British society and left movements in pernicious ways.

Fourth, solidarities are constructed through uneven power relations and geographies. The solidarities with the North were forged through negotiating racialized, gendered and classed spaces of encounter. The terms on which solidarities with American slaves were produced were often characterized by important asymmetries of power. Thus George Howell, a former Chartist, bricklayer and secretary of the London Trades Council during the years 1861 and 1862, denounced the 'vociferous champions of the South', arguing that they were '"enemies of liberty and progress" in the past and would be so in the future' (Foner, 1981: 33).

Foner notes, however, that this did not mean that Howell believed that 'blacks were equal to whites in every area of life'. Howell was convinced, however, that with freedom blacks would overcome these disadvantages: 'give him freedom, surround him with healthier circumstances and you will develop in the slave a manlier life' (Foner, 1981: 103 n16). This emphasizes the racialized and gendered terms on which solidarities were configured. The IMWA also fashioned a distinctively male-centred construction of internationalism. These were also, however, practices through which prejudice could be challenged, reworked and brought into contestation. They generated exchanges and connections which cut across and refused powerful divides.

Finally, there is the sense of solidarities as inventive. They produce new ways of configuring political relations and spaces. This is central to Marx's account in the inaugural address. This shaped ways of thinking differently about working-class political activity. It opened up possibilities for thinking about how working-class and subaltern politics can shape international terrains. This was grounded through specific connections, relations and labour politics. Central here was the construction of political spaces and connections across the Atlantic. These solidarities depended on imaginative ways of understanding place-based politics in Lancashire, such place-based politics being conceptualized in relational terms. It was understood that to break the cotton blockade would have implications for those in the Southern states of the United States who faced the oppressive conditions of slavery. Thus Marx believed that the willingness of Manchester workers to rally in support of the North, even though the 'cotton famine' menaced their own livelihood, showed the moral superiority of a rising class (Blackburn, 2011a: 40).

This 'pressure from without' can reshape the terrain of what is politically possible and what counts or is recognized as political. This contestation produces new ways of generating political community and different ways of shaping relations between places. It is necessary to think seriously about the relations between contestation and solidarity. As the cotton famine example suggests, solidarities can be forged through political antagonisms. The mobilizing of transnational solidarities through working-class anti-slavery politics was inventive. The terms on which these antagonisms were shaped allowed new forms of internationalist political community to emerge.

Solidarities, then, are not just part of the binding together of pre-existing communities. They can be much more active in shaping political contestation than this suggests. In this sense solidarities can be part of the process of politicization. The forging of links in opposition to common enemies such as slaveholders (and Tory prime ministers) can open up new political terrains and possibilities. This allows new conceptions of political subjects and actors to emerge. At stake in the struggles around the cotton famine were different groups such as slaves and working-class men who were denied political rights and representation in different ways, though this is not to suggest the forms of oppression they faced were equivalent.

Engaging with this inventive character of solidarity is central to thinking solidarities politically. By this term I mean thinking solidarity as a political relation that shapes different ways of challenging oppression and inequalities. Political articulations of solidarity are shaped through diverse practices. This book explores the multifarious ways in which such practices are shaped and constituted. The book does engage with the conduct of left political parties and organized internationalist movements. It adopts an expansive sense of the forms of political activity that have shaped left internationalisms.

The book is animated by a concern with the 'subterranean solidarities' forged through political activity (Buck Morss, 2009: 133). I do not envision such solidarities as the product of a domain that is autonomous from official politics. I have sought to trace and engage with the intersections and relations that make up the socially mixed make up of different left movements. Nonetheless it seeks to foreground forms of solidarity and internationalism that have been frequently hidden, silenced and obscured.

Constructing internationalism from below

The book uses this focus on diverse forms of solidarity to assert the important ways internationalism has been created from below. I use the term 'internationalism' because of its direct association with attempts by left political movements to reshape the world on more equitable terms. This differs from terms such as 'transnationalism' which have been less directly associated with explicit political projects. Internationalism has often been written about and theorized through top-down accounts which focus on hierarchical forms of left political organization. These accounts have often excluded the role of subaltern political activity in shaping practices of internationalism.

In the case of the Cotton Famine the oppressive conditions of the cotton operatives did not prevent them understanding the implications of the cotton blockade being broken. This speaks to the importance of subaltern actors in shaping internationalist political cultures. Through interventions in the connections between Lancashire and the United States the operatives constructed agency from below. The pressure they exerted on the material and social connections that linked Lancashire to the USA had significant impacts on the ways in which these relations were constructed. Tracing and asserting the importance of such forms of subaltern agency in shaping political relations between places is a primary concern of this book.

Subaltern political activity has frequently been seen as trapped in place, or as lacking cosmopolitan outlooks. This is to marginalize the diverse and productive ways through which marginal actors have engaged with connection and mobility, albeit often on profoundly unequal terms. This allows subalternity, the diverse forms which marginality can take, to be refigured as being about the 'active determination of society and space' (Chari, 2012; see also Gilmore, 2008a). It is the generative world-making possibilities of subaltern political activity that this book seeks to assert and engage with.

This project draws on long-standing attempts to create histories from below. The recovery of such histories has been an important contribution of left intellectuals and movements for some time. This has shaped powerful re-tellings of the past from movements ranging from the Communist Party Historians' Group in Britain to the Subaltern Studies Collective in India. Drawing attention to such marginalized histories can change the terms on which people understand themselves and their histories. They can also provide important 'usable pasts' for engagements with political activity in the present (see Featherstone, 2008; Phillips, 2007). Experiences of solidarity, as Chitra Joshi argues, can 'become sedimented as part of working class memory, recalled and celebrated in subsequent periods of struggle' (Joshi, 2003: 11).

Hidden geographies are a less commonplace endeavour. I use this term to assert the role of subaltern geographies of connection in constructing internationalisms. This opens up different ways of thinking about the histories and geographies of left politics, and challenges existing ways of narrating the political left. This is usefully illustrated by accounts of the iconic political movements of 1968 by Kristin Ross and Ruth Wilson Gilmore. This was a year when 'revolutionaries around the world made as much trouble as possible in as many places as possible' (Gilmore, 2008b: 24; Katsiaficas, 1987). Ross contests the recuperation of the 1968 movements in France as nothing more than heralding the birth of a radically individualized society by insisting on the importance of anti-colonial internationalisms to these events (Ross, 2002).

Ross argues that throughout the 1960s in France, 'themes of anticapitalism and internationalism were spontaneously combined; the discourses of anti-capitalism and anti-imperialism were woven together in an intricate mesh' (2002: 11). This positions these movements not in solely national terms. Rather, it locates them as part of 'overlapping communities of resistance' which shaped 'opposition to the U.S. war in Vietnam' and 'linked up with anticolonialism and antiapartheid forces on a world scale' (Gilmore, 2008b: 24). These accounts treat the left as a product of different connections and relations. They challenge narratives which contain left politics within fixed containers of the nation-state. This allows something more politically generative to emerge than a depoliticizing story about their role in developing an aggressively individualized society.

This has consequences. Asserting the diverse trajectories and connections shaped by left political solidarities opens up political possibilities. This challenges caricatured and stereotyped accounts of the left as sectional and inward-looking, which, necessarily, foreclose political possibilities in the present and future. This book seeks to tell multiple and contested stories and trace trajectories which have shaped the political left. This opens up a different sense of who and what counts as part of left politics. I adopt the following approach to understanding the histories and geographies of left social and political movements.

First, I challenge nation-centred histories of the left. This draws attention to the importance of political activists, connections, solidarities that do not fit neatly within dominant accounts of the left. Accounts of internationalism still remain

remarkably nation-centred (see Chapter 2). They frequently position agency primarily in the leaderships of particular national
left movements or parties. A key casualty of such nation-centred
accounts of internationalism has been the contributions of anti-
colonial intellectuals, activists and movements to European left
movements.

Important accounts of the history of the left, such as Geoff
Eley's *Forging Democracy*, continue to give a rather marginal
role to the impact of anti-colonial activists on left movements in
Europe (Eley, 2002). Ways of organizing the intellectual history
of left political traditions, such as Perry Anderson's conception of
Western Marxism, similarly obscure such political connections
(Anderson, 1976). To acknowledge the contributions of anti-
colonial movements to European left politics is not just to add
an excluded dimension that develops a fuller or more complete
history. Rather, it is to challenge the very terms on which left
politics is understood and articulated.

Second, I position left political movements as the products
of diverse trajectories and connections. This allows a focus on
diverse forms of labour and agency in shaping internationalist
political activity and assembling connections. This challenges
ways of writing the histories and geographies of left social and
political movements which focus primarily on leaderships and
left elites (Wolford, 2010). Important alternative histories, such
as Vijay Prashad's account of the history of the political idea of
the Third World, have focused on such elites (Prashad, 2007).
This account therefore seeks to decentre the role of iconic left
leaders and figures in shaping internationalist cultures. This is
not to suggest that major figures were not important or did not
shape left political cultures in significant ways. It is to insist,
however, that foregrounding left elites limits an engagement
with the diverse subaltern forms of agency that have shaped
internationalist connections.

Finally, this attention to the diverse forms of labour involved
in shaping, assembling and maintaining transnational solidarities
seeks to foreground the generative conduct of left political

activity. Engagements with political strategy or organizing have often focused primarily on the ways in which these have been theorized. Ernesto Laclau and Chantal Mouffe's influential *Hegemony and Socialist Strategy*, for example, is characterized by a striking absence of attention to the conduct of political struggles and activity (Laclau and Mouffe, 1985). The account of left political activity developed here, by contrast, seeks to be alive to the generative character of political struggle.

Central to the book is an attempt to construct a genealogy of left politics that takes both the geographies and the conduct of political activity and struggle seriously. It by no means attempts to construct a comprehensive history of internationalism from below. Rather, it is focuses on particular events and movements. These have been chosen to illustrate the multifarious and productive character of solidarity. It explores forms of political activity such as anti-colonial networks which created situated connections across deeply uneven geographies. The case studies develop a focus on different forms of internationalist organizing. While they focus on subaltern articulations of internationalism, the movements they describe are often socially mixed and heterogeneous.

There are, of course, many different uses of solidarity by elite and middling as well as subaltern and working-class movements. This book focuses on solidarities forged through direct opposition to inequality and oppression. This project is informed by a political commitment. The book does not seek to provide a solely positive, rosy gloss on solidarity. It also confronts and engages with some of the 'dark sides' of solidarity and the way they have been used to entrench as well as challenge privilege by left movements. It is nonetheless written out of an avowedly partisan position that solidarities can be a powerful force for reshaping worlds in more socially equitable and just ways.

PART I

Theorizing solidarity

CHAPTER I

Solidarity: theorizing a transformative political relation

On 7 October 1935 there was a dispute in the shipping office yard in Bute Place, Cardiff. The disturbance was occasioned by the invasion of Ethiopia by Italian troops under the orders of Mussolini. According to witnesses there were about 100 men in the shipping yard, who reflected the multi-ethnic character of this seafaring community.[1] Harry O'Connell, a militant leader of the 'colonial workers' of Cardiff, was talking with several of the men about the Italian and Abyssinian dispute and was asked 'What can we do?'[2] O'Connell pointed to a photograph in that day's papers showing the police guarding the Italian consulate in London. He is alleged to have suggested that 'if they wanted to show their sympathy for Abyssinia' 'they should wreck' Cardiff's Italian consulate.[3] He was arrested, charged under a statute of King Edward III and found guilty of conduct that was likely to cause a breach of the peace.[4]

O'Connell was a sailor from what was then British Guiana. He had settled in Cardiff around 1910, drawn, like many seafarers from West Africa, the Caribbean, Somalia and Scandinavia, to this hub of the global coal trade.[5] This was five years after strikes and riots involving maritime workers had seriously challenged colonial authority in the port of Georgetown (Rodney, 1981:

190–216). By the early twentieth century the dockside area of
Cardiff, known variously as Tiger Bay and Butetown, had been
transformed into a vibrant cosmopolitan port.[6] An experienced
mariner 'proud of his skill at splicing ropes and rigging ships',
O'Connell became a key figure in the struggles of Cardiff's
multi-ethnic seafarers against the racism of the National Union
of Seamen and the local state.[7] A committed Communist, by 1940
he had been blacklisted for his political activities; the police
withholding the pass that was 'necessary for him to get to the
Docks'.[8] In 1941 the home secretary Herbert Morrison told the
House of Commons that he was 'satisfied that it would not be
in the national interest to allow this man to work on British or
foreign ships'.[9]

The anti-colonial and anti-fascist solidarities forged through
O'Connell's actions were constructed through the relations and
connections that shaped maritime labour. This chapter engages
with the importance of such connections and relations to practices of solidarity. I contend that solidarities are usefully thought
of as transformative political relations. There are no guarantees
about the kinds of transformations wrought by solidarities.
They can entrench as well as challenge privilege and can close
down as well as open up political possibilities and alliances.
Locating solidarities as world-making processes, by tracing the
geographies they shape, contest and rework, however, makes a
significant contribution to understanding their productiveness
and agency. It also presents a set of theoretical challenges which
the chapter seeks to address.

The makings of solidarity

O'Connell's actions in Cardiff were part of a global boycott
of Italian ships and goods in response to the Italo-Ethiopian
conflict. Dockers and seafarers from Trinidad and South-West
Africa, from Durban and Cape Town, from the West Coast of
the United States joined in this action (see Chapter 4). Maritime
workers' refusals to load Italian goods or to crew ships bound

for Italy created political agency. They cut into the flow of trade and goods which Italy depended on, creating vibrant solidarities from below. Through these acts seafarers like O'Connell drew attention to the distant events in Ethiopia, making them visible in port cities across the world.

These solidarities shaped forms of political identification. The transnational response to the invasion of Ethiopia was strongly shaped by the circuits and politics of the African diaspora. Ethiopia had strong symbolic political significance as an independent African state. The terms on which such solidarities were constructed were shaped in distinctive ways by activists like O'Connell. There were struggles over how diaspora solidarities were forged. Thus one of the places where O'Connell's trial was reported was in the *Negro Worker*, the paper of the Communist-led International Trade Union Committee of Negro Workers (ITUCNW).[10] O'Connell was a frequent correspondent with the *Negro Worker*. He described the paper in 1933 as 'the only international champion we have fighting for us' (O'Connell 1933: 25). The paper shaped articulations between anti-colonial struggles in different parts of the world, including the Caribbean and Africa, frequently reporting on struggles and injustices in British Guiana.[11] In 1931 the Surinamese Communist Otto Huiswood, a key figure in the ITUCNW, noted that in the 'struggle of the masses in British Guiana, the International revolutionary movement particularly the British Minority Movement must give every assistance possible' (Huiswood, 1931: 5).[12] This positions O'Connell as part of a radical black internationalist politics which linked anti-colonial politics to the labour struggles and grievances of seafarers and maritime workers.

The actions of O'Connell and other maritime workers in Cardiff were not just making an abstract argument about events in a distant place. Rather, these solidarities were directly concerned with challenging the relations that existed between Cardiff and Italy. Sites of grievance emerged through these actions. The march on the consulate was not a pre-arranged plan, but emerged through discussion in the shipping yard. Targeting such a building suggests how activists sought to make links between Cardiff and Italy localizable and contestable. In what appears to have been a separate incident in Cardiff, seamen boarded an Italian steamer and 'plastered her bulkhead with posters denouncing the fascist aggression' (Nelson, 1988: 170). Harbour workers and coal trimmers in Cardiff 'stopped the loading of coal on the Italian vessel *Rino Carrada*' (Morice, 1936: 25). This action contested the port's strategic importance for the Italian government, which had 'opened a Bureau at Cardiff to buy British coal' (Brockway, 2010: 25).

This mobilized the knowledge that sailors had about maritime networks and trade. Their political activity strategically mobilized knowledge that certain ships were bound for Italy or carried Italian goods. They sought to stop these flows from functioning and to exert pressure on Italian fascism through doing so. This was a politics, then, that was delegated through particular materials. The boycott functioned precisely through attempting to stop particular vessels, coal or munitions from circulating. These solidarities constructed distinctive 'maps of grievance'. I use this term to refer to the dynamic practices through which political activity makes sense of and brings into contestation relations of power (Featherstone, 2008).

There is, here, a double sense in which these solidarities were made. First, the solidarities were politically constructed through political imaginaries that linked different parts of the world through anti-colonial organizing. These imaginations were strongly shaped by translocal political organizing. Second, the solidarities were assembled through contesting particular arrangements of social and material relations, such as cutting into supplies of coal. Such solidarities did not just produce abstracted political ideologies or identifications. Rather, they were interventions in the material relations between places. They intervened in particular relations and networks and attempted to refashion them in more equitable ways.

This focus on the actions through which solidarity is constructed allows agency to emerge from below. This allows a focus on the generative, transformative character of solidarity and how solidaristic practices can shape new relations, new linkages, new connections. This productive account of solidarities challenges accounts where the practices and identities through which solidarities are enacted are seen as primarily 'given'. Accounts of solidarity as 'given' are present in different theoretical traditions and approaches. Thus there is a long-standing tradition of 'humanist' thought which positions solidarity as arising from a shared sense of 'humanness'. Such an identification of solidarity is helpfully unsettled by Richard Rorty, who argues against the contention that human solidarity is based on a 'recognition of a core self, the human essence, in all human beings'. He contests Kant's account of solidarity as a rational expression of a 'common core of humanity' (Rorty, 1989: 192).[13]

At first sight the idea that solidarity is the expression of an underlying human essence might seem incontrovertible and appealing. Indeed it might seem pretty miserly to argue against a solidarity based on such firm foundations. The problem with such an account of solidarity is that it doesn't enable 'movements' or political activity any agency or role in shaping how solidarities are constructed. It assumes that there is a pre-existing 'aptitude' to solidarity underlying human action. This is a poor starting point for engaging with the many contested ways in which solidarities come to be practised and enacted. It also systematically ignores the ways that solidarities are located in and forged through particular contexts.

The formation of solidarities is also treated as given in Émile Durkheim's influential sociological treatises on solidarity. Durkheim makes a key distinction between mechanical and organic solidarity, which he uses to contrast the forms of social organization in 'traditional' and 'modern' societies (Durkheim, 1991). For Durkheim cohesion in 'traditional' societies is generated by 'mechanical solidarity or 'solidarity by similarity' (Durkheim, 1991: 31–67). In such societies each 'segment (clan) is united by a common genealogical heritage' (Ansell, 2001: 11). Here solidarity is positioned as an automatic outcome of social position and is determined by prior allegiance to clan and heritage. Durkheim contends that such solidarity arises because 'a certain number of states of consciousness are common to all members of the same society' (Durkheim, 1991: 64).

Durkheim's conception of organic solidarity is similarly deterministic. He views organic solidarity as arising in societies where there is a developed division of labour. Organic solidarity is positioned as emerging from 'the ties of co-operation between individuals or groups of individuals which derive from their occupational interdependence' (Giddens, 1972: 8). Such solidarities, however, are still not theorized as actively constructed. Rather, the solidarities are viewed as 'spontaneous' expressions that emerge from the specific forms of co-operation of individuals and groups relevant to their position in the division of labour (1972: 8).

In both mechanical and organic variants, then, Durkheim's conception of solidarity is positioned as an automatic reflection of individuals' or groups' social position. This closes down a sense of how forms of identification are crafted and fashioned. Further, he isolates solidarities from the conduct and negotiation of political activity. In similar terms some, though by no means all, versions of Marxism and feminism have positioned those belonging to a particular class or gender as having automatic and innate capacities of solidarity.

In response to accounts which treat forms of solidarity as 'given' there have been diverse attempts to engage with the terms on which solidarities are constructed. This matters. They are in part a testament to key political challenges over the power relations that are generated through the makings of solidarities. Feminist movements, for example, have challenged often unspoken assumptions that position solidarities as solely the product of alliances between male workers. Chandra Mohanty contends that 'the sexism of trade unions' 'has led women to recognize the need for alternative, more democratic organizational structures, and to form women's unions (as in Korea, China, Italy and Malaysia ...) or to turn to community groups, church committees or feminist organizations' (Mohanty, 2003: 163; see also Hale and Wills, 2005). In turn Mohanty's work has powerfully challenged assumptions, often by white Western feminists, of solidarities based around a universal category of sisterhood.

Such interventions crucially question the power relations through which solidarities are constructed. This emphasizes that solidarities are not necessarily unproblematic. They can entrench the position of some groups and further marginalize others, as Mohanty notes in relation to the exclusion of women from some forms of labour organizing. Engaging with the power relations through which solidarities are crafted and conducted is a necessary condition for foregrounding the contested processes through which solidarities are generated. If forms of solidarity are treated as 'given' it is impossible to understand or make visible contestation and disagreement about how solidarities are constructed. As a result this obscures a crucial set of questions. What kinds of relations do they generate between different actors? What kinds of power relations are crafted through solidarities? What kinds of different political trajectories do they shape?

Understanding the tensions and conflicts over how solidarities are constructed is thus a necessary condition for a 'politics of solidarity'. Accounts which position solidarity as 'given' frequently assume solidarities are constructed primarily between actors who are alike. Such accounts of solidarity have a remarkable longevity and purchase. Thus the influential social movement theorists Sidney Tarrow and Doug McAdam have argued that political networks and solidarities based on emulation or likeness are likely to be much more durable than relations generated through difference.

Tarrow and McAdam, however, deal with such processes in rather reductive ways. They argue that 'successful brokerage promotes attribution of similarity, while unsuccessful brokerage promotes the recognition of difference' (Tarrow and McAdam, 2005: 130). Tarrow defines brokerage as the 'linking of two or more previously unconnected social actors by a unit that mediates

their relations with one another and/or with yet other sites'
(Tarrow, 2005: 190; see also Tarrow and McAdam, 2005: 127).
This creates a limited account of solidarity which is reduced to
a process of making connections between those who are already
fundamentally similar. In common with accounts of solidarity
based on rational choice theory, they reduce the functioning of
solidarity to restricted goal-based outcomes (see also Hechter,
1990).

This strips practices of solidarity of their vibrant productive character. Assuming that solidarities are forged through
emulation risks ignoring how likeness is actively produced. Paul
Gilroy usefully adopts the term 'unanimistic solidarity' to refer
to practices constituted through homogeneous notions of 'race'
(Gilroy, 2000: 333). By this term he demonstrates how the adoption and emulation of purified racial categories, such as the forms
of blackness associated with Marcus Garvey's Universal Negro
Improvement Association (UNIA), are actively created.[14] They
are by no means inevitable. Rather, they are produced through
active work of formatting and exclusion so that solidarities are
disciplined within particular limits.

Richard Rorty's account of the relations between solidarity,
similarity and dissimilarity moves beyond the reductive terms
of debate offered by Tarrow and McAdam. For Rorty 'feelings
of solidarity are necessarily a matter of which similarities and
dissimilarities strike us as salient, and that such salience is a
function of a historically contingent final vocabulary' (Rorty,
1989: 192). This stress on contingency situates constructions of
solidarity. It emphasizes that, rather than there being ahistorical
forms of identification, ways of articulating solidarity are always
partial, limited and situated. He argues that a key political
objective should be that 'we should *create* a more expansive sense
of solidarity than we presently have'. We should, he cautions, be
'on the lookout for marginalized people – people whom we still
instinctively think of as "they" rather than "us"'.

This logic is helpful in its insistence that we should think
of solidarities as expansive and not bounded within particular

groups. There are tensions with this position, however. Rorty suggests we need to expand a conception of solidarity to encompass
those we see as different. Crucially for Rorty this is based on
recognition of 'our similarities with them' (Rorty, 1989: 196).
This still traps understandings of solidarity within a reductive
binary of similarity and dissimilarity.

Rorty's account obscures an appreciation of the creative practices of solidarity. Ruth Wilson Gilmore stresses such practices in
her vivid account of the organizing of Mothers Reclaiming Our
Children (ROC), women united by the traumatic shared experience of having children incarcerated in California's burgeoning
prison system. Gilmore's account of the formation and activity
of ROC develops a powerful sense of the productive character
of solidarity. She argues that ROCers 'gradually but decisively
refused to be isolated and began to develop oppositional political
arts centred on creating an order different from the one built
by the state out of more and bigger prisons' (Gilmore, 2008b:
236).

For Gilmore this was a generative process. She demonstrates
that solidarity was actively produced and shaped. She argues that
in 'the context of shared opposition, the activists "discovered" ...
which is to say created – shared values; in turn, that collective
work produced community solidarity, or political integration,
enabling further action'. Solidarity in turn 'increased with increased knowledge about the complexity of how power blocs
have built the new state by building prisons' (Gilmore, 2008b:
238). There is a dynamic sense here of solidarity as a creative
process which speaks to the bringing together of relations and
trajectories. This positions solidarity as actively generating and
shaping shared values and identifications.

Gilmore's account demonstrates the importance of moving
beyond understandings of solidarity as bearing on either similarity or dissimilarity. It challenges the idea that there needs to
be a pre-existing commonality for solidarity to be durable or
effective. Instead she asserts that practices of solidarity generate or negotiate such questions of difference through political

action. For Gilmore solidarity is a creative practice which can involve the making and remaking of identifications. Here the identifications between 'actors' don't simply pre-exist political activity, but instead are actively made through such activity. There is also a keen sense of how such organizing fashions new relations, linkages and knowledges. This project can be developed by tracing the spatial relations through which these practices are made and remade.

Subaltern geographies of connection

In his essay 'Aspects of the Southern Question', written in 1926, Antonio Gramsci, the Italian Marxist militant and thinker, made a major, and oft-neglected, contribution to theorizing the geographies of solidarity. The essay was written in a particular political conjuncture. It was part of a long-standing engagement of the Italian left with the relations between the industrial workers of the North of Italy and the peasants of the South. The questions of the relations between these groups had been discussed in depth in January 1920 in *L'Ordine Nuovo*, the paper Gramsci had set up to organize a radical shop stewards' movement (see Gramsci, 1977: 147-9; Jessop, 2005: 428-9). In *L'Ordine Nuovo* Gramsci had collaborated with anarchists, who had a major impact on working-class culture in early twentieth century Italy (Schmidt and van der Walt, 2009: 276; Levy, 1999). The scrutiny of these connections had been stimulated by the failure of the Italian factory council movement to broaden into a revolutionary force.

In September 1920 hundreds of thousands of metalworkers had occupied factories in Turin, Milan and Genoa (Spriano, 1975: 60-61).[15] This was the 'culmination of two years of intense class struggle'. Workers not only occupied the factories, but put them over to forms of workers' control. At Fiat-Centro in Turin, for example, the factory council assumed all power and called on workers to 'Show that you can run this factory without employers!' (cited by Spriano, 1975: 61). For Gramsci this self-organization elevated workers to a new moral authority. He argued that if 'workers in struggle occupy the factories and decide to go on producing, the moral position of the mass abruptly assumes a different form and value. Union bosses can no longer lead. Union bosses dwindle in the immensity of the perspective. The mass must solve the problems of the factory itself, with its own means, its own men' (cited by Spriano, 1975: 59).

For Gramsci these political activities reshaped the terrain of political possibility and challenged the entrenched power of conservative union bosses. The dissolution of the factory council movement in the face of repression and the rise of fascism, however, threw up significant political challenges (Eley, 2002: 172). Foremost of these was the relation between the industrial workers of the North and the poor and oppressed peasantry of the South. At the time that the factory occupations were ending, workers in Turin and elsewhere failed to form alliances with peasants who were engaged in major occupations of estates and uncultivated lands in the South (Spriano, 1975: 125). The key problematic that Gramsci confronted in 'Aspects of the Southern Question', then, was how alliances and solidarities could be forged across these geographical and social divisions.

To engage with these political tensions Gramsci explored the forms of uneven development that held the North and South apart. He locates the formation of solidarities in relation to the dynamic ongoing, uneven development of Northern and Southern Italy and engages with both the cultural and the political character of that inequality. Further, he positions the 'Southern Question' in relation to the unequal geographies of transnational connection that shaped the South. Gramsci writes trenchantly of the ways in which remittances from migrants in the United States were used to entrench rather than challenge regional inequalities. He notes that

> when emigration took on the gigantic dimensions it did in the twentieth century and the first remittances began to flood in from America ... the emigrants and their families were transformed from agents of the silent revolution into agents for giving the State the

financial means to subsidize the parasitic industries of the North. (Gramsci, 1978: 459; see Chambers, 2010: 2)

Gramsci's political analysis is not just concerned with the spatial inequalities shaped by capital and the state. He is also attentive to subaltern geographies of connection. Gramsci used the term 'subaltern', which he developed in a fascist prison, partly as a code word for class which would evade the prison censors. His usage of the term also brought into serious theoretical engagement the political activity of diverse groups such as 'the peasantry' about which orthodox Marxist accounts had had remarkably little to say. The essay traces the dynamic geographies through which subaltern actors constructed linkages which cut across the divisions of the North and South. This directly challenges the ways in which subaltern groups have frequently been theorized as having more restricted spatialities than the powerful (Calhoun, 2003; Harvey, 1989, 1996).

Central here is Gramsci's account of Sardinian soldiers, from the Sassari brigade, who were sent to Turin, in their words, to 'shoot the gentry who are on strike'. He recounts a conversation between a Sardinian tannery worker from Sassari and a soldier from the brigade bivouacked on the X square in Turin. The 'tannery worker' had approached a young peasant, 'who had welcomed him warmly because I was from Sassari like him'. He managed to convince the peasant-soldier that despite their dress the strikers were far from members of the gentry. Gramsci's account of the encounter gives a strong sense of the ongoing connections that developed between veterans of the Sassari brigade and militants in Turin. He contends:

Did these events have no consequences? On the contrary, they have had results which still subsist to this day and continue to work in the depths of the popular masses. They illuminated, for an instant, brains which had never thought in that way, and which remained marked by them, radically modified. Our archives have been scattered, and we have destroyed many papers ourselves for fear they might lead to arrests and harassment. But we can recall dozens and indeed hundreds of letters sent from Sardinia to the

Avanti! Editorial offices in Turin; letters which were frequently collective signed by all the Sassari Brigade veterans in a particular village. (Gramsci, 1978: 448)

In this account Gramsci foregrounds the practices through which the veterans of the Sassari brigade and the *Avanti!* editorial offices were connected. He notes the importance of the letters, and notes the significance of their collectively signed character, which linked Sassari brigade veterans in Sardinia with militants in Turin. These mark and foreground the ongoing work of making these political connections and solidarities. For Gramsci such connections matter. The 'brains' of the soldiers were marked by their experiences, and were 'radically modified'. As Gramsci notes, 'their songs, though still songs of war, no longer had the same content as those they sang on their arrival' (Gramsci, 1978: 448).

Gramsci's stress on the practices through which solidarities are constructed situates such practices as transformative. This displaces in several significant ways the account of class alliances developed by Lenin in *Two Tactics of Social Democracy*. Lenin's account of the formation of class alliances envisions the production of a '"single will" of the "peasantry" and the "proletariat" in the struggle against counter-revolution' (Lenin, 1968: 105). There is some sense of how such alliances might rework and challenge trade unions and labour aristocracies but little attention is given to the practices through which such connections are produced or generated (Lenin, 1968: 595). Further, the 'masses', both proletarian and peasant, are positioned as 'backward and ignorant' needing to be organized and represented (Lenin, 1968: 582). This produces an account of class-based alliances between proletarians and peasants, envisioned as geographically separate, with fixed and static interests, where alliances are forged from outside by a vanguard party. Alliances are envisioned simply as a strategic means to the greater end of the revolution rather than shaping the terms of militant political activity.

Gramsci's account positions connections between peasants and industrial workers as mutually constitutive. This is partly because he treats the geographies through which solidarities are constructed as productive. He argues that 'the economic and political regeneration of the peasants should not be sought in a division of uncultivated or poorly cultivated lands, but in the solidarity of the industrial proletariat. This in turn needs the solidarity of the peasantry' (Gramsci, 1977: 440). He argues that such connections would have effects such as the reconfiguring of 'craft particularisms' (448). This situates solidarities as practices which generate new trajectories and new experiments with relations between workers, land and technologies (Gidwani, 2008). By attending to the spatial practices through which such articulations are forged, through intervening in them, Gramsci engaged with their relational character (see also Laclau, 1996: 117).

This locates the theorizing of solidarity as part of the conduct of political activity and struggle. Gramsci's political method 'allowed him to pose the emergence of revolutionary critique in the lived consciousness and experience of the oppressed' (Chari, 2012). These links have been marginalized by treatments of left politics which have downplayed the productive character of political organizing and struggle (Saccarelli, 2008). Dominant accounts of left strategizing, such as Ernesto Laclau and Chantal Mouffe's insightful and important work *Hegemony and Socialist Strategy*, have concentrated on political ideas and strategies situating them as rather disembodied and apart from political activity. *Hegemony and Socialist Strategy* is one of the most influential genealogies of the left to be written in the late twentieth century. The account provided a critical rereading of the Marxist canon in the wake of anti-essentialist critiques and of the emergence of what were then termed 'new social movements' (Laclau and Mouffe, 1985). The book asserts an anti-essentialist account of hegemony as a promising organizing logic for left politics (Mouffe, 2010).

In *Hegemony and Socialist Strategy* Laclau and Mouffe characterize 'Aspects of the Southern Question' as a text where hegemony is theorized as constructed between fixed identities. They suggest that this precludes the contingent account of hegemony which characterizes Gramsci's *Prison Notebooks* (Laclau and Mouffe, 1985: 65-8). Their swift dismissal of the essay, however, is only made possible by ignoring the productive geographies of connection which Gramsci makes central to his argument. In Laclau and Mouffe's account of the genealogy of hegemony Gramsci's concern with the geographies through which alliances and solidarities are forged 'is quickly and assertively dismissed' (Sparke, 2005: 181). Gramsci's essay, by contrast, suggests the necessity of interrogating the relations between theorizing political struggle and the geographies through which solidarities are constructed.

It is precisely through engaging with the subaltern geographies of connection through which alliances are fashioned that Gramsci's creative and productive account of solidarity emerges. This opens up an alternative genealogy of left politics that takes seriously both the geographies through which political relations are constructed and the practices and activity of political struggle. The political relations shaped through such subaltern geographies of connection are central to the formation of solidarities from below.

Thinking a transformative political relation

In an open letter written to the socialist historian and peace activist E.P. Thompson in 1983, the Czechoslovak dissident Jaroslav Šabata ruminated on the solidarities that were emerging through the trans-European peace movement. He warned Thompson that

> Solidarity with us cannot be mere solidarity with people who are the victims of certain circumstances. Solidarity must not be motivated solely by humanitarian considerations. Of course such solidarity is important and merits profound tribute. But it is not enough. ... One of the new phenomena is the emergence of the influential autonomous peace movement. We are now confronted with the all-important task of formulating a common, universal, and all-

embracing strategy for the democratic transformation of Europe.
(Šabata, 1983: 70)

Šabata's letter was part of the exchanges between peace activists in Eastern and Western Europe which created a 'non-aligned'
peace movement. These exchanges refused the ideological polari-
ties of the Cold War and were critical of both Communist and
capitalist power blocs (see Chapter 6). Šabata's account presents
an important challenge to the terms on which solidarities are
constructed. He emphasizes that a solidarity characterized by
identification with victims, while important, is not enough. It
forecloses the emergence of solidarity as a genuinely productive, equal and transformative process. Šabata insists that it was
necessary to envision solidarities as part of the process of the
'democratic transformation of Europe'.

The relations that are constructed through solidarities, then,
are not given. Rather, the terms on which they are made are
struggled over and shaped through their conduct. As Šabata
suggests, the geographies of power through which solidarities
are fashioned can bear in significant ways on the character of
the political alternatives they generate. Such geographies are
not passive backdrops to such practices (Massey, 2006). They
can be reworked and reconfigured through the formation of
solidarities in different ways. The forms of political agency forged
through these geographies of solidarity are frequently ignored
or dismissed.

To understand the role of solidarity in shaping and transforming political relations it is necessary to assert the importance
of place-based political activity. One of the key ways in which
solidarity has been understood in geography and beyond is as
part of the scaling up of political activity (Herod, 2001). This
implies that place-based political activity is somehow beneath
the processes through which solidarities are made. It also
isolates places from always already being enmeshed in all sorts
of connections and trajectories, as the Cardiff-Ethiopia example
demonstrates.

Solidarities, then, are worked through and constructed in and between different sites. This allows place-based politics some of the action in constituting solidarities. This distributes in a more generous fashion the agency of who/what gets to shape their formation and challenges accounts which position solidarity, as abstracted universalisms, disconnected from place-based political activity. Such accounts frequently position solidarities as divorced from the ongoing 'real' political struggles in particular places.

The formation of solidarities in and between places can re-shape and bring into contestation power relations within places. The Women Against Pit Closures movement and women's support groups that emerged during the 1984-85 miners' strike in Britain are significant here. The year-long strike was precipitated by pit closures, but came to be also a key struggle over the neoliberal policies of Margaret Thatcher (Williams, 1989: 120-27). Women in mining communities participated in all aspects of the strike, from picketing to the alternative forms of welfare such as soup kitchens which were integral to supporting mining communities during the dispute (Francis, 2009). These linkages were demonstrated by slogans and banners such as 'Your fight is our fight'.

The solidarities and political activity developed by women in mining communities challenged relations within these places. Mining communities, such as the South Wales Valleys, were frequently structured by a pronounced 'focus on men and masculinity' (Loach, 1985: 169). Women were expected to provide the 'invisible' labour that 'propped up the whole filthy business of being a miner' but were generally excluded from political activity (Bloomfield, 1986: 158-9; Massey and McDowell, 1994). For many women their involvement in the dispute and becoming politically active led to a questioning not just of pit closures but also of patriarchal social relations. Betty Cook from Barnsley, for example, recalls that 'I was always told I was thick, the strike taught me I wasn't' (Gillan, 2004). Through the strike there were productive, if at times uneasy, relations between working-class women and (predominantly) middle-class feminist organizations (Loach, 1985: 169).

The testimony of Glynys Evans, who was involved in the Maerdy strike centre in the Rhondda valley, emphasizes the effect of the dispute on her political horizons. She notes that 'you can become quite cloistered in your own little community and you listen to the box and believe everything that's said. Then you meet refugees from Chile, you meet people from Thailand who are trying to set up a working union for the clothing industry. Compared to parts of the world, we don't know what the term oppression means' (Evans, 2009: 61-2). The solidarity networks generated through the dispute also led to productive challenges to the racist and homophobic views of some in mining communities (Loach, 1985; Francis, 2009). The solidarities forged through the dispute linked diverse political trajectories and had effects and consequences.

They did not result in victory, though they clearly were integral to the dispute's conduct and longevity. The solidarities forged within communities involved challenging patriarchal social relations. Other political alliances formed during the dispute also had important effects. In Wales, for example, the alliances developed through the strike partly broke down long-standing antagonisms between the labour movement and Welsh nationalist politics. These tensions mapped onto long-standing cultural divisions between North and South Wales. During the dispute activists from Cymdeithas Yr Iaith Gymraeg and Plaid Cymru, the militant Welsh language society and the Welsh nationalist party respectively, were prominent in offering solidarity (Francis, 2009: 60-63). These solidarities had effects beyond the strike.

Dafydd Elis-Thomas, the first presiding officer at the National Assembly for Wales and a key figure on the left of Plaid Cymru during the 1980s, noted in 2008 that the miners' strike was when the campaign for devolution in Wales 'really began' (cited by Francis, 2009: 55). The solidarities forged during the dispute made possible the alliances that featured in the 1997 devolution referendum (Francis, 2009). Such alliances also decentred and reconfigured the 'traditional labour movement'. Francis writes of the emergence of a 'broad democratic alliance of a new kind' – 'an anti-Thatcher alliance – in which the organized working class had a central role but a role which it would have to earn and not assume' (Francis, 2009: 62). In similar terms, Doreen Massey and Hilary Wainwright noted during the dispute that the miners' strike demonstrated how the 'existing institutions of labour', which 'are old and sectional', could be superseded and challenged 'without abandoning class politics' (Massey and Wainwright, 1985: 168). Drawing on their involvement in the movement of miners' support groups, they noted how 'industrial action' and 'new social movements' could be mutually dependent rather than antagonistic.

The solidarities created during the miners' strike shaped diverse outcomes. They emphasize the open-ended and productive character of the relations and trajectories that can be shaped through practices of solidarity. This is not to deny the enormous loss and destructive consequences of the defeat of the miners by the Thatcher government. It is, however, to insist that solidarities can have significant effects, which are lost by narrowly goal-based accounts. They can have important effects on the shaping of relations and on 'the terms of political discourse' (Thompson, 1996: 100).

The political cultures shaped by Women Against Pit Closures and women's miners' support groups emphasize that solidarities are not neatly 'organic' to places, as accounts of militant place-based political activity sometimes imply (Harvey, 1996; Williams, 1989). This is demonstrated by a dispute relating to anti-apartheid activism in Glasgow in the 1980s. The dispute was occasioned by the singing of 'Rivonia', Hamish Henderson's song of internationalist solidarity with the South African freedom struggle. The song – with its driving, rhythmic chorus, 'Free Mbeki Goldberg Sizulu Free Mandela Free Mandela' – protests the imprisonment of Nelson Mandela and fellow African National Congress (ANC) leaders during the Rivonia trials between 1963 and 1964. The lyrics were set to the tune of the old Spanish

Civil War song, 'Viva la Quince Brigata'. Raymond Kunene, the London representative of the ANC, remarked on the significance of this in a letter to Henderson. He noted that 'there are great similarities between the Spanish struggle against fascism and ours' (cited by Neat, 2009: 190).

The song circulated. Pete Seeger sang it to big audiences in America. Henderson sent it to the ANC office in London. Kunene forwarded Henderson's song to the main office of the ANC in Dar es Salaam, where 'there were ecstatic comments from all the friends there' (cited by Neat, 2009: 191). A recording of the song made by The Corries in 1968 was sent to the 'South African Freedom Fighters in the field' (Freeman, 2003: n.p.). Hamish was 'deeply moved when he heard that black fishermen hauling nets off Robben Island now sang 'Rivonia' in the hope that the wind would carry it to the prisoners breaking stones beyond the prison wall' (Neat, 2009: 191). Atté, 'a group of South African blacks living in London', recorded the song in 1977, radically transforming it by 'providing what is virtually a new tune, and by adding Zulu words' (Crawford, 1977: n.p.). When Mandela went to Glasgow to receive the freedom of the city in 1993 he was to thank Henderson personally for writing the song.

Kenny Caird, a Glasgow folk singer and organizer of the Star Folk Club which had strong links to the Communist Party, sang the song one night in the mid-1980s in the Beaconsfield Hotel in Glasgow.[16] It would have been a central song in his repertoire during that period. On Kenny's singing of 'Rivonia' four white South Africans who were staying at the nearby Youth Hostel left the bar in protest. Kenny in turn was intimidated by the bar manager, an ex-army trainer, who accused Kenny of losing him custom; the pub relied heavily on trade from the Youth Hostel. A heated argument ensued between Kenny and Trish Caird and the bar manager. On another occasion when Kenny sang 'Rivonia' a Conservative councillor left in protest.

This story locates solidarities in contested relations between and within places. Caird's singing of 'Rivonia' was part of a broader set of cultural and political linkages between Glasgow and the freedom struggle in South Africa. This was shaped by many ordinary acts such as the singing of freedom songs or boycotts of South African produce. Such links received institutional support through Glasgow City Council and the Scottish Trades Union Congress (STUC) (Fieldhouse, 2004: 324-5). In 1986 St George's Place, where the South African consulate was located, was renamed Nelson Mandela Place. This mobilization of apartheid, then, was produced through opposing Glasgow's connections with South Africa. This process was contested. The singing of 'Rivonia' by Ken Caird at the Beaconsfield Hotel provoked not solidarity but anger from the white South African drinkers and in turn from the bar manager. This resulted in contestation not just of a distant apartheid system, but also of place-based relations, where radically different and opposing views of apartheid coexisted. The political singer Robb Johnson, a veteran of many political solidarities forged through the 1980s, notes that support for the ANC in South Africa, the PLO in Palestine and the Sandinistas in Nicaragua was also a 'tactical way of fighting back against the government that had systematically set out to destroy the trade unions, local democracy, and even enforced right wing ideology and state control over the Education system' (Johnson, 2009: n.p.).

The connections and trajectories generated through political songs like 'Rivonia' suggest the importance of solidarities in shaping relations between different sites. These connections, as the disputes over them emphasize, were formed through passionate, antagonistic forms of identification. This presents challenges for understandings of solidarity. Solidarity has frequently been understood as bearing primarily on the 'rational economic interests' of workers and other groups. Such practices have also been evaluated in rather functionalist terms, such as whether they advance workers' interests in specific contexts (e.g. Herod, 2001). Solidarity here becomes theorized primarily as a means to specific ends. Locating solidarities as part of the ongoing production of relations between places and sites offers different possibilities.

This challenges conceptualizations of solidarity which are limited to fixed, rational relations. Rather, connections can be shaped in more emotional and intimate ways. The more than rational character of solidarities has been explored by Geraldine Pratt in her account of the visit of a group of nine Canadian human rights activists to the Philippines in November 2006. This international solidarity work was a response to the large number of extrajudicial killings in the Philippines since 2001. Her account usefully foregrounds the embodied and emotional constitution of solidarity. She discusses in vivid terms the experiences of Merryn Edwards, one of the human rights activists involved in the mission.

> Images and stories are lodged in her bones. The muscles of her left eye hold the squint that comes from videoing a woman's testimony to her husband's death, their bodies imaginatively synchronized through deep breaths. ... At the same time, she recognizes her privilege of distance, her capacity to eat, play and joke a short distance from this woman's trauma. She imagines that the military will return after she has flown home to live her life in Vancouver – one day behind, and speculates that her visit will be the focus of a further round of intimidation. (Pratt et al., 2008: 757)

The connections between the Philippines and Vancouver that Pratt traces here are not disembodied, 'rational' or dispassionate connections. Rather, they are embodied and intimate. The images and stories become lodged in Edwards's bones, the stress has bodily impacts. This produces interventions which rework 'static, stable geographies of north/south, west/east, first world/ third world, here/there' (Pratt et al., 2008: 757). These solidarities also had effects on relations in both places. Merryn is dogged by worries that reprisals will follow her visit to the Philippines, especially to those who gave her hospitality.

Following the multiple, contested geographies through which such transnational solidarities are constituted opens up theoretical and political possibilities. As Pratt argues, such 'intimacy and emotionality' are not adequately captured by ethical framings of 'caring from a distance' (Pratt et al., 2008: 757). This also disrupts constructions of internationalism as being about the exoticized struggles of 'distant others'. Asserting the embodied passionate character of connections is a condition for making present and valuing the diverse ways in which solidarities are assembled and fashioned. These may be about providing embodied forms of support, as Pratt's work suggests, or about mobilizing senses of anger, injustice and shame. Such passionate interventions shape the terms on which political antagonisms are mobilized through solidarity work. The political relations forged through solidarities can be decisively shaped through the terms on which they contest and challenge unequal relations.

Conclusion: solidarity as a universalizing relation

In his book *The Coming Community* Giorgio Agamben outlines an account of solidarity 'that in no way concerns an essence' (Agamben, 1993: 17-18). For Agamben it is necessary to move beyond accounts based around unity and fixity, and to consider how solidarities are forged through scattering and generating different relations. This chapter in similar terms has rejected accounts which position solidarity as bearing on linking given, already-formed identities. Instead it has positioned solidarity as a transformative process which works through the negotiation and renegotiation of forms of political identification.

This stress on the transformative potential of solidarity can refigure the relations between solidarity and universality. It highlights a productive aspect of this political relation which has often been closed down. Solidarity has been understood as an expression of underlying 'universalisms'. Jodi Dean contends, for example, that solidarity is necessarily 'underpinned by universalism' (Dean, 1996: 29-30). She argues that what she terms 'reflective solidarity' is 'attuned to the universality within concrete identities as well as to an ideal community of us all'. Dean's account usefully considers the relations between solidarity and universalism. The way it positions universalism as under-pinning solidarity is problematic. It assumes that solidarity is part of an expression of a singular 'community of us all', rather than bearing on fractured and contested political struggles and communities.

Different possibilities are shaped by situating universality as produced through political relations and struggle. C.L.R. James's account of the Haitian Revolution positions universals such as 'equality' and 'liberty' as the product of ongoing dialogues, connections and relations between different revolutionary formations in Haiti and France (James, 1989). He contends that the use of notions of liberty and equality by insurgent slaves dislocated the Eurocentric terms on which they were defined through the French Revolution. Such connections and relations speak to challenges and contestation of the terms on which political universality was configured. This focus on the coeval and often conflictual trajectories through which different notions of democracy, equality or liberty were articulated is important (see also Edwards, 2003). The struggles of diverse interconnected multi-ethnic resistances that traversed the Atlantic world in the seventeenth and eighteenth centuries were productive of 'multi-ethnic conceptions of humanity' (Linebaugh and Rediker, 2001: 352).

This asserts the productive force of solidarity in shaping universalizing practices. Here universalism does not underpin politics. Rather, it is ongoing and created through the conduct of political activity and struggles (Laclau, 1996; see also Hall, 2000). This account positions solidarity as a universalizing political relation. It is part of the means through which political discourses become articulated and universalized. This situates forms of universality as contested, ongoing and under construction. As Judith Butler argues, social movements can produce and struggle over different articulations of universality (Butler, 2000: 162-3). These processes of universalization are partial, multiple and fractured; they are never finished or fully formed, but rather can be articulated and generated in different ways (see also Dikeç, 2012). This account allows political movements some of the action in shaping the terms on which they are shaped.

Understanding solidarity in this way is a condition for engaging with the creativity and productivity of this political relation. It offers important possibilities for engaging with the productive geographies shaped through political struggles. Rather than universality being disembodied and defined against geographical contexts and places, this locates universality as the product of relations between different political trajectories. The forms of universalism constituted by anti-colonial activists, for example, embraced diverse democratic struggles enabling 'an appreciation of their marvellously fluid sense of "we-ness" and the expansiveness of their democratic vision' (Von Eschen, 1997: 23). The next chapter explores how this concern with the generative character of political relations reconfigures accounts of internationalism.

CHAPTER 2

Rethinking internationalism

One of the key sites in Claude McKay's novel *Banjo* is the Café Africain. Located in the Vieux Port, the dockside area of Marseilles, the Café becomes a key meeting point for the transient black seafarers whose lives, music and politics are celebrated by McKay. A key figure in the Harlem Renaissance, the Jamaican novelist and poet had spent time in the French port city during the 1920s. In the novel the Senegalese proprietor keeps *La Race Nègre*, a journal published 'by a group of French West Africans in Paris', 'conspicuously displayed for sale' (McKay, 2000: 62). This gained him the 'disapproval of some colored visitors', who told the proprietor 'they did not think it was good for his business to sell it there'.

It also occasions an encounter between the proprietor and a 'white gentleman'. McKay recounts that

> the proprietor was intransigent about *La Race Nègre* because he had been rebuked for selling it by a flabby bulk of a man who had once been an official out in one of the colonies, and who now had something to do with the welfare of the *indigènes* in Marseilles. The white gentlemen had told the proprietor that the Negroes who published *La Race Nègre* were working against France and such a journal should be suppressed and its editors trapped and thrown

into jail as criminals. The proprietor of the bar replied that he was not in West Africa, where he had heard the local authorities had forbidden the circulation of the *Negro World*, but in Marseilles, where he hoped to remain master in his own café. As the proprietor said that the gentleman from the colonies left the café brusquely and unceremoniously without saying goodbye. (McKay, 2000: 62-3)

McKay makes the colonial geographies of this encounter clear. There are the trajectories of the proprietor's accuser: he 'had once been an official out in one of the colonies' but now 'had something to do with the welfare of the *indigènes* in Marseilles'. There is the 'brusque' manner of the official, which has the unintended consequence of intensifying the proprietor's anti-colonial commitments. Further, the proprietor feels that Marseilles offers possibilities for anti-colonial dissent that is more fully suppressed in West Africa. He emphasizes that in Marseilles he expected to 'remain master in his own Café'.

The passage dramatizes the importance of sites like the Café African to the generation of anti-colonial networks. This positions internationalism as made through specific articulations and connections between different places. These connections were held together by the fragile and contested distribution networks of papers like *La Race Nègre*. The anti-colonial movements they shaped were subject to severe repression by imperial powers such as France and Britain, as indicated by McKay's reference to the suppression of the *Negro World*. This chapter explores the importance of such forms of translocal connection to accounts of internationalism. I argue that the unruly, generative connections that constitute subaltern articulations of internationalism have all too frequently been silenced and ignored.

Internationalism beyond the nation

The discussion of *La Race Nègre* in *Banjo* recalls McKay's own role in bringing copies of radical African American magazines and newspapers, such as the *Crisis* and the *Negro World*, to a club for 'colored soldiers' located in a basement on Drury Lane

(McKay, 1985: 67–8; see also James, 2003: 79–80). During his time London in 1919–20 he frequented the club and collaborated with the radical suffragette Sylvia Pankhurst on the *Workers' Dreadnought*, the paper of the Workers' Socialist Federation. He used this outlet to critique the racism of the British left and to explore solidarities between black struggles and Irish anti-colonialism (see James, 2003; McKay, 1973a; Malouf, 2009). In the early 1920s he visited the USSR, addressing the Third International and influencing the racial policy of the Communist International (Baldwin, 2002). In the late 1920s and early 1930s McKay travelled through Europe and North Africa, the latter being attractive to him for its permissive attitudes to same-sex sexuality and, according to Gary Holcomb, for the distance it afforded from the intelligence agents who had become interested in him (Holcomb, 2007). He was later to become a trenchant critic of Stalinism and distanced himself from left politics more generally, converting to Catholicism in 1944 (see Baldwin, 2002: 25–85; McKay, 1985, 1968).

McKay's presence in Moscow was part of a set of interconnections between anti-colonial and communist politics which are significant and forged generative, if uneven, contested and at times troubling, connections. McKay opened his speech to the Third International in 1922 by stating that he 'would prefer to speak in front of a lynch mob than in front of this great gathering' (cited by Baldwin, 2002: 40). Kate Baldwin suggests this 'declaration set the tone for McKay's awareness of his audience as at once an ally against white supremacy and perilously proximate to that very regime' (40). *Banjo's* focus on seafarers and drifters who refuse disciplined forms of labour organizing is shaped by McKay's rejection of the hierarchical and vanguardist character of the Communist International. The novel marked a 'shift in McKay's political focus away from the proletariat, traditionally conceived, and towards such cosmopolitan, fleeting communities of men' (Edwards, 2003: 199).

Brent Hayes Edwards has termed McKay's novel a form of 'vagabond internationalism'. In doing so he draws on Peter

Linebaugh and Marcus Rediker's work on the motley resistances that traversed the Atlantic world in the early modern period (Linebaugh and Rediker, 2001). This signals the dynamism of forms of internationalism constituted from below. Through his engagement with these 'fleeting communities of men' McKay recovers and celebrates the cosmopolitan trajectories of black seafarers. The mobilities that are foregrounded through the novel are constituted on decidedly unequal terms. McKay sought to 'reveal the ways in which black masculine mobility and freedom were penalized by the larger maritime reach of imperial state forms' (Stephens, 2005: 186). If theirs are cosmopolitan experiences, they are shaped on decidedly subaltern terms.

From the outset of the book these sailor's mobilities are shown to be constituted in subordinate ways. Early in the novel in introducing the character Ginger, McKay notes that of 'all the English-speaking Negro boys, Ginger held the long-term record of existence on the beach. He had lost his seamen's papers. He had been in prison for vagabondage and served with a writ of expulsion. But he had destroyed the writ and swiped the papers of another seaman' (McKay, 2000: 3). Sailors' mobility is impeded and shaped not just by states, but also by white supremacist violence. McKay's discussion of Taloufa, a Nigerian seafarer who had made his home in Cardiff, notes that 'he got a brick wound in the head' 'during the riots of 1919 between colored and whites' (McKay, 2000: 83-4).[1] After the riots he had jumped ship to America, but was deported from the United States after 'the fact of his entering the country illegally' became known.

Michelle Stephens argues that the 'masculine identities of the men in Banjo's crew' are 'shaped and defined by the maritime world on whose periphery they seem to wander' (Stephens, 2005: 179). Her analysis interrogates '*Banjo*'s transnational racial ideologies' 'for their sexual specificity, acknowledging subaltern masculinity, and not just blackness, as itself a globalized racial category' (Stephens, 2005: 168-9). This draws attention to the role played by forms of masculinities in generating forms of subaltern cosmopolitanism. Her work is also keenly aware of the ways in which forms of internationalism and solidarity can be held together by performances of masculinity. Holcomb pushes this analysis further by drawing attention to the dissident sexuality of McKay and exploring how this structures black internationalism articulated through his interlinked novels *Home to Harlem*, *Banjo* and *Romance in Marseilles* (Holcomb, 2007). This challenges the tendency of left historiography to see the relations between masculinities, solidarities and internationalism as given rather than actively constructed.

McKay asserts the injustices that structure the labour and mobility of these seafaring men. Rather than confine these motley figures within narratives of disciplined political activity or organizing, McKay follows the attempt of Banjo, the central character of the novel, and his mates to form an 'orchestra'. McKay writes of Banjo that 'his loud music of life' was 'an affirmation of his hardy existence in the midst of the biggest, the most tumultuous civilization of modern life' (McKay, 2000: 49). Holcomb contends that 'Banjo's art, his lively jazzing – like movement – is the expression of freedom itself, in both its personal as well as political senses' (Holcomb, 2007: 154). These musical endeavours are situated in relation to 'transnational contours of black expression' and histories of oppression (see Woods, 1998, 2007).

Thus Goosey, the character in the novel most sympathetic to Garveyite Black Nationalism, scorns Banjo's choice of instrument. For Goosey 'banjo' is simply 'bondage'. 'It's the instrument of slavery. Banjo is Dixie. The Dixie of the land of cotton and massa and missus and black mammy. We colored folks have got to get away from all that in these enlightened progressive days' (McKay, 2000: 76-7). Banjo's riposte gives a powerful sense of how his music refuses to be contained in the histories and geographies of oppression that for Goosey mark the banjo. 'I play that instrument because I likes it. I don't play no Black Joe hymns. I play lively tunes. All that you talking about slavery and bondage ain't got nothing to do with our starting up a li'l orchestra.' In this regard Banjo's musical interventions produce what Clyde Woods has termed 'blues epistemologies' (Woods,

1998: 16-21). For Woods such blues epistemologies generated alternative ways of understanding and commenting on 'social and economic development and change' (Woods, 1998: 20).

The dispute over the relative cultural merit of the banjo leads to a heated debate about the politics of Garveyism. Goosey articulates his critique of the banjo in relation to a Garveyite politics of racial purity. Banjo responds through reference to Garvey's arrest for alleged corruption: 'And what does he think now they got the fat block of that black swindler in the jail house?' (McKay, 2000: 76-7). It is not just Garvey's corruption, however, that McKay attacks. The very logic of the book, through its affirmation of motley exchange and interaction, is marked by a direct refusal of the cultural purity of race associated with Garveyism. McKay's text challenges the forms of 'unanimistic solidarities' constituted through Garveyism (see Gilroy, 2000: 333). The motley exchanges of those in the Ditch are central to the negotiation of internationalism in *Banjo*. There is coexistence here, but also heated tensions and discussions, over different ways of making and envisioning black internationalism.

McKay's account of black internationalist activity on the Marseilles waterfront offers challenges to nation-centred conceptions of internationalism. Internationalism has frequently been thought of as bearing on the linkages between working-class traditions and movements formed in discrete national spaces. McKay's novel, however, insists that it makes little sense to think of these internationalist connections as the product of working-class movements fashioned in bounded national terms. The connections constituted through such motley exchanges are more unruly than this suggests. The circuits of anti-colonial organizing associated with *La Race Nègre*, for example, exceeded the confining spaces of nation-states. This generated an anti-colonial internationalism formed through cutting into and contesting the relations between France and (francophone) West Africa. As the proprietor of the Café Africain argues, France was seen as offering important potential opportunities for political organizing that were denied in Senegal.

This is an internationalist politics, then, that is worked through particular sites and places. Often internationalism has been constructed as operating at a different 'level' or 'scale' to the politics of local or place-based struggle (see Castree, 2000; Herod, 2001; Waterman and Wills, 2001). This has been a disempowering political narrative. It suggests somehow that internationalism is separate from the 'everyday' or particular contexts; or that it is somehow at one, or several, remove(s) from such places. McKay's account of the Café Africain generates a different sense of situated, internationalist connection. This is a 'networked, practiced internationalism' that 'challenges the dominant geographical imaginary which understands the world in terms of scales and nested hierarchies' (Massey, 2007: 184).

This allows a plural and generous account of the forms of agency involved in shaping internationalist politics. Rather than a focus on elite political figures or leaders this might, for example, accord some of the transient black seafarers agency in shaping internationalism through such acts as passing anti-colonial literature and newspapers through different ports. It also emphasizes how suspicion and refusal of certain forms of discipline and hierarchical relations were also important in shaping the terms on how internationalist connections were forged (see also Hyslop, 2009b).

This presents challenges to dominant ways of theorizing internationalism. The nation has been accorded an unthinking centrality in many versions of internationalism. The political writings of Karl Marx produced through his involvement with the First International are a good example of this. Marx, as the introduction noted, was inspired by the dramatic exchanges and solidarities that were forged during the Cotton Famine. Despite this he still approached working-class strategy primarily in national terms. This was structured by a clear division between national working-class movements and internationalism.

Marx envisioned internationalism as the product of the coming together of national working-class movements which were already fashioned. This process was to be brokered by leaders of national working-class movements. Marx argued that internationalism 'could only be built on the basis of national, working-class organization rooted in the material conditions of exploitation in given national contexts, and aimed at the state apparatuses of various nations' (Foster, 2000: n.pag.). In this regard Marx made a key distinction between the form and content of class struggle. *The Communist Manifesto* implored that 'the struggle of the proletariat with the bourgeoisie is at first a national struggle. The proletariat of each country must, of course, first of all settle matters with its own bourgeoisie' (Marx and Engels, 1978: 482). In the *Critique of the Gotha Programme* Marx contended that it is 'altogether self-evident that, to be able to fight at all, the working class must organize itself at home *as a class* and that its own country is the immediate arena of its struggle' (Marx, 1974: 350).

The centring of the nation here has consequences. It ensures that internationalism is not constructed as an abstracted universalism, built out of nowhere. It also has more deleterious consequences. The focus on national left elites and leaderships gives a restricted sense of the forms of political agency involved in constructing internationalism. This was also reflected in the conduct of the First International. The rules of the International, for example, contain provisions for the creation of strong 'central national organs' (Marx, 1974: 84). Further, Marx's account constructs the nation as a discrete 'container' of political activity, where working-class struggle can be straightforwardly directed. This ignores the ways that 'national' politics are always already fashioned through diverse connections and relations. There is an imagination here that national movements are formed then networked, rather than there being more ongoing negotiations of international contexts (see also Anderson, 2002; Thompson, 1978).

These relations became contested through the activity of the First International, notably through disputes between Marx and Bakunin. Bakunin and other anarchists contested the prominence given by Marx to the state (Schmidt and van der Walt, 2009: 64).

Bakunin argued that 'nationality was separate from the state' and therefore society 'did not need the state for emancipation' (64). The silences of the First International on the links of working-class movements to colonialism are arguably one consequence of this nation-centred approach to internationalism (see Hall, 1992). To engage with the tensions of nation-centred accounts it is useful to interrogate the relations between cosmopolitanism and internationalism.

Subaltern cosmopolitanism and internationalism

Nation-centred approaches to the theorizing of internationalism have had strong legacies. They also persist. A powerful restatement of a nation-centred account of internationalism has marked recent interventions by cultural and political theorist Timothy Brennan (2003, 2006). Drawing on long-standing traditions of left antagonism to cosmopolitanism, Brennan contends that

> *Inter*-nationalism does not quarrel with the principle of *national* sovereignty, for there is no other way under modern conditions to secure respect for weaker societies or peoples. If cosmopolitanism springs from a comfortable culture of middle-class travellers, intellectuals and businessmen, [then] internationalism ... is an ideology of the domestically restricted, the recently relocated, the provisionally exiled and temporarily weak. It is addressed to those who have an interest in transnational forms of solidarity, but whose capacities for doing so have not yet arrived. (Brennan, 2003: 42, emphasis in original)

Here Brennan delineates a strict distinction between cosmopolitanism and internationalism. He positions cosmopolitanism as a 'global representative structure' which is populated by the wealthy/middle class, counterposing this to traditions of internationalism. For Brennan internationalism is a practice born out of respect and interrelation between different 'national' experiences. What is crucial here is that these 'national' experiences are constructed as primarily separate and isolated, before being conjoined through internationalist politics. Further, he suggests that subaltern groups are not able to form transnational forms of solidarity; their capacity to do so is 'yet to come'.

Brennan's work is useful to the extent that it criticizes accounts of cosmopolitanism which all too frequently are unreflexive about who can fashion cosmopolitan relations. There are ways of being cosmopolitan which depend on elite spatial circuits and practices, what Craig Calhoun has referred to as the 'class consciousness of frequent flyers' (2003). Through associating cosmopolitanism primarily with elite groups, however, Brennan and Calhoun close down engagements with diverse subaltern variants of cosmopolitanism. These have had significant political effects and legacies (Kipfer and Goonewardena, 2007). They also provide a useful counterpoint to accounts of internationalism which focus primarily only on national left elite actors. Subaltern cosmopolitanisms frequently cut across, unsettle and disrupt constructions of the nation as discrete bounded spaces.

Brennan invokes Gramsci to support his stark opposition of cosmopolitanism and internationalism. He asserts that Gramsci was 'almost always negative in his usage' of cosmopolitanism, noting his association of the 'phenomenon of "imperial cosmo-politanism" among Italian intellectuals' with elite Catholic uni-versalism (Brennan, 1989: 16, 2003: 43). This focus on Gramsci's straightforward hostility to cosmopolitanism is commonplace in readings of his work (see also Harvey, 2009: 79, 168, 238). Gramsci's writings on cosmopolitan practices, paradoxically, offer resources for a multifaceted and productive account of the relations between cosmopolitanism and internationalism.

Gramsci *is* extremely critical of elite Catholic articulations of cosmopolitanism. He writes of the 'pollution' of the 'Vatican's cosmopolitanism' and associates cosmopolitanism with feudalism (Gramsci, 1971: 63, 249). It would be wrong, however, to use such passages to present Gramsci as univocally hostile to cos-mopolitanism. Gramsci makes a significant distinction between the 'reactionary' forms of cosmopolitanism associated with elite Catholicism and more 'progressive' forms of cosmopolitanism.

He associates such 'progressive' forms of cosmopolitanism with
political and religious exiles, though he makes it clear that these
are still broadly elite in character (Gramsci, 1985: 220; see also
Gramsci, 1971: 274-5). These engagements with cosmopolitanism
are alive to its contested character. This suggests that cosmopolitanism can be mobilized and articulated in different, potentially
conflictual, ways.

Gramsci has a further, and arguably more politically productive, usage of the term. He contends that the Italian people are
the people with the greatest 'national' interest in a 'modern form
of cosmopolitanism'. He continues:

> Nationalism of the French stamp is an anachronistic excrescence
> in Italian history, proper to people who have their heads turned
> backwards like the damned in Dante. The 'mission' of the Italian
> people lies not in the recovery of Roman and medieval cosmopoli-
> tanism, but in its most modern and advanced form. Even indeed
> a proletarian nation, as Pascoli wanted; proletarian as a nation
> because it has been the reserve army of foreign capitalism, because
> together with the Slavic peoples it has given skilled workers to the
> entire world. For this very reason, it must join the modern front
> struggling to reorganize also the non-Italian world, which it has
> helped to create with its labour. (Gramsci, 1995: 247)

Gramsci here uses the term 'modern form of cosmopolitanism'
in a way that is akin to 'proletarian internationalism'. This
articulation of cosmopolitanism is clearly differentiated from
and antagonistic to those associated with 'Roman and medieval'
forms. Gramsci, then, rather than dismissing cosmopolitanism
per se, or constructing it as antithetical to internationalism,
engaged in struggles over how the term could be used and
deployed.

This is a significant move. It suggests that cosmopolitanism
and internationalism might be thought of in relation to each other
rather than as opposites. There are ongoing relations between
different places and workers which unsettle the confining of workers into national left traditions. This suggests the importance
of cosmopolitan experiences of subaltern groups such as labour

migration, exile or forms of mobility such as seafaring (Kothari, 2012). These subaltern cosmopolitan experiences have shaped practices of internationalism in significant ways.

This reconfigures and challenges ways of understanding relations between internationalism and national projects. Linkages between anarchism and anti-colonial internationalism are significant here (Anderson, 2005; Ramnatu, 2011). In the early twentieth century Cuban anarchists sought 'to offer their own agenda for what an independent and internationalist Cuba should look like' in the wake of US occupation (Shaffer, 2010: 278-9). This articulated a distinctive vision of Cuban independence and of anarchist internationalism. Their project was not to destroy 'local and regional autonomy' in the name of an outside notion of 'internationalism'. Rather, they sought to 'Cubanize' international anarchism – that is, to 'blend internationalism and nationality' (278-9). This was a motley, cosmopolitan movement 'made of men and women, old and young, black and white, Cuban- and foreign-born, skilled and unskilled workers, poets, shopkeepers, playwrights and librarians' (278).

Such forms of subaltern cosmopolitanism have been silenced in accounts of internationalism. They have been rendered marginal or ignored. This is partly because such forms of activity often contemporaneously had uneasy or marginal relations with official left parties and organizing practices. The French Communist Party, for example, actively marginalized the forms of anti-colonial organizing that McKay drew attention to in *Banjo* (see Derrick, 2008: 129; Edwards, 2003: 264). Dominant currents in the French left have continued to articulate exclusionary notions of French republicanism. The failure of the French left to articulate a multi-ethnic urban politics is central to Mustafa Dikeç's account of the production of *banlieues* as marginal spaces in French cities. This is memorably captured by political activists from Vaulx-en-Velin in Lyons, as 'this left which is not going to bring the solutions it promised' (Dikeç, 2007: 143-4).

Despite this, such forms of political activity were and are significant in constructing political agency and shaping solidarities in important ways. Tracing forms of subaltern cosmopolitanism and their intersections with internationalism can develop more generous accounts of what counts as internationalist practice. This challenges the problematic terms by which cosmopolitanism has been associated with a transcendental citizenship of the world. Tariq Jazeel has usefully drawn attention to the 'unthinking Eurocentrism' of cosmopolitanism. He challenges its 'planetary geographical imagination' and pretensions to the global and universal (Jazeel, 2011: 77).

There are, however, important distinctions between the geographies generated and envisioned through different articulations of cosmopolitanism. The forms of subaltern cosmopolitanism present in account such as *Banjo* offer different political possibilities to such European-centred geographies. This asserts the importance of subaltern articulations of cosmopolitanism which produce situated forms of worldliness often under harsh and oppressive conditions. Such forms of worldliness cut across spatial partitions such as the West and non-West. Solidarities are constructed by subaltern political activity through forging such connections rather than being 'yet to come'. To develop this position it is necessary to explore the relations between place and internationalism.

Placing internationalism

On the night of 13 October 1937, Elma Francois, one of the founders of the Trinidadian Negro Welfare Cultural and Social Association (NWCSA), spoke at a meeting on the 'Greens' on Piccadilly Street in Port of Spain. Francois was arrested for the political content of her speech and became the first woman in Trinidad and Tobago to be tried for sedition. At her trial in 1938 she 'undertook the greater part of her defence herself' and gave her occupation as a 'clothes washer' (Reddock, 1988: 36-7). She told the court that in her speech she had spoken on 'World Imperialism and the Colonial Toilers'. She continued:

In dealing with my subject I dealt with world conditions linking them up with local conditions; I dealt with land reservations in the Kenya Colony. I explained that a certain amount of land was reserved for the working class and often they were deprived of it and they decided there to organise in order to get their wrongs righted with regard to the question of land reservations, by a Royal Commission. They succeeded in getting a Royal Commission. ... I spoke about the Negro and East-Indian workers who sleep under the Town Hall and in the Square through poverty. I wanted their conditions to be bettered. I referred to the struggle my organisation had carried out against the Trade Tax. (in Reddock, 1988: 36-7)

For Francois it was necessary to link up 'world conditions and local conditions'. They needed to be connected, thought together, rather than seen as separate. Her speech connected diverse places. As well as Kenya, she spoke of conditions in Nigeria. She noted that the 'natives there' were 'protesting against increased taxations'. She 'discussed Germany and Russia also' and pointed to 'the effective method the workers in England used by organising and what they gained'.

Francois's ability to link local and world conditions is a political skill that is integral to internationalism. This skill, as Francois's testimony makes clear, is one that can be embedded in place. In Francois's account understandings of local conditions are illuminated, transformed, by being positioned in relation to 'world conditions'. This is not an internationalism where place becomes, as is so often threatened, irrelevant or immaterial. Indeed the place where Francois spoke was itself a site of contestation. The NWCSA used 'the Greens' on Piccadilly Street for their small public meetings because Captain Cipriani, the upper-class labour leader who was mayor of Port of Spain, had prevented them from using the larger Woodford Square (Reddock, 1988: 22).

Francois's mobilization of this political skill has implications for ways of thinking about the formation of internationalism. Frequently, internationalism has been seen as the domain of abstracted universals; positioned as of more import than 'mere' local issues. The analysis offered by Elma Francois challenges this separation. It suggests the necessity of local and world conditions being thought together. Francois was one of a number of Caribbean activists, including Claudia Jones and Christina Lewis, who connected anti-imperialism and feminism, linking 'labor, black and women's rights' (Davies, 2008: 67). Reddock notes that 'from its very inception the NWCSA set out to attract women members' (Reddock, 1988: 17-18). Through the activity of the NWCSA, Francois and others found ways of acting on this analysis, intervening in both local and international issues.

Seeing internationalism as shaped through place-based politics can usefully broaden the scope of agency of who/what counts in shaping internationalist practices and politics. Dominant accounts of 'international relations' have frequently been grounded in the world-views of elites and policymakers. Gayle Plummer contends, in her study of African Americans and US foreign policy, that international relations scholars from the United States have frequently conflated their 'own authorial voices with those of official Washington'. This actively marginalizes 'non-govermental actors, especially those representing constituencies often deemed peripheral in the domestic milieu'. This exclusion is not accidental. It is 'the imposed product of a particular, integral outlook' (Plummer, 1996: 5; Sharp, 2011).

Accounts of the histories of left internationalisms can similarly be written in rather top-down ways. Vijay Prashad's fine book *The Darker Nations* on the emergence of a politicized conception of the Third World is significant here (2007). Prashad traces the 'internationalist nationalism' formed through anti-colonial struggles (Prashad, 2007: 12). This opens up an important challenge to understandings of global politics by asserting the agency and presence of 'Third World nations' as an independent political force. The importance of this account for reworking understandings of the geopolitics of the Cold War is indispensable (see Chapters 5 and 6). Prashad's account, however, focuses primarily on the activity and perspectives of left elites and leaderships, retaining an account of anti-colonial and left politics which privileges dominant voices and perspectives.

Prashad's book opens with an account of the League Against Imperialism's (LAI) inaugural conference, which took place in Brussels in February 1927, when representatives of 'anti-imperialist organisations from across the planet gathered in the city' (Prashad, 2007: 18). Prashad engages with the ambiguities of the LAI's politics, but doesn't discuss in any depth the rather elite character of the LAI. The League was rather aloof from popular struggles and movements. The conference of the League's executive held in 1929, for example, was dedicated to developing its links to trade-union constituencies.[2] This emphasizes its lack of connections with popular movements. The LAI also depended on diverse forms of labour beyond that of the delegates to the conference whom Prashad discusses. Politicized maritime workers, for example, were integral to the circulation, distribution and smuggling of its literature between diverse sites (see Chapter 3). Engaging with their labour necessitates a distribution of political agency beyond the left political elites that are the focus of Prashad's account.

Here the aim is not to develop an equally problematic construction of all-knowing subalterns with a holistic sense of international affairs and events. Rather, it is to engage with the diverse and situtated practices through which marginalized groups and political activists have constructed solidarities and challenged unequal relations. This involves recovering the ways in which subaltern political activists have constructed solidarities through negotiating translocal flows of ideas, politics and materials. This challenges dominant understandings of the relations between place and internationalist politics.

Places, as Doreen Massey has persistently argued, are not isolated or bounded. Rather, they are the product of diverse connections and relations (Massey, 1991, 2005, 2007). This approach to place is indispensable for rethinking the political practices of internationalism. It allows internationalism to be located not in disembodied or abstracted relations, but in connections that are worked through different places and sites. Further, Massey argues such connections are always in the process of being made. Many such connections have been dominated by powerful forces, such as capital. Their unfinished and in-process character, however, suggests the ever-present possibility that they can be reshaped and reconfigured. This analysis also opens up a sense of how subaltern groups, rather than being isolated from such connections and flows, can be integral to their production. A good example here is the actions of Mary Manning and other workers in the Henry Street branch of the Dunnes Department Store in Dublin. In 1984, in the midst of a recession in Ireland, they launched a strike against the selling of South African goods by the store. Manning, a 21-year-old cashier, spearheaded this action. As the fine song 'Dunnes Stores' recounts, the strike was sparked by her refusal to sell two South African Outspan oranges, clearly labelled 'produce of the Cape'.[3] This precipitated a three-year strike in which eleven shop workers held out against Dunnes Stores, which continued to stock South African goods. The context of economic recession meant that this solidarity action involved risking their livelihoods.

This action usefully illustrates Plummer's argument that it is not only elite actors that can shape the terms of international connection. This was one of many internationalist actions shaped through resistance to apartheid, which took place in diverse places across the globe. It also had effects. It led to the Irish government's decision to 'ban the importing of South African fruit and vegetables until the apartheid regime was overthrown' (Reilly, 2009, n.pag.). This emphasizes how pressure from below can be fundamental in shaping such governmental responses.

Such internationalist action comes not out of disembodied relations, but out of contesting and attempting to change the terms of already existing connections – in this case the export of South African fruit and vegetables to Ireland. Agency is created here by intervening in strategic sites in supply chains to disrupt and transform relations between places. Subaltern forms of internationalism, then, can be generated through engaging with the unequal location that workers and other groups have in relations between places.

Spatial logics of internationalism

Solidarity and internationalism emerge here as distinctive and productive political skills. These are skills which bear on the assembling of relations between places, as Mary Manning's political interventions demonstrate. Indeed, the ways in which internationalisms envision and construct relations between places are not a fixed backdrop to internationalist politics. Rather, the way they are generated can shape the character of the political relations envisioned through internationalism in significant ways. I refer to the terms on which these practices are constructed as spatial logics of internationalism.

For a significant part of the twentieth century one of the most influential ways of articulating internationalism involved an unconditional loyalty to the Soviet Union (Anderson, 2002). This shaped forms of hierarchically organized international-ism. Here there was to be no or little challenge to the political centre of Moscow and the particular lines it dictated. There was also a marked tendency for internationalist politics to become subordinated to the geopolitical interests of the Soviet Union. This depended on and produced particular spatial logics of organizing. These logics were to become progressively chal-lenged through dissident Communist and New Left organizing. Anarchist politics also provided different modes of organizing throughout the twentieth century (Schmidt and van der Walt, 2009). Forms of organizing were generated across the political divisions of the Cold War, as discussed below, which sought to produce more democratic spatial logics of internationalism. Political networks and solidarities were established which sought to contest the hierarchical forms of internationalism centred on Soviet Communism. They forged different political possibilities through so doing.

Crucial to the spatial practices of left internationalisms have been attempts to forge more equal relations between places. This speaks to an important prefigurative aspect of solidarity and internationalism. Such political activity seeks to generate alternatives through their organizing practices. The counter-globalization struggles that have brought neoliberal globalization into contestation at the turn of the twenty-first century have made such logics central to their political practices. One of the key motifs of such organizing has been attempts to construct 'horizontal' modes of solidarity and internationalism.

Horizontality invokes practices of non-hierarchical forms of organizing, which have been seen as characterizing forms of organizing 'from below'. Thus Raúl Zibechi argues that 'elites and masses mobilize in completely different ways, especially in colonial societies. The former do so vertically, closely linked to the institutions. However, the mobilization of the poor, is on the contrary, horizontal and spontaneous' (Zibechi, 2010: 11). Zibechi's stark counterposition of vertical and horizontal modes of organizing is at an initial reading appealing. It ignores, however, the contested organizing practices through which sub-altern groups mobilize. This closes down a sense of the multiple and uneven spaces and relations through which solidarities are constituted.

As Hilary Wainwright has argued, the 'concept of "horizontal-ity" is probably too mechanical for the organic and messy products of social interaction across national boundaries'. She suggests that the concept 'doesn't take account of the hybridity of the "alter-globalisation" movement and the networks stimulated by the World Social Forum – trade unions alongside squatters, political parties in tense but also supportive relations with militant social movements' (Wainwright, 2013). This necessitates engaging with the often difficult and uneven geographies of power through which internationalist connections are constituted.

The most influential attempt to engage with the diverse con-stituencies shaped through these militant political movements has been Hardt and Negri's account of 'the multitude'. Hardt and Negri define the multitude as the 'living alternative that grows within Empire' and position it as composed 'of all the diverse figures of social production' (Hardt and Negri, 2004: iii, xv). For Hardt and Negri the activity of the multitude is constituted through the 'smooth spaces' of neoliberal globalization, rather than being worked through particular places. Their account of the multitude is an attempt to think about diverse forms of political agency. Thus Paolo Virno contends that the activity of the multitude is not reactive to capital. Rather, he suggests that innovations in capitalism such as the emergence of post-Fordist forms of production in Italy in the 1970s 'arose from the tumults of labour-power which was uneducated, uncertain, mobile' (Virno, 2004: 98).

Hardt and Negri's account is significant in its assertion of the dynamism of such movements and through their unsettling of traditional conceptions of class. They contend that the agency and activity of the multitude is 'increasingly autonomous'. They contend that the multitude 'must today be autonomous from either private/capitalist or public/state authority in order to produce and develop the common' (Hardt and Negri, 2009: 302). This usefully asserts the importance of the agency of labour rather than positioning it as secondary to capital. This inversion, however, is problematic. It positions capital and labour as rather fixed entities and either sees one as determining the other or vice versa. Tracing emergent political trajectories positions solidarities as formed through ongoing negotiation of different relations. This allows a sense of how internationalist politics can be constructed through bringing diverse geographies of power into contestation.

This focus on diverse political trajectories challenges binary oppositions of horizontality and verticality. Rather, internationalist political activity is usefully thought of as constituted through the ongoing negotiation of uneven geographies of power. Internationalist political activity, then, can be usefully thought of as the product of unevenly positioned trajectories. This destabilizes claims to 'horizontality'. Indeed, as Chapter 7 discusses, claims that movements are horizontal can actually lead to a silencing or marginalizing of actually existing inequalities. It is more useful to think of attempts to construct non-hierarchical organizing practices as part of ongoing attempts to negotiate and challenge uneven power relations. Viewing internationalisms as the products of different political trajectories can be alive to the productive character of such interactions.

C.L.R. James's account of his time in Nelson, Lancashire, in the 1930s demonstrates this generative character of political connection. James, an Afro-Trinidadian, led one of the extraordinary lives of the twentieth century. Born in Trinidad in 1901, he was a key intellectual and political figure in the pan-African independence movement and fashioned a creative, non-dogmatic Marxism. In the 1930s he was strongly influenced by Trotsky, but later broke with Trotskyism and any notion of a vanguardist politics. He went to Nelson, known as 'Little Moscow', as a cricket reporter following the Lancashire League, living with the cricketer Learie Constantine (James, 1994). In his 80th Birthday Lectures James recounted what he had learned from workers who were involved in the Independent Labour Party (ILP) in Nelson.

> When I told them that I had just come from the Caribbean, I said, 'We want independence, you know, and we hope the Labour Party will give it to us.' Those workers said: 'You make a mistake'. They said, 'Ramsay McDonald, Henderson, Felix Snowdon, Morrison, they never gave us anything and we put them there; why do you think they would give you any? You are making a mistake, you will find out.' That's what I learnt from them in 1932. (James, 1984a: 55)

James's account suggests the importance of exchanges and relations between James and members of the ILP in Nelson. James learned from those workers of their antipathy towards reformist labour leaders like Ramsay McDonald, Arthur Henderson and Herbert Morrison. These workers in turn were to engage with James's anti-colonial work. Harry and Elizabeth Spencer, for example, helped to fund James's trip to Paris to research *The Black Jacobins*, his history of the Haitian Revolution, and he was to dedicate the book to them (James, 1989: v–vii).

This locates internationalism as a dynamic process where different political experiences and contexts are linked. James's activity in Trinidadian struggles for independence, and the involvement of workers in Nelson in disputes such as the General Strike of 1926, become connected. This process of making connections has been usefully termed articulation. Stuart Hall defines articulation as 'the form of the connection that *can* make a unity of two different elements, under certain conditions. It is a linkage which is not necessary, determined, absolute and essential for all time' (Hall, 1996: 141, emphasis in original; see also Hall, 1980, 2003). Hall evokes the productive and situated character of connection. This suggests how political alliances are generative and how their terms can be reworked through political struggle.

James's account signals the importance of thinking such articulations geographically. The connections made between workers in North-Western England and James's anti-colonial politics are made between linking different contexts and experiences. These solidarities are shaped by a common antipathy to a 'British ruling class'. This antipathy is shaped on different terms. But such articulations can rework understandings and political trajectories and have impacts on place-based politics. As James makes clear, these encounters shaped his turn towards a radical anti-colonialism which sought to actively contest, rather than engage with, reformist labour politicians such as Arthur Henderson and Herbert Morrison.

This book, then, understands internationalism as produced through the articulation of different political trajectories. Such articulations are the product of the ongoing assembling of relations between and within different places involving a range of human and non-human actors (Davies, 2012; Hinchliffe, 2007; McFarlane, 2009). This becomes less about creating a 'unity' between two actors or phenomenon, as Hall suggests. It bears on connections and links made between diverse trajectories rather than the coming together of two particular elements. This allows a focus on the temporary, contested and partial practices of articulation shaped between different political trajectories and stresses the ways in which internationalism functions as an inventive process which can create and rework existing forms of political identification.

Conclusion:
recovering connections

In his book *Silencing the Past*, Michel-Rolph Trouillot challenges the silencing of the Haitian Revolution from 'Western History'. He draws attention to the related failure of racism, slavery and colonialism to become central to the writing of history in any Western country (Trouillot, 1995). Trouillot insists on the importance of the relations between the 'uneven power' of historical knowledges and inequalities in historical processes. He suggests the importance of interrogating 'the interplay between inequalities in the historical process and inequalities in the historical narrative' (Trouillot, 1995: 44-5). Nationalist framings of histories have a particular culpability for confining political struggles and movements within 'so many ethnically and econo-mistically defined cemetery plots' (Linebaugh, 1988: 216).

Trouillot does not explicitly interrogate the uneven geog-raphies through which inequalities in historical processes are formed. His argument, however, is extremely useful for scruti-nizing the relations between such uneven spatial relations and unequal histories. One of the key arguments of this book is that particular ways of connecting places that have been central to internationalist political cultures have frequently been silenced or marginalized. The silencing of such histories and geographies has arguably been related to the unequal prominence given to such connections by left movements in particular political presents. The insurgent geographies of connection shaped between anti-colonial activists in metropolitan and colonized contexts, for example, were often marginalized by different European left movements. There are long histories of gendered forms of exclu-sion in the social and political movements of the left.

This opens up a set of challenges that shape the methodological approach of the book. This approach is animated by an attempt to think about the formation of internationalist connection 'from below'. This involves attempting to recover, or, more precisely, to reassert and re-establish geographies of connection which have been silenced, erased, marginalized or downplayed. To do this involves challenging and circumventing the logics of uneven historical production that have shaped histories and geographies of the left. This is inevitably a partial, situated and limited endeavour. It is impossible to develop a full reconstruction of such connections or articulations. It is also inevitable that this account, like others, foregrounds some connections rather than others. The method adopted here, however, attempts to engage with sources and political movements in ways which assert and establish the vibrancy and agency of forms of internationalism from below. Central to this project is an engagement with forms of political activism in both the past and present that have articulated subaltern cosmopolitanisms. This has the following methodological implications.

First, it is necessary to decentre the importance given to left elites and leadership figures within accounts of solidarity and internationalism. This can be a particularly useful contribution of subaltern approaches to internationalist political activity. Wendy Wolford has usefully advocated a 'radical de-centring of leaderships' and 'a probing of those who leave movements, as well as those central to them' (Wolford, 2010: 10-11). Dispersing agency from elite left actors is not just about broadening who is included in accounts of left politics. It can also reconfigure what left political cultures were about. It can alter the political stories and trajectories that are given prominence in accounts of political activity in both the past and the present.

Second, a key methodological challenge is offered by engaging with who/whatever is involved in the labour of connection. Following the labour of assembling and making connections is central here. This can position the construction of subaltern agency within the formation of translocal processes. This is not about implying or fetishizing an unfettered mobility (Pratt and Yeoh, 2003). Rather, it is about engaging with the diverse ways in which subaltern political agency can be formed through contesting the terms on which relations are generated between and within places.

Third, this approach involves positioning sources such as texts, political songs and activist testimonies as part of, not separate from, the conduct of political activity. Rather than seeing such sources as frozen snapshots of solidarities, this situates them as part of the active makings of internationalist political activity (Featherstone, 2009; Ogborn, 2002). Paul Gilroy's vivid account of amassing vinyl records which shaped the 'non-national, cultural and political formations' of 'transnational black movements' is apposite here (Gilroy, 2000: 274). He notes that,

> For a spell, plastic discs stuck with colored paper – 'records' – furnished unlikely and unanticipated vectors for a restless, traveling sensibility. They became part of counter-national culture-making, and their history extends arguments about the role of communicative technologies in augmenting and mediating forms of social and political solidarity beyond the imagined communities achieved via the almost magical agencies of print and cartography. (Gilroy, 2000: 272)

Gilroy evokes the importance of these discs of plastic to the shaping of translocal political connections and imaginaries, powerfully conveying the hold of these transient objects. He notes how he 'probably should have paused at the point at which the printed and illustrated cardboard in which the music was clothed became almost as interesting to me as the sounds inscribed on the ridged surface of the plastic inside its seductive covers' (Gilroy, 2000: 274).

Gilroy emphasises their dynamic role in shaping linkages and affective connections. These recordings are not dry emotion-free artefacts to be analysed and dissected, but are part of the passionate articulations of relations and connections. This approach to sources is, of course, particularly applicable to cultural artefacts such as political song, but is also significant for sources such as letters and newspaper articles and ethnographic engagements with political activity (Davies, 2009). Here this approach is applied to a diverse range of texts, artefacts and instances of political activity such as activist testimonies, pamphlets, the samizdat publications that were important in East-West peace movement connections and material that has circulated electronically.

Fourth, this has implications for how internationalist connections and political cultures are positioned. One influential way in which subaltern politics has been theorized is as autonomous from elite political cultures. Here I reject this approach. My use of the term 'hidden' speaks to the ways in which such political cultures have been silenced and marginalized. Methodologically, however, it makes little sense to treat subaltern political cultures as autonomous (Guha, 1982; Scott, 1992). It is through tracing their engagements with the socially mixed character of left politics and diverse, potentially conflictual political trajectories that agency and dynamic political strategies often emerge. This involves challenging the forms of silencing discussed by Trouillot. It is counterproductive, however, to situate such forms of political activity as outside of uneven and unequal relations. It is through engaging with how such uneven and unequal relations are negotiated and contested that marginalized forms of political agency can be asserted. This is a necessary condition for foregrounding the inventive and transformative political relations constructed through solidarities.

PART II

Colonial and anti-colonial internationalisms

CHAPTER 3

'Labour with a white skin will never emancipate itself while labour with a black skin is in bondage': maritime labour and the uses of solidarity

Arnold Ward, writing in the *Negro Worker* in February 1935, commented that 'events in England as a whole are quiet and for the Negroes the economic situation grows worse everyday.' He observed that

> The one industry where Negroes used to find work occasionally was shipping, but now a great campaign has been started by the National Union of Seamen to oust all Negroes and coloured seamen from working on British ships. At the same time all those Negroes are members of the union as it is impossible to get a job at all without being a member.
> We of the Negro Welfare Association would draw the attention of all workers to the words of Karl Marx written 50 years ago.
> LABOUR WITH A WHITE SKIN WILL NEVER EMANCIPATE ITSELF WHILE LABOUR WITH A BLACK SKIN IS IN BONDAGE.

(Ward, 1935, emphasis in original)

The Negro Welfare Association (NWA), a Communist-led organization affiliated to the League Against Imperialism, was established in London in 1931 (Adi, 1998: 62; Pennybacker, 2009: 28-32). Ward, the Barbadian organizer of the NWA, was one of a number of seamen's organizers from the Caribbean who

articulated connections between anti-colonialism and labour
organizing in 1930s' Britain.

According to a Colonial Office report on Communist activities
written in response to the labour rebellions in Trinidad in the
late 1930s, Ward had been born at Bridgetown, Barbados, in 1886
and had lived in Trinidad between 1903 and 1906.[1] He resided
in Germany from 1907 to November 1915, and like many British
'subjects' living there was interned during the First World War.
Ward was held at Ruhleben internment camp, 6 miles to the
west of Berlin, where he was likely to have been part of a group
of 'black sailors' who arrived from Hamburg in December 1914.
They were accommodated in a wooden barrack, number 13,
which was segregated from the rest of the camp (Stibbe, 2008:
59). He was sent to England in 1915 as medically unfit and by
1930 was, in Colonial Office terms, 'one of the principal negro
agitators in the UK'.

The political resonance that Marx's aphorism had for Ward
is unsurprising. As his contribution to the *Negro Worker* emphasizes, he was involved in organizing black seafarers who
faced harsh labour conditions. This labour was forged through
a double marginality. Black and Asian sailors faced exploitation from shipping lines and institutionalized prejudice from
white labour through the exclusionary organizing practices of
the National Union of Seamen (NUS)[2] (Hyslop, 2009a; Tabili,
1994). There was a strong racial division of labour in the British
merchant marine. Aaron Moselle told the Fifth Pan-African
Congress in Manchester in 1945 that 'as a rule coloured seamen
were given employment only on coal carrying ships, those with
clean cargoes carrying white seamen' (Padmore, 1947: 67).[3] A
'racially segmented shipboard labour system' ensured that black
and lascar[4] sailors frequently did dirtier and harder jobs below
deck, such as the work of firemen and greasers (Tabili, 1994: 43,
1996: 178; Hyslop, 2009a: 56).

While Marx's analysis of race in the USA had significant
resonance for Ward, it would appear to have had markedly less
resonance with leaders of 'white labour', who were its more

direct target. The NUS, as Ward emphasizes, forged exclusionary spaces of organizing shaped by a discourse of 'white labourism'. This linked workers' movements in different imperial contexts, including South Africa, Australia, New Zealand and Britain (Hyslop, 1999). This chapter explores the diverse and contested forms of solidarity constituted in relation to maritime labour. I contend that solidarity functioned in multifaceted ways and generated different geographies of maritime labour and organizing.

Maritime organizing, white labourism and the limits of solidarity

Jonathan Hyslop has argued that the pre-First World War period saw the formation of an 'imperial working class' which 'produced and disseminated a common ideology of White Labourism' (Hyslop, 1999: 399). Such white labourism had distinctive imperial geographies. It was generated through circulations of ideas, workers, movements and organizing practices between South Africa, Australia and Britain. These circulations were generative of political ideas and practices that transcended particular discrete national contexts. Indeed it makes little sense to think of these contexts in narrow national terms (Stoler, 2009).

Hyslop contends that 'white labourism' was produced not by a top-down process, but through the formation of whiteness 'from below' (Hyslop, 1999: 414). By this he means that whiteness was not a given attribute of these workers. Drawing on the work of US labour historians such as David Roediger and Noel Ignatiev, Hyslop argues that this association between labour and whiteness was actively constructed (see Ignatiev, 1996; Roediger, 1994). It was through particular organizing processes and the active exclusion of black and Asian workers from particular labour markets and trade unions that such a dominant association of whiteness and labour was generated and circulated. The circulation of white labourism was cemented by translocal union networks such as the Amalgmated Society of Engineers, which had branches in Britain, North America and across Australasia (Hyslop, 1999: 414-15). This alliance of workers and whiteness reached its nadir with the infamous slogan of the 1922 strikes on the South African Rand: 'Workers of the World Unite for a White South Africa' (see Hirson and Williams, 1995: 228-34).

Solidarity was one of the key political technologies that shaped these exclusionary forms of whiteness. The biggest demonstration of the British labour movement in the early twentieth century, for example, was on 1 March 1914 in Hyde Park. It was called in support of nine leaders (seven of them British) of the South African labour movement, who had been deported to Britain by the government of General Louis Botha and General Jan Smuts for their role in leading 'a white workers' general strike in the Johannesburg area in 1913 and a second attempted one in 1914' (Hyslop, 1999: 399). The march 'manifested the solidarity of British trade unionists and Socialists with the cause of white workers in South Africa' (Hyslop, 1999: 398). These were leaders of unions which 'demanded the exclusion of Black and Asian workers from skilled jobs' (Hyslop, 1999: 399).

What is significant here is the shared understanding of the relations between whiteness and translocal solidarities generated through the labour movement. These solidarities were central to the means through which associations between whiteness and labour were generated and intensified. They depended on the recognition by 'British workers' of the terms of white workers' mobilizations in South Africa. These are solidarities which, after Paul Gilroy, as discussed in Chapter 1, it is appropriate to term 'unanimistic'. They demonstrate that a shared terrain of white labourism was produced around exclusionary logics. Hyslop argues that in 'all the numerous expressions of solidarity that welled up for the South African trade unionists, it is almost impossible to find any British labour concern for the plight of black workers in South Africa, or over the fact that British migrant workers and British unions were helping to enforce the racial segregation of labour there' (Hyslop, 2004: 253-4).

A bastion of white labourism in the early to mid-twentieth century was the National Sailors' and Firemen's Union (NSFU), from 1926 known as the National Union of Seamen. Havelock Wilson, its founder and leader between 1887 and his death in 1929, was an ardent imperialist who argued that no one had done more than 'the British seamen' 'to discover and establish the British Empire, and to develop it' (cited by Tabili, 1994: 81). Under Wilson's leadership the NUS forged a strongly racist agenda, colluding, for example, with government repression of black, Chinese and lascar sailors through the Coloured Alien Seamen Order of 1925 (see O'Connell, 1933; Tabili, 1994). NUS activists like 'Jimmie' Henson lobbied actively, both in and outside the NUS, for state and union policies to bar black seamen from the British labour market (Tabili, 1994: 82). Henson's conduct was contested by black sailors' organizers such as the Barbadian Chris Braithwaite, also known as Chris Jones.[5] Officials from the NSFU were involved in fomenting riots against black and Asian sailors in Cardiff in 1911 and 1919 and in Glasgow, Liverpool, the East End of London and South Shields in 1919 (Evans, 1980; Hirson and Vivian, 1992: 37-42; Jenkinson, 2008a; Tabili, 1994). These riots were part of a 'globally enacted white supremacist attack on blackness' which involved 'international expansion of Jim Crow legislation' and the 'increased lynching of and white labor mob attacks on blacks' in the United States (Harris, 2009: 237). The NUS actively rebuked attempts to contest its racial politics. In 1934, for example, its Executive Committee refused to receive a deputation from the League Against Imperialism 'with reference to the position of coloured seamen'.[6]

The reproduction of exclusionary forms of whiteness was central to the internal organization of the NUS. This can be illustrated by the response of the Executive Committee to the actions of Mr Straker, recorded in NUS minutes as a 'coloured delegate' from Cardiff.[7] In early January 1922 an Elder Dempster boat had come in to port in Cardiff and several 'coloured men' reported that they had a promise of a job in that particular ship. NUS officials, including Jimmie Henson, had gone down to the ship to find out particulars as they understood that white men were to be carried as a result of the Liverpool officials having agreed this with the company. They were 'informed that on no consideration would they carry coloured men'.[8] In response Straker, acting 'on his own responsibility', had called and addressed a meeting of 'coloured seamen' on Saturday 7 January on what he called a grievance, this being that 'the coloured men were not getting a fair shout'. The General Committee of the NUS noted that Mr Straker 'had not consulted the secretary of the Cardiff branch [Mr Jarman] on the matter but called the meeting himself'.

Straker was called to explain himself before the National Executive Committee. He argued that

> the meeting was not called by the officials but by the men and he contended under the rules the men had a right to call a meeting. He stated that he considered Mr Jarman, the secretary, was not doing his duty in staying in the office instead of coming out and helping to fight the opposition. He had asked Mr Jarman to call a meeting but he would not call it. He did not consider that the coloured men had received fair treatment in Cardiff. Some of them had been recently promised a job in an Elder Dempster boat but at the last moment they were not given the job. They started to call the union down, and he invited them to have a talk with him in the union office.

The response of key NUS officials was to bully Straker. 'Captain' Edward Tupper[9] commented 'that Mr Straker knew what Mr Henson had done in trying to get the coloured men everything it was possible. Mr Straker was well aware that there are certain sections of the men who would go for very little wages.' Wilson remarked that 'to listen to the conversation so far it would be imagined there was never a coloured man signed on in the Bristol Channel. He knew that was not the case, and that the coloured men are getting as good a share of the shipping as anybody else.' Wilson had earlier remarked to a deputation led by Harry O'Connell that 'there is not an opportunity the Union did not grab to try and do something for the coloured men to see that they get a fair chance.'[10] The dispute was resolved by Wilson asking Mr Straker if he would be prepared in future to carry out the instructions of Mr Jarman as secretary of the Cardiff Branch. Mr Straker stated he would carry out his instructions but he would not recognize him as a gentleman. Wilson asked Mr Straker to reconsider his statement and to remember that after he had had his growl at a man, 'the Britisher' was willing to forget the incident and carry on. He therefore appealed to the British instinct in Mr Straker, who responded to the appeal, shaking hands heartily with Mr Jarman.

This encounter is indicative of an important set of cross-cutting dynamics between race, class and gender that shaped seafarers' organizing. There is the collusion between some NUS officials and the operation of the colour bar by companies such as Elder Dempster (see also Sherwood, 1997; Frost, 1999). There is the lack of support given to opposition to the colour bar, marked by the foot-dragging of Jarman over organizing a meeting. There is the dismissal by Tupper and Wilson of the grievances of sailors of colour. Finally, in the resolution of the dispute there is a fascinating mobilization of the terms 'gentleman' and 'Britisher'. Straker, whilst happy to resolve the dispute with Jarman at least temporarily, is unwilling to accord Jarman the status of 'gentleman'. This implies that organizing was bound up with particular notions of masculinity, respectability and honour, which Straker insists were transgressed through Jarman's conduct. Wilson's mobilization of the term 'Britisher' is also crucial here.

Wilson positions Straker as a colonial subject who has 'a British instinct' but is not accorded the full status of a Britisher. While he is told by Wilson that this is how Britishers resolve difference, he is not addressed as automatically knowing this. As a result Straker is signalled as having only a subordinate relation to Britishness. This reproduced dominant associations of whiteness and Britishness. In *Banjo* Claude McKay uses the term 'Britisher' to signal a particular imperial articulation of Britishness (McKay, 2000: 127). One of the key issues of contention in the dispute between Straker and Jarman was about the character of the NUS. Straker accused Jarman of being a

desk-bound official aloof from sailor's grievances. These struggles over the character of the union and between the 'rank
and file' of the union and its leadership became dramatically
mobilized three years later.

On 3 July 1925 Havelock Wilson moved voluntarily at the
National Maritime Board for 'a reduction of the already miserable
wages of the seamen'.[11] He noted that 'Last year you were good
enough to give us an advance of £1 per month ... We will give up
that £1 at once without any argument. I hope Mr Chairman and
your gentlemen will recognize that in doing that we are doing
a manly thing.' This offer for a voluntary wage cut on behalf
of the union took place in the context of the hugely increased
profits made by the key shipping lines during the First World
War (Hardy, 1927; Hirson and Vivian, 1992). Wilson, who did not
consult rank-and-file members or seek their agreement through
a ballot, made it clear this was a direct attempt to neutralize
the role seamen might play in concerted working-class action.
He attacked the presence of militants 'sailing on the lines', who
'are a positive danger to the union'. He warned shipowners that
they 'should pay attention' to the threat they posed. 'If you have
an upheaval [with] railwaymen and dockers joining miners you
would have this gang of men, "the danger men", throwing in their
lot against you.' George Hardy, a seamen's organizer with the
Communist-affiliated National Minority Movement, described
this move as 'not only' exposing 'the seamen and their wives and
babies to further hunger and want by giving away their £1', but
akin to throwing 'open the doors of the homes of every worker
in the land to allow black hunger, starvation and death to enter'
(Hardy, 1927: 6).

The response of sailors was a major unofficial strike with an
impressive geographical reach. The strike began in the Port of
London around 17 August. On Sunday the 16th, 2,500 'seamen,
firemen and supporters' had marched through Poplar in the East
End of London behind a banner proclaiming 'Seamen and firemen
are fighting for bread for the kiddies' (Hirson and Vivian 1992:
28–9). In Newcastle seamen refused to sign articles at the lower

rate. For Hardy, a member of the London strike committee, the 'seamen's gallant unofficial strike in Australia, South Africa and Britain showed how deeply the seamen felt the great betrayal' (Hardy, 1927: 6). The strike of British seamen in Australian ports began almost simultaneously, suggesting the mariners' deft skill in executing coordinated international action. The sailors' actions garnered significant solidarity among trade unionists in the ports where the British sailors struck. This was particularly significant in Australia, where 2,500 British seamen were jailed during the strike.

On Monday 17 August 1925 a deputation from the crew of the British Steamer SS *Inkum* approached A.C. Woodfort, secretary of the South Australian branch of the Federated Seamen's Union (FSU) in Adelaide, seeking backing in 'their dispute with the captain of their ship and assistance if they took strike action' (Hirson and Vivian, 1992: 42). At a meeting in Adelaide in support of the sailors H. McKee, who was later elected chair of the strike support committee, congratulated 'the overseas Seamen'

> on their action as it was clearly shown that they were waking up to their position as wage slaves. It was the grandest action taken by them ever since the inauguration of the National Sailors' and Firemen's Union of Great Britain to overthrow the present bludging officials off their backs to obtain freedom. [Furthermore] it was their duty to not only recognize the Union, but to organize for the One Big Union of the Seamen of the World. When that day comes, we will see the dawn of a new era. (cited by Hirson and Vivian, 1992: 44)

McKee's speech demonstrates how the dissatisfaction of the 'British sailors' with their union officials was intensified through these solidarities. It emphasizes the potential of such disputes. The strike is seen as a precursor to the formation of 'One Big Union of the Seamen of the World'. This rhetoric demonstrates the influence of the syndicalist approach to militant unionism associated with the Industrial Workers of the World (IWW), or Wobblies as they were more popularly known (see Bird et al.,

1987; Cole, 2007a). The Wobblies refused to be confined or split along national or craft lines and developed a formidable reputation for organizing migrant and other unskilled workers in the USA. George Hardy had been an influential IWW organizer in the USA (Hardy, 1956).

It is clear through the disputes, though, that this articulation of the One Big Union of the Seamen of the World was shaped through particular exclusionary geographies of labour. In the United States, the Wobblies mobilized an inclusionary notion of the One Big Union in opposition to the frequently segregation-ist practices of the US labour movement (Roediger, 1999). In Australia the IWW challenged the 'White Australia' policy of the Labour Party, championing 'free immigration and the rights of Asians and aboriginal workers', and was the only Australian maritime union to organize non-European Seamen (Schmidt and van der Walt, 2009: 308; Goodall, 2008: 46). Through the conduct of the unofficial strike, however, solidarities were constituted along the routes and grain of white labourism. Hyslop argues the strikes served to reinforce 'the racialization of the politics of British seaborne trade unionism' (Hyslop, 2009a: 63). This white labourism was not just a background to the dispute, but was actively generated and reproduced through it. It isolated Australian unionists and the Left from 'the political concerns of colonised peoples in the region' (Goodall, 2008: 46). Further, it actively shaped, for example, who was being seen as being able to provide solidarity.

This can be illustrated through a note on the dispute in Sylvia Pankhurst's papers. She directly contrasts the Australian sea-men's union, the FSU, with the NFSU under Havelock Wilson's leadership. She asserts that the 'Australian seamen's union comes with the best possible Trade Union reputation'.[12] Pankhurst was a radical suffragette whose East London Federation of Suffragettes was a 'radical, militant, working-class feminist organisation' (Winslow, 1996: 41). Her disputes with Lenin prompted his pam-phlet 'Left Wing Communism, an Infantile Disorder'. Claude McKay described her as 'always jabbing her hat pin into the hides of the smug and slack labor leaders' (McKay, 1985: 77). To contrast the NUS and FSU unambiguously, however, was to overlook the FSU's role as a key advocate of the White Australia policy and its rigid enforcement of the colour bar. Participants in the strike did not contest the relations between the White Australia policy and the FSU. Several ships with 'all-coloured crews and even with mixed crews, defied the call to join the strike' (Hirson and Vivian, 1992: 43). The local unions framed their conflict in terms of their suspicions that the prime minister, S.M. Bruce, was conspiring with British shipping interest to 'reintroduce Asian labour into the Australian industry' (Hyslop, 1999: 402; see also Goodall, 2008).

In Durban the strike intersected with campaigns against las-cars. The response of a Cape Indian Defence Committee meeting organized to defend lascars during the strike underlines the exclusionary forms of whiteness generated through the dispute. Lascars were warned to 'stay away as this was purely a white man's dispute'. The unambiguous colonial positioning of both the sailors and the ship owners was also noted through 'their capacities as voters when on shore, were parties to the repressive legislation passed under the British Crown against their Indian fellow-citizens' (cited by Hirson and Vivian, 1992: 49). This seeded its own counter-forms of transnational mobilization. Worried that employment of lascars as strike-breakers would inflame tensions, Amod Bahayat, president of the Natal Indian Congress, cabled 'prominent persons' in India imploring them to 'keep Indians out of this strike so preserve Indian honour' (Hirson and Vivian, 1992: 49-50). The general secretary of the Indian Seamen's Union, asked officials of the All India TUC to stop any recruiting for South Africa (49-50). This suggests that transnational forms of organizing were generated through attempts to contest, or at the very least circumvent, white labourism (see also below).

Pankhurst's engagement with the dispute was not limited to a critique of the NSFU. She was also involved in attempts to organize women in seafaring communities. Women were active in the dispute in various ways. In Liverpool, for example, women participated in the daily processions of seamen. A procession of strikers with 'red banners and drums' was 'augmented by 100 women bag makers who had taken the day off to show their sympathy with the strikers'. Women were involved in the assault of 'four firemen seen leaving the White Star liner, the *Adriatic*' and shouted 'A scab lives there' when passing certain houses (Hirson and Vivian, 1992: 84). The marchers sang the jingoistic 'Boys of the Bulldog Breed'. Pankhurst attempted to organize women formally in seafaring communities as part of a breakaway union from the NUS.

Pankhurst drafted an appeal to 'Seamen's Wives' to become a part of the women's branch of the Federated Seamen's Union of Great Britain and Ireland. Her appeal implored that 'If you want to get better conditions for your man on board ship and for yourself and children at home you must help to organise the seamen and seamen's wives to stand up for themselves.'[13] Her papers also contain draft membership forms for the branch. The appeal and draft membership forms display a rather patronizing tone, which suggests that unequal class relations were reproduced through these forms of organizing. They hail 'seamen's wives' as not really understanding the conditions of labour of men in seafaring communities or capable of being politically active. Working-class women, such as Edna Braithwaite, were central to shaping multi-ethnic communities and resisting the impacts of the Coloured Alien Seamen's Order (Høgsbjerg, 2011: 40; see also Tabili, 2011, 152–72).

Pankhurst's appeal, however, suggests an important challenge to the all-male constitution of solidarity and trade-union organizing. Her plan sought to open up different gendered spaces of organizing in what was traditionally a male-bound industry (see Creighton and Norling, 1996; Burton, 1999). It is unclear whether Pankhurst's plan for women's branches of the breakaway union was realized. Nonetheless this attempt to construct alternative gendered relations through maritime organizing was an important attempt to break with male-centred forms of trade unionism and solidarity.

While the 1925 dispute was formatted and constituted through discourses and geographies of white labourism, some activists involved in the dispute were committed to a more multi-ethnic conception of sailor's organizing. Hirson and Vivian note that lascars were invited by the unofficial strike committee in London to speak on platforms at meetings, and they contend that in Cardiff the strike committee had no racial barriers (Hirson and Vivian, 1992: 42). In New Zealand the strike committee included a black sailor. Some of the organizers involved in the dispute, such as George Hardy, had a commitment to multi-ethnic labour organizing. This emphasizes that white labourism, while hegemonic within organizing of the British merchant marine, was not the only way of articulating sailors' grievances.

'A fighting international of marine labour'[14]

Writing in a pamphlet published by the International Seamen and Harbour Workers (ISH) George Hardy offered the following analysis of the relations between the NUS and ship owners. He argued that:

> the NUS officials agree with the ship owners to collectively do everything possible to employ the different ratings at whatever wages they can force upon coloured or colonial seamen. What is actually happening is all who dare to fight against inequality, socially or economically prevailing now in British ships and originating in pre-war days are met by the united front attack of the NUS officials and the shipowners backed by the police as at South Shields, Cardiff, Liverpool, etc. (Hardy, 1931: 10-11)

Hardy's analysis contests the interlocking relations of the shipping owners, local state and the National Union of Seamen in the exploitation of 'coloured or colonial seamen'. This emphasises the formidable institutional power behind white labourism. He argues that struggles for equality on board 'British' ships were being met by a 'united front attack' of the NUS and the shipping owners backed up by the local police.

This was clearly an inauspicious context for the formation of multi-ethnic solidarities aboard ship and for challenges to white labourism. That Hardy's pamphlet was written for the ISH signals the contested character of maritime labour politics. The ISH was part of the Red International of Labour Unions (RILU), the Communist-led international of militant unions. The RILU was grounded in the militant 'class against class' approach to labour organizing which defined the Comintern's 'Third Period'. This approach labelled reformist unions and social-democratic parties as 'social fascist' (Padmore, 1931). The ISH sought to organize a 'radical' maritime international defined against both national unions like the NFSU and the International Transport Workers Federation (ITWF), which they lambasted, partly motivated by sectarianism, as being too moderate. The ITWF was also contested by Indonesian anti-colonial activists for its refusal to attempt 'the realisation of the principle of equal wages for equal work for our countrymen on board ship' (Perhimpoenan Indonesia, 1931: 136). In 1928, however, an inquiry by the seamen's section of the ITWF into 'the working conditions of all Asian seamen on European ships' had 'come out strongly in favour of equality of wages and treatment' (Visram, 2002: 245).

The ISH sought to challenge the forms of racialized inequality that structured maritime labour and to develop multi-ethnic spaces of organizing. The ISH's conference in Hamburg in 1932 was addressed by both George Padmore and Garan Kouyaté. Padmore was a Trinidadian activist who organized the International Trade Union Committee of Negro Workers sponsored by the Communist International (Comintern) and was the founding editor of its paper, the *Negro Worker*. Padmore was later to break with the Comintern over its subordination of anti-colonial work to the geopolitical interests of the USSR. He became a key figure in pan-African politics, collaborating with C.L.R. James (see Baptiste and Lewis, 2009; Padmore, 1956, Schwarz, 2003). Kouyaté, from the French Sudan, led the Paris-based anti-colonial group 'Ligue de Défense de la Race Nègre', editing its paper *Le Cri des Nègres* (Edwards, 2003: 244; see also Derrick,

2008: 221-6; Pennybacker, 2009: 80-81). Harry O'Connell also attended the conference representing the Cardiff Seamen's Minority Movement.[15]

The publication of the pamphlet by the RILU locates Hardy within networks of Communist-led transnational labour organizing. Hardy himself was the product of a multi-continental radical trajectory (Hardy, 1956). Born in Yorkshire, he worked as an agricultural labourer before emigrating to Canada in 1906. He joined the IWW after meeting a Swedish lumberjack in British Colombia, whom he describes as the first socialist he ever met. In the early years of the twentieth century the IWW became an important force in US and Canadian labour politics, developing a remarkable reputation for organizing dispossessed itinerant workers, who were excluded from established labour unions. Hardy was to become a significant figure in the leadership of the Wobblies in the USA. He was one of a 112 IWW members tried in Chicago in 1918, receiving a sentence of a year and a day's imprisonment. He left the Wobblies, siding with the Communists in the acrimonious disputes over whether to affiliate to the Communist International that followed the Russian Revolution. According to his autobiography he was attracted by the discipline and leadership offered by Communism (Hardy, 1956: 123-48; see also Kornbluh, 1964: 352).

Hardy's involvement with the Wobblies signals an important exposure to political trajectories which were antagonistic to white labourism. The Wobblies were inventive and produced forms of multi-ethnic organizing in opposition to the exclusionary official labour movement in the USA. W.E.B. Du Bois, a noted critic of the segregationist policies of unions such as the American Federation of Labor, wrote in 1919 that 'We respect the Industrial Workers of the World as one of the social and political movements in modern times that draws no color line' (Du Bois cited by Bird et al., 1987: 139).[16] The IWW's actually existing experiments with multi-ethnic organizing, however, were situated, limited and partial. Their most successful engagement with interracial unionism was through Local 8 of the IWW Maritime Transport

Workers Union (MTW) on the Philadelphia docks (Bird et al., 1987; McGirr, 1995; Cole, 2007b). Here approximately 'half of the peak membership of four thousand was black, with the remainder composed mainly of Poles, Lithuanians, and Latin Americans from various nations' (Cole, 2007a: 1). Ben Fletcher, the most important African American leader to emerge within the ranks of the IWW, was one of the key organizers of the local.

Central to the success of Local 8's maritime organizing was an innovative deployment of and commitment to multi-ethnic solidarity. The local adopted innovative forms of organization. The local chairmanship was 'rotated monthly between blacks and non-blacks' (Bird et al., 1987: 177-8). The testimony of James Fair, a black Southerner, who moved to Philadelphia and joined the IWW to get work, signals the importance of solidarity to the conduct of Local 8. He argued that,

> As far as blacks were concerned, things were rough. To my knowing the IWW was the only union, at that time, accepting black workers freely. They advocated just one thing – solidarity. Ben Fletcher would tell us we had to live together and work together. His pet words were: 'All for one and one for all.' Solidarity was the main thing. That sank in with a lot of us. (Fair, 1987: 184).

Fair here emphasizes Fletcher's insistence on solidarity as bearing on living and working together. One of the key achievements of Local 8 was to translate these solidarities to the workplace. It did not make much sense to have an 'integrated' union if labour practices were segregated.

Prior to the organizing of Local 8, work practices on the Philadelphia docks were segregated, a policy which continued to shape labour organizing on East Coast docks until well into the twentieth century (Davis, 2002). African-American longshoreman Abe Moses contended that foremen, who were all white, 'encouraged segregated work gangs to compete with each other in unloading ships, simultaneously increasing company profits and fomenting animosity among the workers' (Cole, 2007b: 14). In contrast Local 8 'imposed integrated gangs on a waterfront that had been segregated, a system that had been supported by both employers and workers' (Cole, 2007b: 173). This was in marked contrast to the racial politics of the American Federation of Labor, which placed the responsibility for 'race-mixing on the employer' (Roediger, 1999: 142). Peter Cole argues that breaking down such segregation in the workplace was central to the longevity and success of the local (Cole, 2007b). This was particularly remarkable given the segregation of the local residential spaces in Philadelphia. W.E.B. Du Bois's study *The Philadelphia Negro*, published in 1899, demonstrated that 'prejudice against the Negro' shaped the spatial relations of the city, keeping 'him and his children out of decent employment, from certain public conveniences and amusements, from hiring houses in many sections, and in general, from being recognized as a man' (Du Bois, 1996: 322).

Local 8 was configured in relation to translocal solidarities as well as through powerful solidarities within the workplace. This reflected the importance of internationalist syndicalist networks. James Larkin, the influential Irish syndicalist who led the Dublin lockout in 1913, spoke to the local in February 1915 during its dispute with the Charles M. Taylor Company. Larkin pledged the 'support of the Irish Transport Workers if necessary'. He promised 'to present the situation in this port of dockers across the sea with a request that they hold themselves in readiness and refuse to discharge any grain or cargo from ships loaded by scab labour' (Fletcher in Cole, 2007b: 66-7).[17] This was particularly significant given the historic tensions between the Irish and African Americans in Philadelphia (Ignatiev, 1996).

During the local's six-week strike in 1920, Argentinean dockers and sailors, who had strong traditions of anarchism and syndicalism, offered their support (Cole, 2007b; de Laforcade, 2010). This reflected the Atlantic connections maintained and generated by the Spanish anarchists Manuel Rey and Genaro Pazos, who organized Spanish sailors, shipping out of Philadelphia, 'into a foreign-language branch of local 8' (Cole, 2007b: 66, 91, 104-105, 120). A letter to the local from G. Malvido, secretary of the Organizing Committee of the Buenos Aires MTW, looked forward to 'overthrowing our enemy the vampires of capitalism' (cited by Cole, 2007b: 105).

This positions Local 8 in relation to the translocal syndicalist political cultures which shaped the maritime organizing of the IWW. Ben Bright, a Welsh seafarer involved with the Wobblies, recalled being 'active in the MTW (Maritime Transport Workers)' and 'helping to organize the seamen against the crimps in Buenos Aires' with a 'fella called Tom Barker' (Bright, 1980: 22). Barker had been deported to Chile from Australia for his leading role in the opposition of the IWW to World War I. He landed in Valparaiso in 1919, where the IWW (Trabajadores Industriales del Mundo) 'controlled the whole waterfront' (Barker, 1965: 34). There was also a strong IWW presence on the waterfront in Santiago (DeShazo, 1983: 181-2). Deported by the Chilean government to Argentina, he was involved in organizing MTW branches in Buenos Aires and Rosario with Julius Muhlberg, an Estonian comrade he'd known in Sydney, before he was again deported by the Argentinean authorities (DeShazo, 1983: 318 n2). Barker spoke of the militancy of the union culture in Buenos Aires at the time, arguing that they were 'largely syndicalist and they were always spoiling for a fight' (Barker, 1964: 34).

Such translocal organizing circuits shaped the conduct of Local 8. During the 1920 dispute Local 8 gained support from radical sailors from the syndicalist Shop Stewards' Movement in England. John Gannon, the delegate of the British freighter *Haverford*, entered Local 8's hall 'followed by thirty other members of the crew' and 'proudly declared that in the name of international solidarity, they would not handle scab cargo' (Cole, 2007b: 115). Jack Tanner, a leader of the Shop Stewards' Movement, also addressed Local 8. Tanner had represented the movement at the second congress of the Third International in 1920, urging that 'there was no need to establish a Communist Party in Britain since the Shop Stewards' movement already organised the politically conscious vanguard of the proletariat' (Hinton, 1973: 324). George Hardy enlisted him into a plan for 'a British campaign of solidarity with the sore-pressed American workers' during the repression of the IWW in the late 1910s (Hardy, 1956: 126). Such solidarities were reciprocated. During the 1920 miners' strike in Britain Local 8 'worked with other Wobblies to prevent coal from being shipped to Great Britain' (Cole, 2007b: 143). The Shop Stewards' Movement developed formalized ties with the IWW. In May 1920, at the 12th IWW Convention arrangements were made for the interchange of membership cards between the two organizations (Thompson and Murfin, 1955: 135).

The practices of solidarity adopted by Local 8 shaped particular place-based organizing and political cultures. The spaces through which maritime labour were organized had effects. Hardy argued for a fighting seamen's union where branches were organized on ships themselves (Hardy, 1927). This challenged the social and physical distance of union organization from sailors' experiences and grievances clearly articulated by Straker and in the 1925 dispute. Hardy's analysis also contested white labourism. As David Roediger's engagements with the relations between race, class and gender in the IWW caution, however, it is necessary to attend carefully to the ways in which 'progressive' unions configured such relations. Roediger notes that 'even the rare labour paper that did support full equality for African Americans ... necessarily cast its appeals in terms of the interests of its largely white readership and in instrumentalist terms' (Roediger, 1994: 140-41). Roediger also problematizes the importance of appeals to shared masculinities in cementing such multi-ethnic solidarities (Roediger, 1994: 127-8).

Hardy's approach is not dissimilar to such white-centred logics of multi-ethnic solidarity. Hardy's pamphlet for the National Minority Movement articulates a critique of the conditions of 'Lascar, Chinaman, Arab or West African Negro' in the following terms:

> No fellow seamen! Notwithstanding the desire of shipowners to reduce wages to the level of the lowest paid seamen, it is not foreign competition that is wholly responsible for the loss in wages,

overtime and conditions. Neither is the Lascar, Chinaman, Arab or West African Negro to blame. They have been prevented from organising by force and anti-trade union laws. In the pursuit of the 'Lion's share' the 'patriotic' British shipowners have made them even greater slaves than those of the 'bulldog breed'. With the aid of Havelock Wilson they would have you blame Eastern and African seamen for the rotten conditions, etc. The policy of the shipowners is 'divide and conquer'. Ours is to unite internationally, East and West, for as long as your arguments are directed at Eastern and African seamen the Western shipowners will grab that 'lion's share'. Remember: an injury to coloured seamen is a blow struck to British seamen. (Hardy, 1927: 26)

Hardy here seeks to configure solidarities between multi-ethnic sailors and to challenge the white labourism of Havelock Wilson. At the same time, however, it simultaneously reproduces a strong division between British seamen and seafarers of colour. There is a clear logic of an instrumentalist solidarity here. The primary reason for practising solidarities with 'Lascar, Chinaman, Arab or West African Negro' is clearly to defend 'British sailors'. Note Hardy's injunction that 'an injury to coloured seamen is a blow struck to British seamen'. Further, it is clear that by the way he invokes the term 'fellow seamen', Hardy positions 'Lascars, Chinaman, Arab or West African Negro' outside this imagined political community of 'fellow seamen'.

The ISH, however, was part of attempts to construct multi-ethnic spaces of organizing and solidarity. At its conference in Hamburg in 1932, George Padmore emphasized 'that it is the task of the ISH and its affiliated sections to give the Negro workers active help in breaking through the barriers set up by imperialist, terror and reformist treachery to strengthen their already existing organizations and to create new ones in the colonies' (Padmore, 1932: 25). Padmore, through the *Negro Worker* and other black internationalist networks, was integral to a further set of challenges to white labourism and one which more centrally challenged its 'imperial' logic. These were the forms of black internationalism constructed by West Indian and West African seamen's organisers.

Black internationalism and maritime labour

In 1938 Chris Braithwaite, the then London-based Barbadian seamen's organizer and pan-African radical, announced in the journal *International African Opinion* that he would be writing a column 'Seamen's Notes'. The journal was published by the International African Service Bureau closely associated with C.L.R. James and George Padmore. Braithwaite, who wrote under his alias Chris Jones, noted that the column would 'discuss the problems and grievances affecting coloured seamen and invite the co-operation of all those who are interested in airing the disabilities of those who earn their living on the sea' (Jones, 1938). He argued that

> It is up to us, therefore, as coloured seamen, to enlighten our fellow colonial workers during our travels that we underdogs have nothing to gain by fighting in the interests of the imperialist robbers. This is a task which we must not shirk.[18]

For Braithwaite the mobility of 'coloured seamen' made it possible for them to play a key strategic role in enlightening 'fellow colonial workers'. He articulates a powerful argument that this form of marginal, exploitative labour afforded opportunities for constructing translocal solidarities. The 'narrowness of colonial economies gave relatively small numbers of workers in transportation and commercial nodes and in mines the possibility of disrupting an export-import economy' (Cooper, 2005: 205).

Braithwaite had come to Britain from Barbados via New York and worked as a sailor and docker. He was involved in protracted struggles against racist NUS officials and was a leader of the Colonial Seamen's Association, which opposed the institutional racism of the NUS.[19] He was also involved in the leadership of the International Association of Friends of Abyssinia, had links with figures in the Independent Labour Party, such as Reginald Reynolds, and was a friend of Nancy Cunard (Høgsbjerg, 2011; Padmore, 1956: 145; Reynolds, 1956: 118–20; Derrick, 2008: 283–4; Joannou, 2004). Ethel Mannin drew on her friendship with Braithwaite in her satirical novel about the left, *Comrade O Comrade*. She noted that 'the socialist and anti-imperialist struggle lost a valiant fighter by his death' (Mannin, 1945: 5).

Such subaltern articulations of black internationalism were significant. They were marginalized within some forms of pan-Africanism centred on the 'talented tenth' and through the relative elitism of left internationalist organizations like the League Against Imperialism. Politicized maritime workers were central to the production and distribution networks of papers like the *International African Opinion* and the *Negro Worker*. The labour of seafarers from West Africa and the Caribbean in the 1920s and 1930s was central to ensuring the distribution of radical newspapers and correspondence through translocal anti-colonial networks. This subaltern agency in constituting black internationalist organizing is illustrated by the conduct of political activists such as Ronald Sawyer and Jim Headley.

Sawyer was a seafarer from Sierra Leone who was active in anti-colonial politics in London in the 1930s. Like Arnold Ward he had been interned during the First World War. He was held at Wiesbaden, before being released in 1915 on medical grounds. In 1917 he is alleged to have been in touch with a 'member of the Liberty League of Negro Americans, organised by West Indian and American Negroes'. According to a Colonial Office report on 'Communism and the West Indian Labour Disturbances' written in 1938, Sawyer had taken 'literature issued by the League Against Imperialism and the International Trade Union Committee of Negro Workers' from London to Jamaica 'while working as a fireman on one of the Elder and Fyffe's ships'.[20] At a meeting held in London under the auspices of the Negro Welfare Association in December 1936 Reginald Bridgeman, the head of the British section of the League Against Imperialism, had re-emphasized 'the importance of colonial seamen as channels of communication between communists in this country and native colonial people'.[21]

Jim Headley, a Trinidadian, was 'based for some years in the United States where he had been a ship's cook' (Reddock, 1988:

13). He had been active in the radical National Maritime Union and the Young Communist League and had come into contact with George Padmore. Headley corresponded with the *Negro Worker*, the paper of the International Trade Union Committee of Negro Workers sponsored by the Communist International (Comintern).[22] Central to the *Negro Worker* was a configuring of anti-colonial struggles with labour grievances. Padmore described the *Negro Worker* as 'a much needed popular journal, taking up the broad international problems of Negro workers' (cited by Edwards, 2003: 257). This was a 'notable departure not just in its unprecedented internationalism but also in its aspirations as a "popular" publication driven by the "fullest co-operation" of black workers around the world' (Edwards, 2003: 257-8). C.L.R. James contended that 'tens of thousands of black workers in various parts of the world received their first political education from the *Negro Worker*' (James cited by Edwards, 2003: 259; see also James, 1984b: 251-63).

In a letter to the paper in 1932 Headley argued that it was only

> by unity of purpose and solidarity can the workers go forward to smash the barriers and free themselves from a life of degradation and starvation. Not only by Indian Solidarity, nor by Chinese or African Solidarity, but by the world-wide solidarity of all Colonial workers and oppressed workers of all nations marching forward as a united whole against Capitalism and for the establishment of workers and peasants rule. (Headley, 1932: 19)

Headley's articulation of solidarity here owes much to the variant of anti-colonial Marxism which was the hallmark of the *Negro Worker*. These connections with the ITUCNW were to have a major influence on the direction of the Negro Welfare Cultural and Social Association (NWCSA) (Reddock, 1988: 13). According to police files, in 1932 Headley was a committee member of the Negro Welfare Association in London, along with Ronald Sawyer, Chris Braithwaite and Nancy Cunard.[23]

Padmore depended on a network of contacts like Headley to distribute the *Negro Worker* (Edwards, 2003). This involved

circumventing the legislation, policing and repression that colonial powers employed to stop the circulation of radical newspapers
and correspondence. In 1932 Governor Hollis, described by the
Negro Worker as 'Trinidad's Mussolini', prohibited the 'importa-
tion and circulation of the *Negro Worker*' into Trinidad under
the Seditious Publications Law. This was designed to 'discourage
and suppress the organisation of Trade Unions in the British West
Indies'.[24] The banning of the paper from Trinidad was contested
in the UK Parliament by R.C. Wallhead, the Independent Labour
Party MP for Merthyr Tydfil, and James Maxton the former chair
of the League Against Imperialism.[25]

Such repression exerted considerable pressure on the spaces
of anti-colonial organizing. In 1933 the Nigerian activist Ladipo
Solanke, who had emerged as a key spokesman of the growing
numbers of West African students in Britain, was warned to
discontinue his association with the *Negro Worker* after a copy
he had sent to the editor of the Nigerian *Daily Telegraph* was
discovered in a raid by the Nigerian police (Adi, 1998: 24, 50 n72).
Many delegates directly from 'the colonies and semi-colonies
– South and Central America, Africa, India – were prevented
from attending the conference of the International Seamen and
Harbour Workers in 1932. They were 'either detained on their
way or unable to obtain passports' (Padmore, 1932: 23). There
was similar targeting of delegates travelling to the International
Conference of Negro Workers organized by Padmore in Hamburg
in 1930 (Worrell, 2009: 27).

The *Negro Worker* and *International African Opinion* articulated black internationalism in different ways. Padmore
collaborated with C.L.R. James on *International African
Opinion* after breaking with the Comintern over its subordination of anti-colonial organizing to the geopolitical interests
of the USSR (see Hall and James, 1996: 23-4). Padmore was
viciously denounced in the *Negro Worker* for so doing. The
intersections between anti-colonialism and labour grievances
that were articulated through the *Negro Worker*, and through
Chris Braithwaite's columns in *International African Opinion*,

drew on long-standing connections between anti-colonial politics and the labour grievances of 'colonial workers'.

There were dynamic relations between resistance to white supremacist violence in port cities in Britain and anti-colonial struggles in the Caribbean. On 17 July 1919, sailors arrived back home in Trinidad who had been subject to the white supremacist terror in the Cardiff riots of June that year. Lynch mobs composed primarily of demobilized white servicemen, including Australians, had attacked black, Somali and Malay sailors, killing a young Arab man, Mahommed Abdullah (Evans, 1980; Fryer, 1984: 303-9; Jenkinson, 2008a).[26] There were also attacks on communities and seafarers of colour in Glasgow, Liverpool, the East End of London, Newport, Barry and South Shields (Jenkinson, 2008b). In 1932 the *Negro Worker* was to describe these events as 'pogroms' (Bressey, 2011: 128).

In Trinidad returning sailors made public the 'atrocities which had been visited upon the black population in Britain' (Martin, 1973: 314). The militant paper the *Argos* carried a report of 'how a white mob in Cardiff had attacked a black man's funeral, cut off the corpse's head, and used it as a football' (318). They swiftly set up the 'Returned Soldiers and Sailors Councils', 'held public meetings and propagandized their grievances to the people'. The grievances of sailors intersected with those of soldiers returning from the British West India Regiment. This included soldiers who had mutinied in Taranto, Italy, in December 1918 in protest at their degrading and humiliating treatment at the hands of racist white officers (James, 1998: 62-3; Martin, 1973: 318).

During 'peace celebrations' in July, 'several British sailors from the H.M.S. *Dartmouth* "were wantonly and severely assaulted, as were several other European members of the community" and "very lewd and disparaging remarks were freely made about the white race and about their women folk," and the Deputy Inspector General and an Inspector Carr of The Constabulary were stoned' (Martin, 1973: 318). This unrest fed into a major dock strike four months later that almost 'brought the Empire to its knees' when 'the governor persuaded shipping agents to grant the strikers' demand for a 25 per cent wage increase' (Williams, 2002: 171; Fryer, 1984: 312). On the night of 18 July there was a disturbance in Kingston which 'included some ex-British West Indies Regiment men and sailors' in a 'determined attack' on 'some sailors of HMS *Constance* resulting in about five or six of them being wounded by razor cuts and stabs'. The acting governor of Jamaica noted that this 'was subsequently stated to be due to the treatment which had been received by coloured sailors at Cardiff and Liverpool'.[27]

These connections between resistance to the riots in Cardiff and Liverpool and anti-colonial sentiment and labour organizing in Trinidad and Jamaica assert the dynamic relations shaped through subaltern political activity. The ITUCNW sought to discipline and lead such popular struggles and movements. The *Negro Worker* counselled the Kikuyu Central Association in Kenya to avoid 'isolated and spontaneous action', to conduct its 'organizational activity on a wider regional scale', to 'promote peasant revolts against colonial taxation' and to form trade union groups which excluded tribal chiefs and other government agents (Wilson, 1974: 217). Considerable pressures were certainly exerted by such vanguardist and hierarchical conceptions of internationalism. This does not mean, however, that seafarers' organizers like Harry O'Connell were mere 'Comintern dupes' or lacked agency in shaping the terms on which black internationalist connections were constituted.

This is underlined by the account given by Jan Valtin, an alias of Richard Krebs, of his encounters with O'Connell during Valtin's time as an enforcer for the Comintern. He was sent to discipline the Communist Party of Great Britain (CPGB) and to deal with the failures of its attempts at organizing maritime workers. He commented in a letter to Theodor Lender that the 'English movement, measured by the standards obtaining in Hamburg, is a dung heap'.[28] Valtin had apparently received instructions to 'break' George Hardy and his fellow maritime organizer Fred Thompson 'with every means at my command' (Valtin, 2004: 291). He found O'Connell harder to deal with.

Valtin describes O'Connell, in aggressively racialized terms, as 'an energetic individual, very dark of skin, but with the nose of an Arab horseman and the chin of a pugilist' (Valtin, 2004: 292).[29] He recounts that his mission

> ended in bleak defeat. I journeyed to Cardiff. O'Connell was willing to accept the money I offered to support his organization, but he stubbornly insisted that the West Indies were one thing, and Moscow another. Bluntly he told me: 'I represent my negro brothers; you want me to represent Russia among the West Indians. I cannot be a servant to two masters. My conscience rules that out.' (Valtin, 2004: 292-3)

It is difficult to square Valtin's assessment with St Clair Drake's detailed ethnographic descriptions of O'Connell. St Clair Drake depicts O'Connell as a diehard Communist who sat down for meals with his Welsh wife under a picture of Stalin.[30] He stood for the council in Cardiff's Adamstown ward for the Communist Party in 1950 (Sherwood, 1991). Valtin's account underlines the aggressive political masculinities through which such internationalist networks were policed and disciplined. There is evidence that Valtin exerted pressure to ensure that O'Connell's role in the Cardiff branch of the ISH was limited to 'colonial work'.[31] Valtin's account also suggests, however grudgingly, that activists like O'Connell were able to use the political resources afforded by the *Negro Worker* to carve out political space and could stand up to Comintern enforcers like Valtin while still remaining loyal to the party. Robin Kelley has argued in similar terms that African-American communists in the 1930s used the CPUSA to develop political presence, space and dignity despite Communist Party paternalism towards black communists (Kelley, 1990: 92-116).

Other seafarers were less patient with party discipline. Bill McCormick, who like O'Connell was from British Guiana, was expelled from the Communist Party in 1945. He had gone to Cardiff in the early 1920s after spending some time in Portuguese East Africa where he was jailed for 'stirring up the natives'.[32] Charged with reading Trotskyite literature, he told the purge committee that he didn't know he was joining a 'bloody Catholic Church with an index'. The unofficial geopolitical knowledges gleaned through maritime work could disrupt as well as intensify political commitments (see Davies, forthcoming; Hyslop, 2009b). Ted Bryce, an official of the Coloured International Athletic Club in Cardiff, was a vociferous critic of the USSR and would not associate with left-wingers. He had observed conditions in Russia on several trips to the Arctic ports and 'was particularly critical of Archangel [Arkhangelsk] using the term "slave labour" to refer to the situation there'.[33] He told St Clair Drake, 'I've told these darkies here that the Reds are no good, but they won't listen. They ought to all go and see. That would teach them.'

The formation of black internationalist networks consolidated resistance to white labourism in port cities like Cardiff. This militancy became particularly acute around the mid-1930s in the context noted by Arnold Ward at the start of the chapter when the NUS had colluded with the local state and shipping lines to force 'coloured workers out of the labour market'. This institutional racism and white labourism was opposed by the formation of Colonial Defence Association in Cardiff. The multi-ethnic solidarities shaped through this resistance were signalled in the *Negro Worker*:

> As soon as the 'proving of nationality clause' began to be worked a committee of coloured seamen was formed in Cardiff to fight against it. On the Committee sat spokesmen of Malayan, Arab, Somali, West-Indian and African workers. From the first meeting of the committee a delegate was sent to see the officials of the NUS. Mr Reed secretary of NUS told the deputation that they [the NUS] did not assist in the making of the new regulations and that they would help the colonial workers in their fight against injustice. But now the facts are starting to come out – that those very people Messr's Spence and Keep, sat on a body called the Trade Union Parliamentary Committee for Shipping and Waterside Industries. (Cardiff Coloured Seamen's Committee, 1935: 10–11)

This account emphasizes the forms of subaltern cosmopolitan-ism that shaped organizing in Cardiff in the 1930s. O'Connell's article suggests how organizing against the racism of the NUS brought together 'Malayan, Arab, Somali, West-Indian and African workers'. These alliances were mobilized against the NUS. Reed, despite his claims to help the 'colonial workers', had publicly called for the repatriation of what he termed the 'thousands of coloured men [that] had been "imported" to Cardiff'.[34]

Similar alliances were forged in London. In November 1936 the first annual conference of the Colonial Seamen's Association (CSA) was attended by fifty-one workers – drawn from 'Negroes, Arabs, Somalis, Malays and Chinese'. It was addressed by Chris Braithwaite, the chair of the CSA, and the secretary, the lascar leader Surat Alley, who had links to the Textile Workers' Union in Bombay and the All-India Seamen's Federation (Visram, 2002: 219). The conference passed a motion denouncing 'the pernicious colour discrimination which is deliberately fostered by the employers and the Government in order to divide and rule the seamen of all countries in the interests of the ship owners'.[35]

This suggests how such place-based solidarities can be productive of forms of 'progressive localism' (Featherstone et al., 2012). These solidarities shaped local politics in Cardiff in important ways. The networks forged through these struggles in the 1930s were integral to the defeat of attempts to introduce Jim Crow housing into the city in 1945 (Adi and Sherwood, 1995: 160). Officials in the local state were 'inspired' by segregationist policies elsewhere. In 1929 the chief constable of Cardiff had advocated legislation like the 'recently passed 1929 Immorality Act in South Africa' (Derrick, 2008: 404). The report of the First All-Wales Congress of the Communist Party in 1945 notes that 'Jim Nurse (colonial seaman) of Cardiff' spoke at the Congress on 'the need for unity with coloured workers' (Welsh Committee of the Communist Party, 1945: 17).[36] The Congress received fraternal greetings from the United Committee of Coloured and Colonial People's Organisation and the Colonial Defence Association (27). Tensions over how black internationalism was to be configured, however, also impacted on place-based politics. The United

Committee of Coloured and Colonial People's Organisation in Cardiff split over the decision to send delegates to the 1945 pan-African Congress in Manchester. O'Connell told St Clair Drake that 'I smashed it up when I saw that we were being led to affiliate with Trotskyite Pan-Africans.'[37]

Conclusion

This chapter has engaged with the multifarious uses of solidarity constructed through maritime labour politics in the interwar period. Competing and potentially antagonistic solidarities were constructed through these forms of labour organizing. At stake in these struggles were alternative ways of envisioning geographies of maritime labour. Imperial articulations of white labourism were central to the forms of solidarity envisioned by maritime unions such as the National Union of Seamen. Further, the solidarities shaped through unofficial action like the international strike of 1925 were similarly forged through the translocal contours and circuits of white labourism.

White labourism was not the only, or an uncontested, way of articulating maritime organizing. Translocal solidarities were constructed through multi-ethnic spaces and organizing. Important intersections of anti-colonial politics and maritime labour were forged by political activists like Harry O'Connell and Chris Braithwaite. Their actions played a key role in challenging the imperial articulations of labour organizing and linked anti-colonial politics in labour struggles in important ways. These solidarities were integral to contestation of white labourism and contributed to the decolonizing of labour movements in diverse contexts. The forms of agency they constructed are easily marginalized through terracentric and nation-centred histories. Their struggles over the limited, exclusionary solidarities forged through white labourism, however, shaped different ways of envisioning a politics of labour.

CHAPTER 4

'Your liberty and ours':
black internationalism and anti-fascism

In 1937 Salaria Kee, an African American nurse from Akron, Ohio, travelled to Spain with the Second American Medical Unit. The unit was attached to the Abraham Lincoln Brigade, the brigade of around 3,000 men and women who joined the struggle against the fascist coup that attempted to depose the Spanish Republican Government on 17 July 1936. Led by General Franco, the coup was authored by a 'brutalized and interventionist officer elite' who had fought and won the colonial war in Spanish Morocco (Balfour, 2002: x). For the next three years Franco fought, with the support of troops and munitions from Hitler and Mussolini, to defeat the diverse forces that rallied to the support of the Republic.

In Spain, Kee 'met and nursed Spanish, English and Czechs, and Irish and Scotch, and poor whites from Georgia, and Ethiopians from Djibouti and Negroes from Haiti and Africa and America' (Negro Committee to Aid Spain, 1938: 124). Kee served with the Second American Medical Unit, only after being turned down by the Red Cross, which told her 'that they didn't have any place for colored nurses'.[1] In New York she had worked in the Seaview Hospital, where together with other nurses who 'were not considered white' she had been made to work in tuberculosis wards, which white supervisors refused even to enter. There she became involved in struggles against white supremacist health officials. She recalled in 1980 that she had gone to Spain because she had read 'about nuns working here and working there, in these poor places and they had to take care of the patients, when they got sick, they taught them and they did'. She also notes that 'it was because I had received so much help and this was my greatest ambition, to be a nurse because I thought I could do so much more.'

Kee was part of what Robin Kelley has described as a significant 'Pan-African presence in the international brigades'. About ninety African-American volunteers joined the Abraham Lincoln Brigade to fight on the side of the Republicans in the Spanish Civil War (see Collum, 1992; Kelley, 1992; Robinson, 1983). This pan-African presence also included Nyabongo, a Ugandan, and Ahmed din Josef, an Ethiopian volunteer who as part of the Garibaldi Battalion of the International Column fought against Italian Fascist troops in Spain.[2] Prominent African-American left intellectuals, cultural figures and activists such as Paul and Eslanda Robeson, Louise Thompson and Langston Hughes visited Spain as part of the international solidarity with the Republic. This chapter explores the maps of grievance and articulations of internationalism configured through these solidarities.

Anti-fascist trajectories

Salaria Kee, like many other African Americans who travelled to Spain, first came to anti-fascism through her involvement in organizing against Mussolini's invasion of Ethiopia in 1935. She had been involved in 'gathering the first two tons of medical supplies and dressings sent from this country to Ethiopia' (Negro Committee to Aid Spain, 1938: 127). James Yates, originally from Brown Settlement in Mississippi, who volunteered with the Abraham Lincoln Brigade, was likewise involved in the organizing efforts around Ethiopia before deciding to go to Spain. In his autobiography *From Mississippi to Madrid* he recalls roaming Chicago 'collecting food and clothing to be sent to the victims of the bombs. In addition to passing out leaflets denouncing the war we gathered signatures and sent them to President Roosevelt, entreating him to stop Mussolini' (Yates, 1989: 87).

The actions of Kee and Yates were part of the major organizing efforts across the African diaspora that mobilized from the outset of the build-up of Italian troops on the borders of Ethiopia. Ethiopia had a particular symbolic resonance both because it was, along with Liberia, one of the two surviving independent states in Africa, and because a 'sacral belief in Ethiopia's importance was widespread in the black diaspora' (Plummer, 1996: 38). Italy had attempted to colonize Ethiopia in 1896, but had been defeated by poorly equipped Ethiopian forces (Caprotti, 2011: 386). The Second Italo-Ethiopian war was defined by a 'horrific campaign' which utilized mustard gas and machine guns against poorly armed troops and employed aerial bombardment of civilians (Atkinson, 2000: 94; Caprotti, 2011: 385). The invasion was an integral part of Mussolini's attempt to construct an Italian imperialist Fascist project that also included the colonization of Libya (Plummer, 1996: 40).

The invasion provoked significant pan-African organizing. This linked the struggles in Ethiopia to a broader anti-colonial imaginary and had a transnational impact. In Nigeria, for example, a mass meeting held at Glover Memorial Hall in Lagos on 20 September 1935 was attended by over 2,000 people. It was chaired by Eric Olawu Moore, the vice president of the Nigerian National Democratic Party; Peter J.C. Thomas, a businessman who had attended the 1921 Pan African Congress, was among the speakers (Derrick, 2008: 333). On 22 August in Paris 2,000 'Muslims, Black and Coloured' attended a big rally organized by the LDRN and ENA. The anti-colonial militants Tiemoko Garan Kouyaté, Paulette Nardal and Hedi Noira were among the speakers (341).

The response among the African diaspora in the USA was vociferous. In New York there were riots and street brawls between

International African Friends of Abyssinia
demonstration in Trafalgar Square, 1935

African Americans and Italian Americans, including violence
after the defeat of the boxer Primo Carnera by Joe Louis on 26
June 1935 (Harris, 1994: 98). The leading African-American
Communist James Ford noted that in the 'Harlem upsurge' of 19
March 1935 'the Negro people expressed their hatred of Italian
fascism and its plans for war against their Ethiopian brothers.
Italian liquor shops were smashed with cries of, "Down with
Mussolini!"' (Ford and Gannes, 1935: 3). There were boycotts
of Italian businesses in Harlem and elsewhere, which drew on
broader black resentment against Italian Americans (Plummer,
1996: 42).

In London, C.L.R. James co-founded the International African
Friends of Abyssinia (IAFA), acting as chairman. Its committee
had a strong pan-African make-up, with Peter Milliard (from
British Guiana) and T. Albert Maryshaw (from Grenada) vice
chairmen, Jomo Kenyatta (from Kenya) as secretary and Amy

Ashwood Garvey (from Jamaica) as treasurer, and with strong involvement from George Padmore (see Derrick, 2008: 334-7; James, 1974).³ The IAFA organized a major demonstration in Trafalgar Square in 1935. Speakers included Chris Braithwaite, Amy Ashwood Garvey, George Padmore and C.L.R. James. C.L.R. James made significant contributions to the political responses within the British left (and beyond), particularly in relation to the Independent Labour Party (ILP). ILP leader Fenner Brockway describes James as making a 'typically torrential speech' during ILP debates on Abyssinia (Brockway, 2010: 326). Brockway notes that the fact that James had appealed as 'a black worker for help for the black population of Abyssinia' was used to dismiss his case as nationalist rather than socialist (Brockway, 2010: 326). This emphasizes how left politics could be formatted/policed in ways which excluded or downgraded anti-colonial discourses.

James also contributed to *The Keys*, the publication of the politically moderate League of Coloured Peoples. His article 'Abyssinia and the Imperialists' asserted the importance of solidarities with Ethiopia for bolstering pan-African political feeling. James argued that

> Mussolini, the British Government and the French have shown the Negro only too plainly that he has got nothing to expect from them but exploitation, either naked or wrapped in bluff. In that important respect this conflict, though unfortunate for Abyssinians, has been of immense benefit to the race as a whole. (James, 1936: 40)

The terms of James's argument, here, emphasize how pan-African discourses could be rather dismissive of the experiences of Africans/Ethiopians themselves (see also Padmore, 1937; Schwarz, 2003). His phrasing belies an almost cavalier disregard for the 'unfortunate' Abyssinians subordinating their 'plight' to the broader aims of building a pan-African movement.

The IAFA shaped the terms of international debate around opposition to Mussolini and around pan-Africanism and anti-colonialism. Their attempt to form an 'International Brigade' to fight fascism created a 'political stir' (Høgsbjerg, 2006: 23;

James, 1974: 159). Padmore and James shaped an anti-colonial resistance which was doggedly sceptical of the USSR's claims to be at the forefront of anti-colonial politics. The integrity of Communist support for the Ethiopian was undermined by the failure of Max Litvinov, the Soviet Union's delegate to the League of Nations meeting of April 1935, to condemn Italian aggression (see Kelley, 1992: 18; Naison, 2005: 156). Padmore had by the mid-1930s broken with the Comintern over its attitude to colonialism. He argued in May 1935 that 'the Soviet Union would be quite willing to sacrifice Ethiopia to Italy if it served Soviet interests' (Asante, 1977: 44).

Figures like Padmore were part of black internationalist networks which linked the USA, West and Southern Africa, the Caribbean and cities like London and Paris (Edwards, 2003). Padmore had extensive contacts in West Africa such as Alfred John Ocansey, nationalist businessman, keen supporter of the Aborigines' Rights Protection Society, and proprietor of the *Gold Coast Spectator*, and the Nigerian Nnamdi Azikwe, editor of the *African Morning Post* (Asante, 1977; Derrick, 2008). Padmore noted in correspondence with Ocansey that the European powers were happy to '"direct Mussolini's aggression towards Africa" in the hope of maintaining the status quo in Europe as long as possible' (Asante, 1977: 51). Such geographies of connection shaped translocal solidarities and organizing circuits in important ways. In Trinidad, Elma Francois and other activists involved in the NWCSA became interested in the war in Ethiopia after receiving and reading copies of the *New Times and Ethiopian News* edited by Sylvia Pankhurst (Reddock, 1988: 18–19).

Pankhurst's campaigns developed a distinctive feminist socialist approach to anti-fascism. She sought to make public, for example, the forms of gendered violence deployed by Mussolini's troops. In a letter to the press in 1935 she argued:

> Though the terrible events which have taken place in Ethiopia since the fall of Addis Ababa have been veiled by Italian press censorship, sufficient information has come through to show that the aggressors

have acted with ruthless brutality. Particularly disgraceful have been the atrocities perpetuated against women. Women of all classes, even the highest, have been cast without mercy among the Italian soldiers to be raped and misused and many of them have died of their maltreatment.[4]

As with Pankhurst's campaigns around sailors' wives discussed in the preceding chapter, there is more than a hint of class-based prejudice here, with a use of the phrase 'even the highest'. Pankhurst's analysis, however, suggests a direct engagement with the gendered politics of fascism and colonialism, which were frequently marginalized by broader left discourses.

The mobilizations in Trinidad around the war in Ethiopia had significant effects. The NWCSA activist Dudley Mahon argued that the 'Abyssinian War awakened the consciousness of the Trinidad working class' (cited by Reddock, 1988: 18-19).[5] The NWCSA organized a mass meeting on 10 October 1935 in Port of Spain, where

> speakers denounced France for its lukewarm attitude and also renounced England for refusing to sell arms to Ethiopia. They called on all Negroes to boycott French and Italian goods and stevedores were asked to refuse to unload Italian ships. A demonstration marched from the meeting to the office of Seconi, the representative of Italy in Trinidad and Tobago, shouting 'Down with Mussolini!' The meeting unanimously passed two resolutions – the first condemned the 'shooting and bombing of thousands of defenceless men, women and children for the purpose of glorifying Italian fascist imperialism', while the second 'criticized the prohibition of meetings and marches as a direct attack upon the political rights of the working class by a government incompetent to solve the unemployment crisis'. (Reddock, 1988: 18-19)

The forms of organizing here recall the tactics used by Harry O'Connell in Cardiff in contesting Italian fascism, as discussed in Chapter 1. There is the targeting of the Italian consulate and attempts to disrupt Italian maritime trade, which resulted in dockers refusing to service Italian ships in Trinidad (Harris, 1994: 37). On 15 November 1935, for example, dockers in Port of

Spain refused to unload the Italian ship *Virgilo*.[6] This disruption of maritime trade was a key way in which internationalist solidarities around Ethiopia were enacted. It was also a means through which decidedly subaltern groups became involved in forging such solidarities.

Tim Hector, the Antiguan pan-Africanist, argued that C.L.R. James, through the International Friends of Ethiopia, was able to organize 'through waterfront workers and longshoremen around the world an international boycott of Italian goods'. Hector contended that it was effective because it was 'imposed by workers around the world, and not by States!' (Hector, 2002: n.pag.; see also Quest, 2009: 121-2). Hector's assessment perhaps overly stresses James's role. What is significant, though, is his emphasis on how such international action was constituted despite, rather than through, nation-states. Maritime workers' actions drew on their location in international trade networks. They created distinctive anti-fascist agency through seeking to prevent the flows of trade sustaining fascist practices and colonial regimes.

This emphasizes the argument made by Chris Braithwaite in his 'Seaman's Notes' column, noted in the previous chapter, that black seafarers could use their strategic positions in maritime networks to further anti-colonial politics. Maritime workers' articulations of anti-fascism had consequences. The prominent African-American communist Harry Haywood, who served as a political commissar in the Abraham Lincoln Brigade, notes in his autobiography that when 'Italian fascists invaded Ethiopia, National Maritime Union seamen refused to sail steel-laden ships to Italy' (Haywood, 1978: 501; see also Ford and Gannes, 1935: 30). In Cape Town, Garveyites such as 'Emile Wattlington, Zach Masopha and A.J. Maphike became particularly active in the Hands off Abyssinia campaign. The campaign raised funds for Abyssinian war refugees, refused to offload supplies for Italian ships and created a united front against fascism during the Italo-Abyssinian conflict, as well as leftist and trade unionist organizations in the 1930s and 1940s' (Vinson, 2006: 302). Dock workers also refused to handle Italian goods in Durban (Derrick, 2008). A meeting in Calcutta passed a resolution condemning the Italian imperialist threat and assuring the Abyssinian people that 'their fight for independence is the fight for all oppressed peoples against Imperialism'.[7]

In South West Africa, then a German colony, 'a hundred Liberian, Ovambo and Karro dockworkers ... refused to work on Italian ships' (*Baltimore Afro-American*, 5 October 1935, cited by Robinson, 1985: 62). Asante notes the expression of protest by association of market women in Ibadan and Lagos and of the Sailors' Union in Freetown (Asante, 1977: 129). At the port of North Shields, in north-eastern England, Sierra Leonean crew members of the SS *Holmea* 'protested against the Italian threat on Ethiopia in a resolution which the captain of the ship was made to sign before the ship could set out for Sierra Leone' (Asante, 1977: 130). The Californian Seamen's Union temporarily succeeded in delaying 'all West Coast ship departures when it believed outbound vessels carried strategic materials for Italy' (Plummer, 1996: 50). Longshoremen in San Francisco refused to load the Italian ship *Cellina* and 'adopted a resolution not to work any ship carrying material for the fascists to continue their war in Africa' (Morice, 1936: 25). In San Pedro longshoremen and seamen refused to load or man the SS *Oregon*, because they were suspicious that although it was bound for Singapore the 'aviation fuel it was carrying could be transhipped to the war zone' (Nelson, 1988: 171). These maritime workers shaped how anti-fascism and anti-colonialism moved and had important effects on the terms on which anti-fascist internationalism was articulated.

The effects of such boycotts against Fascist Italy were noted by Claude McKay in an article for the US socialist paper the *New Leader* in 1939. McKay participated in the boycott of Italian businesses across North Africa during the time he spent in Morocco in the 1930s. The boycott was a significant part of the political response to Italian Fascism across North Africa and to notorious incidents such as the bombing of the Senussi tribe in

Libya and the annexation of their fertile land by Italian farmers
(see Atkinson, 2000). McKay noted the detestation that 'North
Africans' felt towards Fascist Italy due to the 'ruthless measures
Italy employed in its conquest of Tripoli' (McKay, 1973b: 288).
He argues that 'the native boycott of Italian business which grew
out of this incident, a boycott in which I participated ... started
in Egypt and spread all through North Africa.'

> Italian farmers could not obtain native labor. Italian groceries and
> cafes depending on native patronage had to be liquidated. Perhaps
> it was the effect of that boycott more than anything which prompted
> Mussolini to pretend that he was a friend of Islam. (McKay, 1973b:
> 288)

McKay here suggests the impact of the boycott of Italian businesses and some of the dynamics through which it spread across
North Africa. McKay's intervention signals the importance of
black internationalist intellectuals in shaping understandings
of fascism and anti-fascism.

This engagement with the terms on which fascism has been
understood and contested is significant, but has rarely been
accorded the significance it deserves (Gilroy, 2000). For writers
and political activists like McKay, James and Padmore it was
impossible to understand fascism without relating it directly to
colonial practices and imaginaries.[8] Eric Hobsbawm has argued
that 'Italian fascism ... lacked at least two characteristics that
were likely to make it unpopular among intellectuals: racism
(until 1938) and hatred of modernism in the arts' (Hobsbawm,
2007: 129). This is to ignore the importance of colonialism to
Italian Fascism and to dismiss the connections between race,
Fascism and colonialism that were integral to the invasion of
Ethiopia in 1935. Hobsbawm's analysis thus ignores both the
invasion of Ethiopia in 1935 and the translocal anti-colonial
resistance it generated. Influential accounts of the politics of
fascism also adopt a territorially limited focus (Bauman, 1989).
Zygmunt Bauman's treatment of the relations between modernity and the Holocaust, for example, does 'not extend to the

genocidal activities of Theodor Leutwein and Lothar Von Trotha among the Herero people of German South West Africa' (Gilroy, 2000: 87).

The importance of an anti-colonial understanding of fascism for anti-fascist practices was made clear by George Padmore's contribution to a *Left Review* pamphlet 'Authors Take Sides on the Spanish War' published in 1938. This short commentary develops a sharp anti-colonial analysis of the Spanish Civil War. Padmore argues that

> The sympathy of Africans and other colonial peoples naturally goes out to the toiling masses of Spain in their heroic struggle against Fascist-barbarism, for they have not forgotten Abyssinia. And precisely because of this, it is so regrettable that democratic Spain, by failing to make an anti-imperialist gesture to the Moors, played into the hands of Franco. This should be a reminder to the European workers that: 'No people who oppress another people can themselves be free'. (Padmore, 1938: n.pag.)

Padmore's contribution foregrounds the contested geographies through which anti-fascism was constituted and articulated. He draws out the important continuities between anti-fascism in Ethiopia and Spain and relates the solidarity of Africans and colonial peoples for the cause of Spain to the Spanish, not forgetting 'Abyssinia'. His support for anti-fascism in Spain, however, is tempered by strong criticism of the Republic's failure to develop an anti-imperialist stance in relation to Morocco.[9] In *Africa and World Peace* Padmore commented that 'had the People's Front Government made a gesture to the Moors by pointing out to them that the new regime was the defender of their economic and social interests, then we feel certain that Franco would never have been able to have deceived these African tribesmen into supporting his cause' (Padmore, 1937: 266).

Spain's imperial connections with Morocco had been contested by independence struggles and by the Spanish left. In 1909 a general strike was called in Catalonia 'to protest at the flare

up in the colonial war in Morocco through the second Rif war
and especially at the sending of reservists' (Smith, 2002: 38).
Martial law was declared in Tarragona, Gerona and Barcelona
and 104 workers were killed across Catalonia; the events became
known as the *Semana Trágica* or Tragic Week (Smith, 2002:
38). Paul Trewhela argues that this was the 'one occasion' where
'the proletariat in Europe rebelled and shed its blood against
imperialism in Africa' (Trewhela, 1988: 50). This resistance
was shaped by strong anarchist hostility to imperialism, which
was also a major influence on anti-colonial political cultures
in Italy. The Italian invasion of Libya in 1911 was greeted with
demonstrations against the war and a partial general strike by
anarchists and syndicalists (Schmidt and van der Walt, 2009:
214). There was 'an explosion of verbal protest from every working class and many peasant centres and a ripple of direct action'
(Williams, 1975: 37).

Attempts to forge anti-colonial alliances in the early weeks
of the 'Spanish Revolution' were shaped by such anarchist
anti-imperialism. The anarcho-syndicalist CNT prepared with
'certain Moroccan groups' plans for 'an insurrection in Spanish
Morocco' (Schmidt and van der Walt, 2009: 319). These plans
were put on hold, however, as the anarchists and syndicalists
moved towards the Popular Front. In September 1936, Pierre
Besnard, the international secretary of the syndicalist International Workers' Association, 'advised the CNT to ensure
the success of the revolution by the internationalization of the
struggle through promoting rebellion against the pro-Franco
regime in Portugal and fomenting a Moroccan uprising' (319).

These alliances drew on already existing connections between
North African and European left movements. The Étoile Nord
Africain (ENA), Algeria's 'first mass-based leftist party', which
was founded by Algerian immigrants in Paris, was significant in
this regard (Thomas, 2005: 1040). Representatives from the ENA
had spoken at the conference of the League Against Imperialism
in Brussels in 1927. On 31 July 1936 a resolution organized by the
ENA in Paris declared that those present 'Send their fraternal

greetings to their Muslim brothers of Morocco, who are suffering under the boot of Fascism, and call on them to place themselves on the side of the Republicans of the Spanish Popular Front, against the rebel generals' (cited by Derrick, 2008: 363). There were other attempts to forge connections and alliances. Spanish and French Trotskyist activists argued for the necessity of links between revolution in Spain and North Africa (Derrick, 2008: 363; Trewhela, 1988: 50). An interview with Moroccan leaders by Nancy Cunard was published in the *Afro-American* (Padmore, 1937: 266 n1).

The Republican government, as Padmore implies, failed to develop an anti-colonial position. This facilitated the recruitment of Moroccan soldiers to fight as part of Franco's forces. The Republican government did not promise independence to Morocco or engage with the grievances of its inhabitants. An attempt to negotiate a deal with Moroccan nationalists after the outbreak of the Civil War was blocked by France (Balfour, 2002: 273). France, as the other colonial power in Morocco, was concerned about the destabilizing effects of ceding independence to Spanish Morocco. The French Popular Front avoided a significant engagement with anti-colonial politics in Morocco and 'liquidated its native sections' (McKay, 1973b: 289; see also Cohen, 1972).

Claude McKay expressed in withering terms the consequences of this failure. He argued that 'Spanish reaction first strengthened itself in Morocco by forcing the young Republic to betray the native workers in the colony before it began its offensive against the Spanish workers at home.' For McKay the 'lesson' was 'plain', as the title of his article indicates: 'Native Liberation Might Have Stopped Franco's Revolt' (McKay, 1973b: 289). These intellectual engagements through which anti-fascism and anti-colonialism were decisively linked were a significant contribution of black internationalist politics. These linkages and the translocal organizing around Ethiopia shaped the political imaginaries of African-American volunteers in the Abraham Lincoln Brigade in important ways.[10]

Black internationalist maps of
grievance of the Spanish Civil War

Albert Chisholm, from Spokane in Washington, noted that he
'signed up to go to Spain because in that era fascism was on
the march. Italy attacked the country of Ethiopia ... It was sort
of a primitive society, but nonetheless it was something that
black people throughout the world could look up to because it
was governed by a black administration' (Chisholm, 1992: 147).
His comments about Ethiopia's backwardness suggest some of
the uneven geographies through which diasporic connections
were forged and imagined. The movement of Italian troops from
Ethiopia to Spain underscored the connections between these
struggles. James Yates observed, in an interview with Cedric
Robinson, that 'when Ethiopia was invaded and Italy overran
it, those same troops left there and went to Spain. This was a
time and a chance for especially the Blacks to volunteer and
get back at the fascists that had invaded Ethiopia' (Robinson,
1985: 62).

For Yates the decision to join the Abraham Lincoln Brigades
to fight in Spain, however, was much more difficult to come to
than a decision to go to Ethiopia. He argues that:

> I had been more than ready to go to Ethiopia, but that was different.
> Ethiopia, a Black nation, was part of me. I was just beginning to
> learn about the reality of Spain and Europe, but I knew what was
> at stake. There the poor, the peasants, the workers and the unions,
> the socialists and the communists, together had won an election
> against the big landowners, the monarchy and the right wingers
> in the military. It was the kind of victory that would have brought
> Black people to the top levels of government if such an election had
> been won in the USA. A Black man would be Governor of Mississippi.
> (Yates, 1989: 112)

Yates's account gives a sense of both the difference and the
connectedness of the struggles in Spain and Ethiopia. This
shift in identification from Ethiopia to Spain signals an inventive engagement with anti-fascism. Central here is an ongoing

engagement with the shifting maps of grievance through which fascism was contested. Thus Yates connects the conflict in Spain both to struggles against racism in the USA and to anti-colonial politics in relation to Ethiopia. He also emphasizes the inspiration afforded by the political changes that had happened in Spain prior to the outbreak of the Civil War.

These maps of grievance generated productive solidarities between struggles in Spain, Ethiopia and the USA. The translation of black internationalist anti-fascism from Ethiopia to Spain was a significant political intervention. Some Black Nationalist leaders such as Marcus Garvey generated black diaspora politics which were constituted and formatted in part through Garvey's stress on racial homogeneity and purity and through anti-Semitic narratives (Garvey, 1990: 389; see also Gilroy, 2000; Holcomb, 2007; James, 1985; James, 1998). The solidarities constructed by African-American volunteers in relation to Spain challenged the racially purified articulations of solidarity associated with Garveyism.

The political context that volunteers went to in Spain was, as signalled by Yates, an inspiration to many. The Republican government and popular uprisings, especially in Catalonia, threatened powerful interests, which, coupled with the shaky foundations of Spanish democratic culture, bred fertile grounds for right-wing reaction. The left forces that rallied to the defence of the Republic, however, were divided and factionalized (Paniagua, 2007). There were at least four major strands of the left in Spain in the 1930s. The Socialists were linked to the major trade-union confederation, the UGT, and had an important presence in the Republican government. The weak Spanish Communist Party was massively bolstered by the international support of the Brigades/Comintern. The significant anarcho-syndicalist movement the CNT was based primarily in Aragon, Valencia, Andalusia and industrial Catalonia (Eley, 2002: 273). Finally, the POUM articulated a militant, independent and anti-Stalinist left politics. The POUM was to be repressed as 'fascist' 'in a disgraceful copy of the Soviet purges' by the Communist-led forces in the Civil War, despite the POUM joining the fight against Franco (Eley, 2002: 273; Orwell, 1938).

Black internationalists had different relations with the diverse political groupings on the left in Spain. C.L.R. James contributed a foreword to *Red Spanish Notebook* by Mary Low and Juan Breá in which he praised the 'revolutionary heroism' of the POUM (James, 1937: vi; Scott, 2004: 25). The majority of African-American volunteers, however, had strong Communist affiliations. This was in line with the leading role that the Comintern took in organizing the Brigades; this included the vetting of volunteers by Communist Party officials for their 'political reliability' (see Francis, 1984). The African-American brigadists were diverse and 'included Northerners and Southerners, the college-trained and semi-literate, unemployed workers and self-styled intellectuals'. Kelley argues that 'most were Party members or supporters who interpreted communism through the lenses of their own cultural world and the international movement of which they were a part' (Kelley, 1996: 124). Some volunteers, such as Mack Coad and Harry Haywood, had studied at the Lenin School in Moscow. Haywood had made important connections there with anti-colonial political figures such as M.N. Roy, from India, Tan Malaka of Indonesia, Ho Chi Minh of Vietnam and the Irish militants Sean Murray and James Larkin Jr (Haywood, 1978: 205; Perkins, 1990: 298).

Volunteers had diverse experiences of political organizing and struggle in the USA, which shaped their approach to the conflict in Spain. James Yates directly linked the rise of fascism in Europe to his own harsh experiences of racism and oppression in the USA.[11] He had grown up in Mississippi, fleeing to the North with a number of friends to escape the Klan. Angered and shocked by the existence of racism and oppression in Chicago, he became a union activist with the Pullman Porters until he was blacklisted during the Depression and moved on to New York. Yates contends that the geography of racism in the USA shaped the involvement of other African Americans in Spain. He recalls meeting Admiral Kilpatrick, a volunteer from Cleveland, while in Spain and asking him why there were so many African-American volunteers from Ohio. Kilpatrick 'began to explain by drawing a map of Ohio':

> 'The fight against slavery began early in Ohio, it was the major route for slaves en route to Canada. Despite the work of abolitionists like Harriet Tubman and Sojourner Truth, Ohio was one of the most racially bigoted states north of the Mason–Dixon line. Even today Blacks are segregated. Black unemployment and poverty are chronic.'
>
> Through learning these facts I came to understand why so many brave young Black men and women from Ohio went to Spain: Walter Cobb, Claude Pringle, Bernard Rucker, Edward Johnson, Leroy Collins, Salaria Kee, Abraham Lewis, Walter Dicks, Admiral Kilpatrick. (Yates, 1989: 127)

Yates directly relates the geography of participation in the Abraham Lincoln Brigade, here, to experiences, understanding and contestation of racism in the USA. It emphasizes that these forms of solidarity were constituted in relation to the political geographies of this oppression. Yates's invocation of the abolitionists Harriet Tubman and Sojourner Truth also positions the struggle in Spain in relation to histories of translocal black feminist organizing.

These geographies of oppression and white supremacy shaped how African-American volunteers made sense of the conflict in Spain. In Langston Hughes's autobiography he recounts how Ralph Thornton, an African-American volunteer from Pittsburgh, described a fascist sniper in Aragon, who 'turned out to be the vice-president of the local Falangists', the Spanish fascist movement, as 'a Spanish Klansmen' (Hughes, 1993: 357). Hughes recalls Thornton saying that he 'wished he'd shot him'. Vengeance and anger towards white supremacist organizations like the Ku Klux Klan shaped these translocal anti-fascist solidarities and volunteers' understandings of the dynamics of the Civil War in Spain. This challenges understandings of solidarities as only being forged through positive identification. It emphasizes how desire for vengeance and anger could be central to the construction of solidarities between different struggles and geographical contexts. This also underscores the violent constitution of anti-fascist maps of grievance through the conflict in Spain.

The anti-colonial maps of grievance constituted by some volunteers unsettles Robin Kelley's assertion that they joined the movement solely 'out of their concern for black people' (1996: 124). Admiral Kilpatrick had been involved with the Industrial Workers of the World before becoming a Communist.[12] He cites an anti-colonial position towards the USA as being central to his decision to fight in Spain. He recalls that 'the US was at that time carrying out its own type of diplomacy. There ain't no use anybody trying to kid themselves ... this country carried those types of diplomacies so damn far, until they actually made slaves out of the Latin American people, that went back to the early parts of the 1900s.' He argues that 'these types of actions' were 'uppermost in my mind when I went to Spain'.[13]

Oscar Hunter, a volunteer from Orange County, New Jersey, who was working in the stockyards of Chicago before he went to Spain, was politicized by experiencing the US South with the outlook of a Northerner. He recounts that his mother was 'mostly Indian' and his father, from South Carolina, was 'mostly French' (Collum, 1992: 78). On the death of his mother, when he was in the fourth grade at school, his brother raised him and 'took up with a woman who was from the south'. He makes his negotiations of the difference between the North and South of the USA clear: 'now you have to understand, I'm not a southern black or whatever I am, I'm a northerner and that's a thing I've lived with all my life. I went south but I was not southern. I had never seen Jim Crow until the war became more intense and they began to bring blacks up from the south.' Hunter attended the Hampton Institute in Virginia for five years, became politicized, leading a student strike and meeting Hampton faculty member Louise Thompson, who was later to become a prominent Harlem activist and reported from Spain.

Hunter's decision to become involved in the Spanish Civil War was shaped by the translocal circuits of opposition to fascist violence and of anti-fascist refugees. He recounts meeting a

German refugee at the John Reed Club, an important gathering place for left activists in Chicago:

> A bunch of us were going downstairs to the John Reed Club and we had a German refugee with us, a woman, and as we went down the steps, we could hear the kids down on State Street calling out an extra of some kind. As we got down the steps, I went across the street to get one of the papers, I came back and it showed that the Fascists had beheaded a certain number of communists and I don't know, I felt the paper being taken from me, this refugee woman and she says this is my man. This is my husband. Oh man!

This testimony emphasizes how connections with refugees fleeing from Germany to US cities such as Chicago and New York had effects on the political outlooks of volunteers. Italian brigadists in the USA included refugees and political exiles from Mussolini's regime in Italy (Ottanelli, 2007). Hunter's account also signals the significance of brigadists' encounters with violent repression of anti-fascism and left politics in Germany.

Michelle Haapamaki has argued that during the 1930s there was an important shift in the left from support for pacifism, which was particularly significant in the wake of the First World War, to support for 'just war' in Spain. She argues that mobilizing particular forms of heroism and reproducing associations of violence and masculinity were integral to this shift (Haapamaki, 2005). Haapamaki develops a useful scrutiny of the relations between gender, violence and solidarities, which are often not interrogated adequately in left historiography. Hunter's account of his political trajectory, however, positions his activism in relation to diverse histories and geographies of political violence, which undermine the idea of a straightforward shift. Rather, he emphasizes the violent repression meted out to left political alternatives in early- to mid-twentieth-century USA. He recalls the importance of meeting coal miners who had been involved in the West Virginia Mine Wars. The miners

> had come from West Virginia, now if you read American Labour History, there is a famous revolt after the first world war that took

place in the coal mines of West Virginia and it's called the Armed March where these coal miners got a hold of guns and marched on Charleston West Virginia and I met these guys too. And they're all full of these stories and then they had to get out of the state, and that's how they got to Cleveland. But I mean they were my heroes, these guys.

Hunter argues that the experience of meeting these miners decisively shaped his political understandings. The West Virginia mine wars were part of the violent confrontations between unionized miners and mine owners' militias and guardsmen in the early-twentieth-century United States. They convulsed the coalfields of states such as Colorado and West Virginia with 'shootouts and assassinations, executions and ambushes' (Andrews, 2008: 1). At the Battle of Blair Mountain in 1921 a rising of 10,000 armed miners was only quelled by police, strike-breakers and the US Army using guns, poison gas and aerial bombers (Blizzard, 2010). Hunter's account emphasizes how the conflict in Spain wasn't seen as being neatly separate from circumstances of political organizing in the USA that were seen as peaceful.

The effects of racialized and gendered violence on his life are a key theme of James Yates's autobiography. His response to seeing his friend Herman Wolfowitz 'standing on a park bench, speaking to a crowd on the danger of the rise of fascism' was to note that 'We Blacks had our own fascism to contend with. The Ku Kluxers and lynchers here at home were an ever present threat. While Herman spoke, I saw myself as a boy seeing five men and four women dangling from a bridge – lynched' (Yates, 1989: 87). This linking of lynching and fascism emphasizes the diverse forms of violence that shaped the lives of volunteers who fought in Spain and that can easily be erased by a shift from pacifism to violence. The violent repression of labour and African-American movements and the diverse forms of racialized and gendered violence, particularly in the South, shaped the political trajectories of volunteers in decisive ways.

Mack Coad, a black Communist and organizer of the Share-Croppers Union (SCU) in Alabama, for example, was 'caught in a shootout with police' within weeks of the SCU's founding (Kelley, 1992: 12; see also Haywood, 1978: 391-415; Kelley, 1990: 41-2). Sharecropping was 'wrapped in violence and fraud'; those who 'challenged this year-in and year-out system of exploitation often found themselves or their family members imprisoned beaten or murdered' (Woods, 1998: 93). Police violence was used in the repression of organizing around Ethiopia, with repression of the 'Hands Off Ethiopia' march in Chicago and arrests and beatings of prominent activists including Harry Haywood and Oliver Law (Haywood, 1978: 447-57; Yates, 1989).

In this context some volunteers spoke of their time in Spain as affording possibilities denied to them in the USA by the effects of racism and oppression. Crawford Morgan argued that 'from the time I arrived in Spain until the time I left, for that period of my life, I felt like a human being, like a man' (Morgan, 1992: 176). Tom Page noted in similar terms that 'Spain was the first time in my life I was treated as a person ... I was a man! A person! And I love it very much' (Page, 1987: 55). Morgan's and Page's testimony demonstrates the way that internationalisms generated political masculinities that worked differently in different places. It also emphasizes how solidarity and masculinity could be co-constitutive. Their testimony emphasizes that Spain, despite (or maybe because of) it being a war, afforded possibilities that the USA denied. Yates contended that in Spain he was able to 'stand and fight' in ways that he hadn't been able to in the USA (Yates, 1989).

Forging solidarities in Spain

Oscar Hunter, in his short story '700 Calendar Days',[14] gives a striking sense of the significance of the Brigades to black volunteers. In the story, Jay, an African-American volunteer, discusses his reasons for fighting in the Brigades: 'I tried to tell what it meant to us Negroes in the original Lincolns. Being part of the first mixed American Battalion of black and white men to go into battle together. Told him that if a black man had it in Spain the comrades could and would use it' (Hunter, 1952: 299). Hunter emphasizes the importance of the Abraham Lincoln Brigade as the first integrated military unit in the history of the United States. His reference to how the comrades would use the story of this integrated unit suggests the resonance of the Brigade to African-American politics.

The integrated character of the Brigade was of particular significance for those who, like Harry Haywood, had fought under segregated, Jim Crow, conditions in World War I (Haywood, 1978: 36–80).[15] Many volunteers, such as Crawford Morgan and Thomas Page, would go on to fight, again under Jim Crow conditions, in World War II (Collum, 1992). These solidarities were forged under political circumstances that African-American volunteers saw as markedly different to those they faced in the USA. This is in part illustrated by the diverse roles that African volunteers played in Spain. Many African-American volunteers served as foot soldiers at the front. Others like James Yates, who worked as a driver running supplies to the front, performed important support roles (Yates, 1989). Admiral Kilpatrick served as a mechanic and in an international interrogation unit to stop the sabotage of loyalist trucks. Oliver Law, who died in Spain, was the first African American ever to command an integrated American military unit (Nelson et al., 1981: 187). Harry Haywood, the highest ranking African-American Communist to serve in Spain, was a political commissar charged with political development/ enforcement. His conduct, however, was bitterly contested by rank-and-file volunteers, and he described his time in Spain as 'a personal crisis' (Haywood, 1978: 489).

The Brigade was headquartered at Albacete in south-eastern Spain. Yates describes the Albacete he encountered in early spring of 1937 as 'a United Nations of a special kind. Men and women of all different tongues and nationalities, young and old, all came together to fight side by side with the Spanish people' (Yates, 1989: 122). The Welsh brigader Alun Menai Williams recalled this cosmopolitan character of the International Brigades in his autobiography: 'We were there in a foreign land, men of all nationalities, of colour, creed, race, religion and cultures. From all parts of the world; Iceland to Australia, from the tortured lands of Central Europe to the affluent democracies of the West' (Williams, 2004: 180). He celebrates this 'international force of volunteers' as 'in itself a unique event'.

The solidarities forged between these international volunteers were generated through small acts and friendship, as well as shared political convictions. Oscar Hunter speaks affectionately in his oral history testimony of an English brigader called Topsol.[16] He recalls that 'one night with some Englishmen going home, they were going home and I was going to Albacete, and one of them was named Topsol and all the way down, I'll never forget, he sang all these filthy English ballads ... Topsol was something.' Hunter's account of his friendship with Topsol emphasizes that the Brigade nourished very different relations to the racial politics of the USA. His account of Topsol's 'filthy ballads' and sailor's songs suggests that these friendships were forged through a very 'manly' sense of freedom.

The racial politics of the Brigades, however, were not experienced in uniformly positive ways. The Abraham Lincoln Brigade officer Lieutenant Conrad Kaye told Paul and Eslanda Robeson that there had been tensions with Southern white Americans and British on the 'Negro question'. Kaye noted that 'the really difficult ones [were] the British', who refused 'to eat in dining rooms with the Negroes' and had to be 'drastically re-educated, because neither the Spaniards nor the International Brigade will tolerate such heresy' (cited by Duberman, 1989: 219-20). This account emphasizes how racist conduct could be challenged through the Brigades. Salaria Kee's testimony of her time in Spain gives a strong sense of the entrenched prejudice she encountered from senior medical staff.

Kee's difficulties with the head of the medical unit, a Dr Pitts, who was a white Southerner from Alabama, started on the voyage to Spain. She recalls her experiences on the SS *Paris*, a Cunard liner, in the following terms:

I got on the ship and it came time to eat. There was a long table, and they told me that I was to sit with this group, because this was the second group going to Spain from the United States of America, doctors and nurses. There were twelve of us. Doctors and nurses. And I was to sit with them. I went to the table and I had met some of the nurses, because I had known them, because we had – our paths had crossed – and we were all very happy – and Dr Pitts, he was the top doctor, he was in charge of the unit. I was like the fifth person sitting by him. And he looked at me and he wouldn't sit down. And we can't sit down until our doctor, top person, sits down. So when the waiter came and asked him if there was any problem, he says yes. He says, 'I have never sat to the table with a n— wench and I'm not going to start now'. And the French waiter ran away and I could hear all the dishes around the place going on the floor and all like that – people jumping up and looking because he screamed it. And I was the only Black person there – looked all over the place. Nobody as Black as me was there.[17]

The head waiter returned with the proprietor of the Cunard line and his daughter, Nancy Cunard, the renegade heiress to the Cunard Line, who had diverse contacts among black internationalists and had edited the *Left Review* pamphlet in which George Padmore presented his anti-colonial analysis of the Spanish Civil War.[18] In defiance of Dr Pitts, who again refused to sit down with Salaria, the ship's captain took her up to first class where she roomed with Nancy Cunard. Kee recalls that Cunard said she would 'be her roommate and all those French people just took me in ... they made a postcard of the two of us, and that went all over France, all over Spain'. This, however, was not the end of Salaria Kee's difficulties with Pitts. She recounts how on a number of occasions while in Spain Pitts left her unnecessarily in dangerous situations.[19] She directly attributes this to malicious intent on the part of Dr Pitts.

Kee's testimony here is overlaid with a clear sense of intersecting class/racial/gender superiority. Tensions bearing on class differences within the African-American volunteers emerged through the conduct of the Brigades. This marks the testimony of Eluard Luchells McDaniels, who had grown up on the West Coast of the USA and had been adopted by a wealthy bohemian family. He developed links to the Communist Party through involvement in the battles of longshoremen in San Francisco.[20] He notes strong class and regional differences between himself and other black brigaders. recalling that though the other volunteers 'treat me nice' he seemed 'different from the rest of the people. But that was the way with the Lincoln Battallion'. One of his explanations for this difference was that 'most of these Negroes are of the East'.

Oscar Hunter's testimony gives a dramatic sense of the differences that class background could make in negotiating the harsh conditions and terror of life at the front. He recalls the significance his background and that of his friend Doug Roach from Provincetown, Massachusetts, made to a routine act such as digging a trench. The context of the trench-digging was the 'Battle of Jarama', where the Lincoln Brigade suffered huge losses. 'So you know the Spanish soil was very hard, and Doug and I didn't give a damn, we had a pickaxe and a shovel that's all we need, and we're digging all the time.' 'Doug and I' were 'workers, not high school kids, not college boys', 'from New York but workers', and 'we start digging, and Doug and I dug, we really dug, see, and we did it as long as we were at the front together, they'd always say when you'd get to the part of the trenches where Douglas and Oscar are, be sure and have a ladder cause you're going to have to climb down. It was funny as hell, but we survived and they didn't.' Hunter notes that at 28 he was also older than most of the other brigaders and that 'a lot of them were high school kids, almost, Jewish kids ... going to go up there and fight the enemy they never had a chance'.

The extremely heavy casualties among the Abraham Lincoln Brigade at Jarama, and at other battles such as Brunete, led to significant dissension within the brigade (see Nelson et al., 1981: 187) The International Brigades became notorious for the use of poorly equipped and trained volunteers. Throughout Hunter's account of his time in Spain there is a profound sense of disenchantment with the organization and military strategies of the Brigades.

But then the tragedies started, you know. In the first place, none of us knew a god damn thing about guns. Oliver Law said he knew all about machine guns. He never proved it to me. He died I understand pulling one. One of those Gorki things. ... I also knew that we didn't have five guys in the whole Lincoln Battalion who knew what the hell to do with a gun. It was obvious we didn't know and it was also obvious they were going to move us up.

Yates writes of the trauma of having to deal with the death of his friend Alonzo Watson at Jarama in what he describes as 'unbelievable' conditions at the Brigade headquarters in Albacete. He writes that 2,000 volunteers were housed within a barracks built in the sixteenth century to hold no more than 300 soldiers (Yates, 1989: 123).

In these conditions the relations between political violence, gender and solidarity were contested. Volunteers who didn't conform to particular ideal ways of performing military masculinities could face censure or ostracism. Langston Hughes's account of the conduct of a 'colored officer in charge of a mixed unit of several nationalities in the Brigades' at the battle of Brunete is a good illustration of this. The African-American officer 'had taken shelter with his men in a hillside cave during a terrible day of long Fascist bombardment' and had refused an order to charge, arguing that 'it was crazy' (Hughes, 1993: 355). He describes the African-American officer as 'the greatest "disgrace to the race"' he encountered in Spain, reproducing associations of military prowess and 'racial pride'. Harry Haywood, arguably the officer referred to by Hughes, contended that he was ostracized for critiquing the 'brutal incompetence and irresponsibility' of General Gal and Lt Colonel Vladimir Copic, division and brigade commanders at the Battle of Jarama (Haywood, 1978: 477; see also Baxell, 2004: 66). The conduct of Haywood himself, who had a privileged position as a political commissar, however, was bitterly contested by rank-and-file African-American volunteers, such as Oscar Hunter and Eluard Luchells McDaniels. McDaniels recalled that 'he spent most of his time around women and dressed up and stuff like that'.[21]

Paul Gilroy has argued that Marcus Garvey's politics were forged through particular 'masculinist values of conquest and military prowess' (Gilroy, 2000: 233). Arguably, such masculinist values were reworked and foregrounded rather than challenged through the Brigades. This speaks to the violent constitution of political solidarities. This refigured violent masculinities as central to left politics, raising questions about how anti-fascist politics was generated and produced. There were also tensions in the ways in which the Communist Party of the USA (CPUSA), the key institution through which volunteers were enrolled into the Abraham Lincoln Brigade, constructed anti-fascist maps of grievance. Despite the Communist Party's explicit commitment to multiracial politics there were ongoing tensions over racial politics in the party and a high turnover of black members (see Naison, 2005).

Hunter, for example, problematizes the way that he was treated as a black member of the Communist Party in Chicago. This indicates how internationalist political activity can involve challenging place-based forms of organizing.

> You know people are very strange to me, for instance, why should someone who's a member of the CP in Chicago know more about blacks and the history of blacks than I did and I'd spent all those years almost seven years in the South and not as a Southern but as a Northern kid who had gone down there and been trained, all those marvelous people had been training me and you know they couldn't stand me, I was always in trouble. I was *always* in trouble, I didn't have the correct line, I didn't have the correct approach, I didn't have this, I didn't have that. I kept right on anyhow, I didn't give a damn, you see. I didn't care. One thing I did have, I knew how to get on the floor, on the kill floor, on the soap floor, I mean on the floor where the work was and that's my specialty.

Key figures in the CPUSA formatted and shaped anti-fascist maps of grievance in ways which closed down linkages to anti-colonial and anti-racist struggles. There were significant differences in the maps of grievance constituted by those like Earl Browder, the leader of the CPUSA, who constructed a patriotic American anti-fascism, and those like James Yates or Oscar Hunter who directly related contestation of fascism in Spain to contestation of racism in the USA.

The articulation of anti-fascism in relation to the Spanish Civil War promoted by Earl Browder, the leader of the CPUSA, explicitly articulated forms of left patriotism in line with Popular Front policies elsewhere (see Browder, 1938a). Browder argued that 'we will not be able to raise our heads as Americans, who have fulfilled the traditions of Jefferson in giving aid to other democracies, until this embargo has been lifted, and we observe our treaty obligations to Spain, which we now violate' (Browder, 1938b: n.pag.). For Kilpatrick, such a patriotic construction of US Communism, the idea that it was carrying on 'the traditions of Lincoln, Jefferson and Douglas', was 'a lot of bull'.[22] These articulations of the conflict continued to be contested. Hunter ends his oral history with a reflection on how the CPUSA had memorialized the Spanish Civil War, accusing the CP of ignoring the deaths of volunteers. 'I was astounded, really it's such an insult. Imagine here guys at Gandesa, died. And you never know they did it. I was at Jarama, dying in the snow, you'd never know we did it ... but all that dying, nobody dies. It's a fantastic document. Nobody dies.'

Conclusion

In 1954 Crawford Morgan was hauled up before the Subversive Activities Control Board (SACB) and questioned on his experiences in Spain. The SACB was in the process of declaring the Veterans of the Abraham Lincoln Brigade (VALB) a 'subversive organisation' (Collum, 1992: 87). In these repressive circumstances Morgan made a powerful articulation of anti-fascism. On being asked if he had an understanding of the issues connected with the war before going to Spain, his response was:

I felt that I had a pretty good idea of what fascism was and most of its ramifications. Being aware of what the Fascist Italian government did to the Ethiopians, and also the way that I and all the rest of the Negroes in this country have been treated ever since slavery, I figured I had a pretty good idea of what fascism was. (Morgan, 1992: 175)

Morgan's testimony suggests the importance of the way volunteers configured relations between anti-fascism, anti-colonialism and the racial inequalities of the USA. It suggests that these articulations of anti-fascism continued to be politically subversive and challenging in the USA. This emphasizes the importance of the black internationalist contribution to understandings of anti-fascism. These were the products of innovative political linkages and seeded important geographies of solidarity and connection. The context in which Morgan spoke emphasizes the increasing repression that left activists faced in the United States in the 1950s. Veterans faced intimidation and harassment, as well as their veterans' organization being proscribed. These were indicative of the pressures on the forging solidarities and internationalisms which were to become entrenched during the Cold War. The pressure exerted by the CPUSA on the imaginative connections made by black internationalist intellectuals and activists is a further testament to this.

PART III

Solidarity and Cold War geopolitics

CHAPTER 5

'No trade with the junta': political exile and solidarity after the Chilean coup

In October 1973 an article appeared in the illegal Czechoslovak opposition monthly *Narodni Noviny* entitled 'Against the Terror in Chile and Elsewhere'. The article offered solidarity to those imprisoned in the wake of the military coup led by General Augusto Pinochet on 11 September of that year. The coup, which received the backing of the CIA, had deposed the democratically elected socialist president, Salvador Allende. La Moneda, the presidential palace, was strafed by Hawker Hunter jets. Allende took his own life and in his last radio address from the besieged palace pledged: 'You must know that, sooner rather than later, the grand avenues on which a free people walk will open and a better society will be at hand' (cited by Cooper, 2001: 39). In the coup and the immediate period of repression that followed it there were at least 1,823 deaths and disappearances.[1] These were predominantly of left-wing activists and trade unionists.

The article's author was Jiří Pelikán. As director general of Czechoslovak Television between 1963 and 1968 he was a central figure in shaping the liberal/reform communism associated with the 'Prague Spring'; the extraordinary flowering of dissent which was crushed by Soviet tanks in August 1968 (Eley, 2002: 493; Pelikán, 1972). Pelikán went into exile in Rome after the

Soviet invasion and was stripped of his Czechoslovak citizenship. He continued to be active in politics, publishing the dissident magazine *Listy*. The repression of the Prague Spring directly shaped Pelikán's expression of solidarity with those in Chile. He argued that:

> President Allende, the Chilean equivalent of Dubček, is dead. But what has followed his death is – except for the killings (but the Soviet armies contributed to that in our country as well) – so similar to Czechoslovakia that it must be obvious. The methods of putschists are the same, whether they come from a Russian steppe or South America.
>
> Fascism is simply fascism, no matter under which label it operates, whether it rages in Chile or Czechoslovakia. That is why we are united with the Chilean people and that is why we should protest, not only against the threat to the life of Luis Corvalán (who, by the way, approved of the occupation of our country in 1968), but against the sacking of people from work, against censorship, against infringements of privacy, against the ban on freedom of association, against the ban on certain books, against the abolition of trade union rights. All this must feature in our protests. We must understand that we are against it, no matter where in the world it is happening, and we must fight against it. (Pelikan, 1976: 208-9)

In line with a dissident socialist position, Pelikán compares Allende with Alexander Dubček, the reforming leader of Czechoslovakia who was deposed by Soviet invasion in 1968. His account draws attention to the shared experience of political repression in Chile and Czechoslovakia. He posits this as a key reason for expressing solidarity with the Chilean people. He also ensures that the terms on which solidarity is constructed are broadened beyond Luis Corvalán, the leader of the Chilean Communist Party, who he notes supported the Soviet invasion of Czechoslovakia, to all those suffering political repression.

Pelikán also offers a trenchant attack on the Soviet response to the coup. He argues that the 'decisive problem of supplies (which arose when the [Chilean] transport workers declared their destructive strike) could have been solved with aid from the socialist countries, if they had been prepared to give it.'

Further, he contends that 'the USSR was in fact content, in spite of its formal protests, with what happened in Chile (so was the USA of course).' For Pelikán the 'meticulous preservation of democratic processes in the process of building a socialist society' that characterized Allende's Chile 'were a thorn in the flesh of the Soviet Union'.[2] Unidad Popular, the democratic social- ist coalition headed by Allende, was a 'beacon of inspiration' to many on the left, demonstrating that 'radical social change' was possible through 'democratic, peaceful and legal means' (Cooper, 2001: x). Washington's assault on Allende was in part prompted by the realization 'that he would not turn Chile into a Cuban-style Soviet satellite' (Grandin, 2004: 175; see also Thompson, 1982a: 23).

The terms of these solidarities constructed between a Czech dissident and those subject to repression in the aftermath of the Chilean coup suggest the tensions and pressures of constructing solidarities amidst the Cold War; the entrenched geopolitical divisions around the US/USSR blocs between the late 1940s and 1989. This chapter engages with the diverse forms of internation- alism and solidarity produced in response to the Chilean coup.

Constructing solidarities
and the geopolitics of the Cold War

Pelikán's analysis of the Chilean coup demonstrates that there were attempts to construct solidarities which explicitly chal- lenged, refused and sought to transcend the geopolitical divisions entrenched through the Cold War. Sharad Chari and Katharine Verdery have usefully challenged the effects of these 'spatial partitions' on intellectual imaginaries and divisions of labour (Chari and Verdery, 2009: 18; see also Sharp, 2000). Contending that the Cold War was 'quintessentially an organization both of the world and of representations and knowledge about it', they argue for an approach which transcends the legacies of these divisions (Chari and Verdery, 2009: 19). They argue that one of these key legacies is the partitioning of intellectual work so that 'areas emerging from European colonization go to postcolonial studies and areas emerging from behind the Iron Curtain to post-socialist studies'. In opposition to such divisions they articulate an agenda of 'bringing together postsocialist and postcolonial studies toward rethinking socialist and anti-colonial values simultaneously' (Chari and Verdery, 2009: 29).

This section of the book, following Chari and Verdery, traces political trajectories and solidarities which cut across and refused the polarizing logics and spatial partitions demarcated by the Cold War. The Cold War exerted considerable pressure on various forms of political activity, such as the organizing of international union federations into rival blocs (see Herod, 2001). Following political trajectories and solidarities that refused to be defined by the binary oppositions of the Cold War can be productive. Indeed, forms of internationalism which were generated through contesting and refusing Cold War binaries were significant in both challenging the Cold War and leading to its end.

Such solidarities also challenge the spatial partitions between so-called Third, Second and First Worlds that are contested by Chari and Verdery. As Pelikán's solidarities between Czechoslovak dissident communism and Chilean socialism suggest, political solidarities were crafted which brought together struggles in different parts of the world in ways that both worked across such spatial partitions and unsettled the logics that held them apart. This approach destabilizes the primary focus of Cold War scholarship on the USA and USSR, which has other countries and places relegated to playing secondary roles.

Vijay Prashad asserts the importance of post-colonial countries in shaping the geopolitics of the Cold War in his valuable study of the political concept of the Third World. Prashad argues of the Bandung Conference of newly independent post-colonial states held in 1955, for example, that 'the colonized world had now emerged to claim its space in world affairs, not just as an adjunct of the First of Second Worlds, but as a player in its own right. Furthermore, the Bandung spirit was a refusal of both economic subordination and cultural suppression – two of the major policies of imperialism' (Prashad, 2007: 45-6). Prashad asserts the generative force of anti-colonial/post-colonial countries in shaping global political geographies. This approach is crucial to understanding some of the geographies of solidarity constructed in relation to Cold War geopolitical divisions.

To analyse these solidarities it is necessary to trace linkages and connections to the USA/USSR blocs and to explore how these were negotiated. However, it is crucial not to treat such solidarities as determined by such linkages and contexts. As James Dunkerley argues of US–Central American relations, 'however crucial and iniquitous the role of Washington in Central America, it is by no means the whole story' (Dunkerley, 1988: xi). Right-wing elites in Central America drew on diverse political and religious influences to shape a virulent regional articulation of global anti-communism. Counter-revolutionaries on the Guatemalan right, for example, borrowed from Spanish fascism to promote 'a potent Catholic folk nationalism based on social harmony, deference and duty' (Grandin, 2004: 75).

The repressive dynamics of the Cold War quickly exerted pressure and terminated the 'fragile, democratic firmament that took shape throughout Latin America between 1944 and 1946' (Grandin, 2004: 4). In Guatemala the October Revolution of 1944 'sparked by urban protests' and 'invigorated by the Allies' impending victory in World War II' had deposed General Jorge Ubico, bringing to an end one of the Americas' 'longest and most repressive dictatorships' and ushering 'in a decade of unprecedented reform, including an ambitious land reform' (4). This is a testament to the role of the left in opening up processes of democratization on the continent.

Guatemala, however, was to suffer 'the United States' first Latin American Cold War intervention'. In 1954 Jacobo Arbenz, the left-leaning democratically elected president of Guatemala, was deposed in a coup which was 'almost exclusively US-directed' and was prompted by the challenge posed by a left administration in the region (Dunkerley, 1988: 149-52; Slater, 2013). This intervention set the tone for the USA's ferocious role in aiding and abetting dictatorship and repression in Latin America in the second part of the twentieth century. Grandin notes that military dictatorships 'murdered 200,000 people in Guatemala, 30,000 people in Argentina, 50,000 in El Salvador and at least 3,000 in Chile. Security forces throughout the continent tortured tens, possibly hundreds, of thousands more. To a large degree, it was the expertise supplied by the United States ... that made such industrial terror possible' (Grandin, 2004: 74). Opposition to this repression drew on histories of anti-imperialist struggle against US intervention in Latin America that Admiral Kilpatrick invoked as a motivating factor in his decision to fight in Spain.

The well-documented support given to the Chilean Junta by the CIA is the most obvious geopolitical context to the coup that deposed Allende; support that was fundamental to ensuring the coup's success (Cooper, 2001; Haslam, 2005). CIA involvement was sanctioned at the highest level by Henry Kissinger, then Richard Nixon's special adviser for national security affairs. The coup was shaped by transnational circuits of anti-communism. Before the coup there were references to 'Djakarta' on the walls of suburbs of Santiago and in the right-wing press. This referred to 'the systematic massacre of Indonesian Communists in a country-wide pogrom in 1965' (Roxborough et al., 1977: 226). During the assault on the Indonesian Communist Party (PKI) the island of Bali 'lost about 8 per cent of its population, or a hundred thousand people' (Prashad, 2007: 154). This built on colonial histories of anti-communism. In response to the PKI-led revolt of 1926 the Dutch colonial governor Jonkheer De Graeff pledged to 'exterminate communism' (Hatta, 1928: 32). Right-wing elites constructed such anti-communist repression as the only viable strategy for opposing Unidad Popular.

US involvement in the coup was central to this geography of anti-communism. Henry Kissinger contended that he didn't 'see why we need to stand by and watch a country go communist due to the irresponsibility of its own people' (cited by Cooper, 2001: 23). The CIA continued to provide significant support to Pinochet's regime after the coup, despite the assassination of a diplomat on US soil by DINA, the murderous Chilean secret service set up by Pinochet (Cooper, 2001). The military coup was an 'exceptional event for a country of almost unbroken democratic constitutionalist tradition' (Collins, 2010: 61).

The US support for the coup built on long-standing engagements and interests in the country. Chile was the showcase for John Kennedy's 'Alliance for Progress' in the 1960s, which sought to deter Latin American countries from embracing communism (Taylor, 2006: 20; see also Grandin, 2004: 10). Under the Christian Democrat administration of Eduardo Frei, Chile 'was the recipient of over US$1 billion of direct US aid, resulting in a higher aid per capita ratio than any other Latin American country' (Taylor, 2006: 20). In 1968 the United States possessed $964 billion in direct investments in Chile, mostly in copper production (Haslam, 2005: 12). The USSR had its own interests in Chile. The Chilean Communist Party had played a key role in helping the Soviets to 'understand' Latin America (7).

One of the most significant and enduring influences of US-Chilean connections, however, was through the impact of the influential group of US-trained economists who came to be known as the 'Chicago Boys'. This group had trained at the University of Chicago with Milton Friedman, the high priest of neoliberalism. Influential agreements, funded by USAID and the Ford Foundation, between the Universidad Católica de Chile and the University of Chicago led to the education of around one hundred Chilean economics students at the University of Chicago from 1957 to 1970 (Valdés, 1995: 13). This resulted in 'an organized transfer of ideology from the United States to a country within its direct sphere of influence' (Valdés, 1995: 14). This 'ideological transfer' produced the first 'actually existing' experiment with neoliberalism.

In the wake of the coup the 'Chicago Boys' were integral to the adoption of neoliberal economic policies by the military Junta.[3] Pinochet handed control of the economy to the Chicago Boys after inflation had spiked at 370 per cent in the first year of the Junta (Peck, 2010: 108). This neoliberal project was constructed under hugely repressive social and political conditions. As David Harvey notes,

> Working alongside the IMF, they restructured the economy according to their theories. They reversed the nationalizations and privatized public assets, opened up natural resources (fisheries, timber, etc.) to private and unregulated exploitation (in many cases riding roughshod over the claims of indigenous inhabitants), privatized social security, and facilitated foreign direct investment and freer trade. The right of foreign companies to repatriate profits from their Chilean operations was guaranteed. Export-led growth was favoured over import substitution. The only sector reserved for the state was the key resource of copper. (Harvey, 2005: 8)

The relation between this economic restructuring and the political terror employed by Pinochet was direct. An assault on organized labour was central to the Pinochet regime's use of political violence. That the first organization to be banned by the military Junta was the Central Única de Trabajadores de Chile (CUT), the Chilean 'TUC', is indicative of the vehemence of the assault on the Chilean labour movement.

Political violence was mobilized not against an armed opposition but through 'a one-sided drive to eliminate political enemies' (Collins, 2010: 62). The primary achievement of repression 'was the decapitation of organized labour, the destruction of autonomous and politically active social movements, and the general suppression of political opposition including the established political parties' (Taylor, 2006: 32). This 'decapitation' was crucial to the establishment of the Chilean neoliberal project. The political violence and human rights abuses perpetrated by the regime, then, were foundational, not secondary, to the emergence of neoliberalism in Chile.

The CUT did not, however, cease to function in the wake of the coup. It reconstituted itself in exile, maintaining links to underground movements in Chile and instigating and shaping international solidarity networks. This was part of sustained transnational organizing which ensured that in 'a matter of months the Chilean left had been replicated in dozens of countries around the world' (Wright and Oñate, 2007: 39). The women's committee of the Unidad Popular, for example, set up organizations in thirty-five countries (Wright and Oñate, 1998). The leaders of the CUT, Luis Figueroa and Eduardo Rojas, went into exile in France and Sweden respectively. Offices were set up in cities such as Paris and London. The CUT in exile gained the recognition of the International Labour Organization (ILO), the International Congress of Free Trade Unions and the British TUC as the 'only authentic organisation representing the Chilean Trade Union Movement'.[4] The ILO rejected 'the credentials of the pseudo-trade unionists nominated by the military junta'.[5]

The CUT played a key role in garnering international solidarity. In January 1975, for example, Luis Figueroa and Eduardo Rojas visited Britain at the invitation of the British TUC.[6] Figueroa also attended the Conference of the Scottish Trade Union Congress in Aberdeen in 1975. These connections shaped the 'International Solidarity Platform of the Chilean TUC'. This proposed that 1975 should be the 'Year of international solidarity with Chile and with all peoples in the fight against fascism'. The platform was shaped by a radical, anti-colonial internationalism. It argued that the

> Chilean workers know that their cause is not the cause of Chile alone. The struggle of the working class and of the people of Chile is one part of the struggle of the peoples of the under-developed countries, of the peoples of Latin America, and of the exploitation, misery and oppression, so that the way will be opened for democracy and social progress.[7]

The platform drew on and sought to develop the 'broad and deep web of solidarity actions that took place across the world' in response to the coup (Jones, 2007: 209-10). It outlined a fourfold approach to international solidarity with the Chilean struggle: to 'Increase the international isolation of the dictatorship', to 'Develop the economic blockade against the Junta', to 'Develop the boycott against the Junta' and to 'Step up direct solidarity with the people of Chile'. These internationalist solidarities emphasize that the neoliberal experiment in Chile was contested through translocal organizing from its inception.

Some of the dynamics through which solidarity work was constructed can be gleaned through the boycott of Chilean vegetables proposed by the CUT in 1977. In March 1977 Pedro Cornejo, the representative of the CUT in Britain, wrote to British trade unionists appealing for support in a planned boycott of Chilean fruit and vegetables. His appeal notes that 'At this moment the Fascist Junta in Chile is Planning to ship massive amounts of Fruit and Vegetables (mainly onions) ... to Europe.'[8] The rationale for the boycott is set out in the following terms:

> Foreign trade is the Junta's lifeline and we have been asked by our colleagues in the Trade Union Movement in Chile, fighting as they are under conditions of the most severe political and economic repression, to appeal on their behalf to the British Trade Union Movement to boycott this trade.
>
> This trade does not benefit the Chilean people. The only reason that this produce is being exported is because the economic policies of the Junta have reduced the standard of living of the mass of Chileans to such levels that they cannot afford these goods.
>
> These goods are known as 'Non-trad' exports. In the past our country never produced enough of these goods, fruit, vegetables etc. to supply our own people, let alone to export them. ... It is taking the food out of our people's mouths to export it.

This appeal sets out a clear economic rationale for the targeting of Chilean fruit and vegetables, setting out to break the Junta's lifeline of foreign trade. The exiled CUT committee drew on underground trade unionists' unofficial knowledge of what exports were economically important to the Junta. The boycott also intervenes in the unequal geographies of power shaped by the trade. The appeal makes it clear that to boycott Chilean fruit and vegetables would not cause harm to ordinary Chileans. Rather, such exports took 'food out of our people's mouths'.

This suggests some of the connections that shaped the internationalist strategies of the CUT. The CUT played a strategic brokering role through articulating, maintaining connections between underground trade-union activists in Chile, and forging connections with trade-union and other political activists in countries like the UK and France. Activists in the UK helped to draw up lists of suppliers involved in the import of Chilean fruit and vegetables. These solidarities in turn had effects on organizing within Chile. Luis Meneses Aranda and Julio Valderrama Rios, who were on the CUT's exterior committee in France, noted that 'the wide movement of International Solidarity has contributed in an important manner to the development of interior struggles'. They argued that 'the mere existence of this great growing movement' is evidence of the 'Junta's failure in reaching its main objective: to destroy the organization of working class and popular parties, to isolate popular mass movement, to liquidate all democratic forces and [to get] permanent control of power.'[9]

The strategies of the CUT in exile emphasize the political skill of the Chilean left in reproducing itself through transnational organizing under conditions of exile. The exiles were successful in keeping 'the regime's dark side in the news and the public consciousness and in achieving repeated condemnations of the regime in international forums' (Wright and Oñate, 1998: 151). This depended on the construction of diverse forms of translocal solidarity. It is necessary, then, to follow practices of solidarity, which were pressured and confined in all sorts of ways by Cold War contexts and divisions, but which were certainly not determined by them. The next section explores some of the practices through which such solidarities were made.

'Now the generals rule Chile / And the British have their thanks / For they rule with Hawker Hunters / And they rule with Chieftain Tanks'[10]

On 21 May 1974, Harold Wilson, the UK prime minister, made a statement about 'Government decisions regarding the supply of arms to Chile and South Africa'. Wilson noted that

The Government have now completed their review of the contracts covering supply of engine spares by Rolls-Royce (1971) Ltd. to the Chilean Air Force and have been in touch with Rolls-Royce. So far as overhaul is concerned, the contract between the company and the Chileans provides for determination on three months' notice. Rolls-Royce will exercise this contractual right at the Government's request. The policy on spares for these aircraft and their engines should obviously be consistent with the policy on overhaul, and contractual obligations to supply spares will also therefore have to come to an end.[11]

Wilson's statement was greeted with cries of 'Disgraceful!' from the opposition Conservative benches. This response was indicative of the significant, and lasting, divisions in British political opinion over the coup and the Pinochet regime. These divisions were to re-emerge dramatically in 1998 when Pinochet was arrested for human rights abuses in London on an Interpol warrant which alleged that between 1973 and 1983 he committed atrocities against Spanish citizens. After his arrest he was visited by Margaret Thatcher, who had been influenced by Pinochet's adoption of neoliberalism. Other leading Conservatives such as Norman Lamont, chancellor in John Major's administration, also gave public support to the dictator.

A dispute over the servicing of jet engines might seem a rather obscure issue for a prime ministerial statement. The statement is indicative, however, of the high profile that solidarity movements with Chile (and also with South Africa) had in Britain in the 1970s. What is significant here is how the engines of Hawker Hunter jets became 'matters of concern' in political terms (Latour, 2004: 25). The prime-ministerial statement owed something to pressure from within his cabinet. Tony Benn describes the statement in his diaries as a 'total victory' (Benn, 1995: 289). Benn also notes how Wilson circumvented the attempts of the Foreign Office to 'get round the Cabinet proposals on the Chilean air force contract'.

The central impetus for the statement, however, was the concerted boycott or 'blacking' of the engines by workers in the Rolls-Royce factory in East Kilbride, just outside Glasgow. The Labour MP Ernest Fernyhough compared their action to the Manchester workers' solidarities during the Cotton Famine. Workers at the plant had swiftly registered their opposition to the coup. On 14 September 1973, Bob Somerville, one of the convenors for the Amalgamated Engineering Union (AEU) in the plant, submitted a motion to send telegrams to the Foreign Office and the Chilean embassy in London, protesting 'against the *junta* takeover of the democratically elected Chilean Government' (Beckett, 2002: 148). The motion was 'passed unanimously'. In the months after this, workers at the plant discovered that eight Avon jet engines which had been sent to the plant for routine maintenance belonged to Hawker Hunter jets from the Chilean Air Force.

Hawker Hunter jets held a particular political significance. They had been used during the coup to attack and bomb La Moneda, the presidential palace. As Andy Beckett notes:

> On 22 March 1974, the union committee spread the word across the shop floor that work on them was to cease. For the next four and a half years, despite threats from Rolls-Royce and fury from Chile, court rulings, and interventions by successive Prime Ministers, half the engines (the other half were sent to another factory and then back to Chile) slowly rusted in their crates in a small yard towards the back of the East Kilbride plant. (Beckett, 2002: 148).

This action was to have significant ramifications. As Wilson's statement suggests, the engines became a national political issue. Rolls-Royce attempted to exert pressure on the union branch. Chilean officials made the engines a cause of diplomatic contention between Chile and Britain. Perhaps most significantly, however, the news of this action travelled. When Hortense Allende, Salvador Allende's widow, went to Glasgow in 1975, as part of her campaigning to promote international solidarity, she personally thanked those involved in blacking the engines. She described their actions as 'a beacon of light to those in Chile' (Somerville, 2003: 11).

The 'blacking' of the eight Avon jet engines by workers in the East Kilbride plant suggests how solidarities can be crafted from below through intervening in the linkages between places (as with the boycott of Mussolini's Italy discussed in Chapter 4). In this instance what would have been a routinized transaction between the plant in East Kilbride and the Chilean Air Force through maintenance work on the jet engines became instead something that was disrupted with significant political implications. This also emphasizes how agency constructed through particular place-based activity can have significant translocal impacts.

The engines were reworked through these solidarity actions. One of the key actions the workers took was to place them out in a small yard at the back of the plant. This allowed them to be vigilant against the many attempts to remove the engines from the plant so that they could be refurbished elsewhere. This also exposed the engines to the vagaries of the Scottish climate. Further, they refused to allow them to be taken out of their containers so that 'they could be sprayed with preserving fluids' (Beckett, 2002: 152). By the time the four remaining engines were taken away by 'Harvey Haulage', a firm that did not exist and that used false plates, it would appear they were rusted beyond use (154). This was after the Callaghan government had controversially approved the export of the engines, in a move that 'split the Labour Party' (Dodds, 2002: 111).

Politicized shop stewards from the AEU were involved in blacking the engines. Bob Somerville, for example, was a Communist, part of a tradition of engineers in the Communist Party of Great Britain so strong that Raphael Samuel termed it a 'party of engineers' (Samuel, 2006: 189).[12] The blacking of the engines, however, received broad backing in the plant. Somerville recalls that his motion condemning the coup was seconded by one of 'the most right wing' officials 'in the Mid Lanark district' of the AEU (Somerville, 2003: 10-11). This 'gelled the workforce in East Kilbride'; a particularly significant achievement given the notoriously factionalized politics of the AEU. The blacking of the engines was supported by Hugh Scanlon, the left-leaning leader of the AEU, and key Scottish labour movement figures such as Jimmy Milne, the general secretary of the STUC.

The disabling of the engines generated relations and connections with those struggling against the Pinochet regime in Chile. These solidarities had enduring effects. Their significance was powerfully articulated by Bob Somerville at a witness panel on Scotland and Chile convened to commemorate the thirtieth anniversary of the coup. Somerville recounted the story of a visit to the East Kilbride plant in 2003 by Sergio Rueda, a Chilean who had come to meet some of the men who 'took part in the blacking of the Avon Jet Engines'. Rueda had been taken away blindfolded and tortured after the coup and kept at Tres Alamos prison camp in Santiago until November 1976 (Beckett, 2002: 156). Sergio recounted that while being tortured he was passing the guards' office and they had inadvertently left a radio on.

> He heard on the radio of an act of solidarity with the Chilean struggle in Britain, somewhere in Scotland, thousands of miles away, of the blacking of the engines for the Chilean Air Force of Hawker Hunter, the Avon Engines. He says he was at his lowest at that stage, he was ready just to give up, but hearing this solidarity with him so many thousands of miles away gave him hope, gave him back the will to survive, and that he was not alone in his time of darkest moments. (Somerville, 2003: 10)

This account gives an extraordinary sense of the reach that local solidarity action can have. The accidental playing of a radio within earshot of a tortured prisoner allowed him to find out about the solidarity action of those in the Rolls-Royce plant. This emphasizes the diverse and often unexpected trajectories and linkages shaped by solidarities. In this case these linkages were important in cultivating and renewing a sense of hope and survival in the bleakest of circumstances.

The solidarities shaped by workers in the East Kilbride plant were not just part of broader transnational webs of solidarity. They were part of, and shaped, broader cultures of solidarity in relation to Chile. Gideon Ben-Tovim, Liverpool community activist, labour councillor and academic, recalls that solidarity with Chile was part of broader internationalist left cultures, including the Free Angela Davis campaign and the anti-apartheid movement (Tovim cited by Frost and Phillips, 2011: 85). This had effects on the response to the significant number of Chilean exiles/refugees who went to Scotland. By January 1977 more than 1,350 Chilean refugees had moved to the UK.[13] The testimony of Phil O'Brien, then a lecturer at the University of Glasgow, gives a strong sense of the networks of support for Chilean refugees:

> everybody thought that what you did, you arrived here, you were immediately rushed off to Rolls Royce who was immediately responsive and gave tremendous assistance, or you went to the shipyards, there was a whole group of people in the shipyards, the miners, and in order to just build up solidarity in order for what they thought would be only a short time military coup. (O'Brien, 2003: 4)

O'Brien gives a sense of the dense relations of support that the Scottish labour movement and others gave to Chilean exiles. His account also suggests the way that many exiles struggled to cope with the fact that this wasn't to be the short duration of exile that they thought it would be. He argues that 'a lot of people never quite sort of accepted that they were going to live their lives here' (O'Brien, 2003: 4). Many suffered serious adjustment problems, particularly those who were exiled beyond Latin America and 'suffered high rates of depression, divorce, alcoholism, and suicide' (Wright and Oñate, 2007: 38).

Solidarities with Chilean refugees often led to dramatic short-notice reworking of domestic spaces and relations. Sandy Hobbs, a member of the Chile Committee for Human Rights, recalled being 'aware of the Allende government coming into power', people varying 'in their reaction of how well Allende was conducting things' and being 'horrified by the coup'. He notes that 'most significant in my memory, is that suddenly at very short notice we were confronted with a request to give very specific help to the Chilean refugees'.

Lois and I living in a household of four, at very short notice became a household of nine, because a Chilean family, Eduardo and Sonia Godoy and their three children came to stay with us, prior to being housed in Glasgow, in Drumchapel specifically and that was a very dramatic experience, it was also a very difficult experience because they spoke no English and we spoke no Spanish. (Hobbs, 2003: 2)

This account of housing a Chilean family gives a sense of the difficulties involved in the formation of solidarity. It also suggests the tensions of coexistence generated through such connections – of families having to share the same space without sharing a language. What is clear, however, is that such difficulties were negotiated (see also Buchan, 2003).

Such exiles were often coming from incredibly harsh conditions in Chile. Oscar Mendoza had been imprisoned by the Junta for two years in a secret military detention centre before being expelled and going to live in Scotland (Mendoza, 2003). Mendoza, talking in 2003 about his welcome in Scotland, spoke of 'the flames of solidarity, of brotherhoods, the common links of humanity, that brought together very different people under very different circumstances, but who were able to come together for the common good' (Mendoza, 2003). The process of exile was also often traumatic. Maria Figueroa, who settled in Newcastle, describes having experienced harsh treatment by UK immigration officers, who refused to use her correct name (Figueroa, 1990: 35).

Tensions within the Chilean left were reworked through exile. Rivalries and fissures that had existed in Chile were 'exacerbated by the blame-laying for the UP's defeat. Communists, Socialists, MIRistas, and other groups developed their own theses, and groups often divided over the differing interpretations. Nonetheless, most of the groups were able to work together on the exiles' common political goals' (Wright and Oñate, 2007: 38). Different left movements had contrasting political attitudes to exile. The MIR, the Movement of the Revolutionary Left, had a strong presence in Europe with more than a thousand MIRistas scattered in different countries. The MIR 'took active status away from all of those who exiled themselves rather than being expelled. So that they had a great guilt complex' (Patricio Rivas cited by Wright and Oñate, 1998: 161).

The solidarities generated through links with political exiles had important effects. Exiles shaped the cultures of the political left in Scotland and the UK. Chilean refugees, for example, played a significant role in shaping solidarities with the political struggles in Central America in El Salvador and Nicaragua. Maria and Victor Figueroa, who settled in Newcastle and became founder members of the Red Herring food co-operative, were key activists in the city's Nicaraguan Solidarity Campaign.[14] Maria Figueroa recalls the impact of the Sandinista revolution:

> they were teaching us a lesson, even that small country, was poor, and with the strength to go through and when they triumph – it was on the television – you can't imagine how we felt here; it was magnificent. We went to the University, distributing leaflets and demonstrating outside the Union, it was wonderful. (Figueroa, 1990: 70)

Solidarities were also forged with political movements struggling against the neoliberal onslaught in the UK. Notable here was the involvement of Chilean exiles/refugees in support groups during the miners' strike of 1984-85. The Ollerton Colliery Women's Support Group, from one of the pits in Nottinghamshire where few miners had come out on strike, had significant support from Chilean exiles who had settled in Norwich. Linda King, of the Support Group, gives a strong appreciation of these solidarities:

> The Chilean people have been great to us. You see, they know what it's like to go through this, better than we know ourselves. They are lovely people. After the strike, there is no way we are going to lose touch with them, and the people in Norwich who helped us. All the things they've done for us – they took the kids down for a week's holiday. ... Whatever happens, we can't let the contacts go. There are people we have got to know, things we have learned that would never have happened if it hadn't been for the strike. None of us are the same as we were before. (cited by Stead, 1987: 23)

King's testimony suggests some of the productive connections that were shaped through these solidarities. Central here is the sense that 'they know what it's like to go through this, better than we know ourselves'. There is a strong recognition here that both Chileans and mining communities were dealing with similar processes.

Through these solidarities women in mining communities learned 'about the monetarist political system in Chile and at what cost in terms of imprisonment and torture it had been imposed' (Stead, 1987: 22). The experiences of women involved in the strike dramatically changed their understandings of international politics. Stead notes that 'what was happening in Soweto, in Chile or at Greenham Common became relevant to them, they said, because they saw very strong links with their own situations' (Stead, 1987: 22). These solidarities shaped the transnational circulation of opposition to neoliberalism. They also demonstrate the contested linkages between the emergence of neoliberalism and Cold War geopolitics.

Folk music has no borders[15]

In 1973 the Nicaraguan singer Carlos Mejía Godoy recorded his song 'Pinocho, Pinochet' on his debut album *Cantos a flor de pueblo* (Mejía Godoy, 1973). The song compares Pinochet to Pinocchio. The chorus observes

Este pinocho ... pino, Pinochet
es un buen chico, como lo veis, amaestrado, bien alienado
habla español, pero piensa en inglés
¡Oh yes!

(This Pinocchio... pino... Pinochet / he's a good guy as you can see, well trained, very crazy / he speaks Spanish but he thinks in English. / Oh yes!)

The song satirizes Pinochet in directly anti-imperialist terms. Pinochet is ridiculed for his subservience to the USA and portrayed as someone who talks in Spanish but thinks in English.

The chorus continues:

hace tan bien las poses gorilistas
que le enseñó su tío imperialista
que ya parece todo un chimpancé

(He is so good at the gorilla poses / that his imperialist uncle taught
him / that he seems like a real chimpanzee).[16]

This use of the term *gorilista* positions Pinochet as part of a
tradition of Latin American putschists and strong men (see Nef,
1974: 64). The farcical lyrics are set off by the accompaniment
of a 'dainty waltz performed with flute and an electric keyboard
set to the celeste stop whose timbre is reminiscent of a child's
wind-up toy' (Scruggs, 2002: 60).

'Pinocho, Pinochet' demonstrates the transcontinental Latin
American solidarities shaped in opposition to Pinochet. The
song also indicates the significant reach of the Chilean new song
movement (*Nueva Canción*). Mejía Godoy was one of a number of
political singers in Central America who were influenced by the
Nueva Canción movement. A supporter of the Sandinistas, the
Nicaraguan revolutionary movement, he wrote songs instructing
the civilian population how to handle the rifles the insurgents
were winning from the Somoza dictatorship (Scruggs, 2002:
65). This hostile caricature of Pinochet by a Nicaraguan singer
shows the role of political song in shaping transnational political
cultures and solidarities.[17] Songs such as 'Pinocho, Pinochet' can
be a significant practice through which political movements forge
relations and solidarities between and within places.

Nueva Canción emerged in the 1960s, beginning 'as a fusion
of traditional musical forms with socially relevant lyrics' (Morris,
1986). From the outset it had a strong political and anti-imperial
agenda. This ethos was partly a reaction to US-dominated forms
of popular music and was a key way in which the geopolitics of
the Cold War were negotiated and challenged through cultural
politics. The movement is most strongly associated with the singers Victor Jara, Angel and Isabel Parra, Rolando Alarcón, Patricia
Manns and the groups Inti-Illimani and Quilapayún (Reyes

Matta, 1988: 451). Many of the movements' key protagonists had links to the Chilean Communist Party (Riesco, 1999: 121). *Nueva Canción* involved the use of traditional Chilean instruments such as the charango, cuatro, quena, bombo and leguero. Fernando Reyes Matta argues that this interweaving of musical instruments fulfilled a 'dream of Latin American integration' which could not be achieved by political or economic decisions (Reyes Matta, 1988: 451).

Nueva Canción Chilena's nexus was an 'artistic co-operative established at the Pena de Los Parra in Central Santiago by Violeta Parra's children Angel and Isabel' (Lynskey, 2010: 280). *Nueva Canción* drew on the research into folklore undertaken independently by Violeta Parra and Margot Loyola in the 1950s and 1960s (Party, 2010: 673). While Parra's 'oeuvre was openly critical of the social inequality and the political regime of her time', such political commitments were developed more explicitly by musicians like Victor Jara and the bands Quilapayún and Inti-Illimani (Taffet, 1997: 97). The movement was dominated by male musicians despite the role of Parra and Loyola in instigating *Nueva Canción*. This tended to reinforce the 'image of the dedicated young *barbudo*, who risked everything in the name of revolutionary justice' (Mallon cited by Party, 2010: 674).

Nueva Canción was a central part of the democratic socialist coalition that brought Salvador Allende and Popular Unity to power. During one victory speech Allende stood 'in front of a banner reading: "You can't have a revolution without songs"' (Lynskey, 2010: 285). *Nueva Canción* singers were not just important in the high-profile campaigning they did for Allende during his presidential bid. They shaped the distinctive popular and democratic socialist character of the Unidad Popular coalition, which allowed Jiří Pelikán to compare the Allende regime with the Prague Spring. It was also a significant factor in the international appeal of Unidad Popular.

The *Nueva Canción* movement challenged the organizational forms of music, in terms of both participation and distribution. *Nueva Canción* singers saw their work as part of a broader democratic political process, rather than just performing to passive audiences. The participatory ethos of the movement is articulated by Jara in terms which suggest the linkages between his ongoing cultural work and his involvement in Allende's election campaign of 1970. In 1971 he wrote:

> In every place where we perform we should organize, and if possible leave functioning a creative workshop. We should ascend to the people, not feel that we are lowering ourselves to them. Our job is to give them what belongs to them – their cultural roots – and the means of satisfying the hunger for cultural expression that we saw during the election campaign. (cited by D'Ambrosio, 2004: 203)

The political activities of *Nueva Canción* writers and artists meant that they faced severe repression during and after the coup. The murder of Victor Jara in the National Stadium in Santiago, after he had been tortured – his hands smashed because he was a guitarist – became one of the most notorious atrocities perpetrated by the Junta (Jara, 1983). After four days of torture Jara managed to sing 'a verse of the hymn of popular unity, 'Venceremos' to his fellow prisoners before being dragged away to his death' (Jara, 1983: 249). Jara's grave in the General Cemetery of Santiago would, however, 'never be without flowers'. Unknown people risked arrest 'to climb up and tie tins and pots with bits of wire and string in order to leave their offerings' (Jara, 1983: 1). Eduardo Carrasco, a member of the group Quilapayún, who were exiled after the coup, recalls that in their first week the military government 'called a meeting of the most prominent folklorists to inform them that certain folkloric instruments like the quenaa and charango were prohibited' (cited by Morris, 1986: 23). To be found 'with records of Victor, of the Parras, of Quilapayún, Inti-Illimani, if the military came to search the house, meant almost certain arrest' (Jara, 1983: 257).

Despite the ferocity of repression against the *Nueva Canción* movement in Chile, it continued to be influential and shaped 'transcontinental' political solidarities. One of the key ways that this was done was through forging counter-strategies of dissemination (Reyes Matta, 1988: 449). Fernando Reyes Matta argues that 'despite being rejected or ignored by the recording transnationals and great regional networks' New Song 'generated its own independent dynamics to attain social significance'. This significance was achieved through various practices, particularly the distribution and sale of cheap and pirated CDs and cassettes and the 'support of students, workers, poverty-stricken city dwellers, rural workers, and many other grass-roots and base organizations' (449).

These strategies were used by New Song adherents in diverse parts of Latin America. The Salvadoran band Cutumay Camones, who were supporters of the Farabando Martí Liberation Front (FMLN) in El Salvador's civil war,[18] for example, 'played live in zones of popular control (and in Santa Ana, San Salvador, and San Miguel in 1988)'. They 'broadcast nationally over the two rebel radio stations, and disseminated clandestinely by cassette tape and mini-songbooks within the revolutionary and popular organizations' (Almeida and Urbizágastegui, 1999: 20). Among Cutumay Camones's songs was 'Radio Venceremos', 'a kind of advertisement' for one of the two rebel radio stations linked to the FMLN (23). Radio Venceremos developed extraordinary ingenuity in circumventing the attempts of the USA to block their transmission using goniometers. The station's engineers hooked the transmission of the radio station up to the numerous barbed wire fences that cut across the landscape of Morazán, one of the strongholds of the FMLN. 'The quality was still inferior, but not that bad. The music did sound a little metallic' (López Vigil, 1995: 174-5). The crew of Radio Venceremos itself had an internationalist character, including an engineer from Venezuela.

Nueva Canción movements across Latin America shaped trans-regional solidarities with the struggles in Nicaragua, Guatemala and El Salvador during the 1980s. These were key sites of conflict in the region, which were directly linked to Cold War dynamics. In November 1982 a number of political singers met in Varadero, Cuba, for the First International Nueva Canción. The context was 'the struggles for recovery or achievement of democracy and a free destiny for Central America' (Reyes Matta, 1988: 459). The meeting led to the creation of the *Nueva Canción* movement's International Permanent Committee. Its inaugural declaration pledged its 'solidarity with the popular struggle for total liberation in Latin America and the Caribbean, Africa, Asia, including the industrially developed capitalist countries; against yankee influence in El Salvador and Guatemala and the threat of imperialist intervention in those countries that have decided to determine their own destiny' (cited by Reyes Matta, 1988: 459). Artists signed from Brazil, Uruguay, Chile, Nicaragua, Angola, GDR, Mexico, Argentina, Cuba and the USA. The anti-imperial analysis developed through the declaration emphasizes the role of *Nueva Canción* movements in shaping connections between diverse struggles. The institutionalization of *Nueva Canción* through the international permanent committee also suggests the influence of the Cuban state in shaping the terms of these internationalisms.

Anti-imperial solidarities drew on transcontinental linkages between political militants. Patricio Rivas of the MIR had been exiled in Western Europe before returning to 'active service' in Chile. He was pulled out of the group and sent to take 'charge of the clandestine relations in Central America, with the Frente Sandinista [the Sandinistas in Nicaragua], with the FMLN, with the Guatemalan guerrillas, with the movements in Colombia' (Wright and Oñate, 1998: 161). Rivas recounts that these 'organizations demonstrated extraordinary solidarity with us especially the Salvadorans'. He attributes this solidarity to the fact 'that none of these groups followed the line of the pro-Soviet Communist parties and decided to support us' and that the MIR were the only group trying to open up a guerrilla front in the Southern Cone of Latin America (Wright and Oñate, 1998: 161). There were also more organic invocations of the Sandinistas in Chile. During street demonstrations in 1983, 'teenage boys and girls, their faces covered with bandanas' stood guard 'with slingshots and sharpened wooden poles' and spoke of becoming 'Chilean Sandinistas' (Cooper, 2001: 74).

The performances of exiled Chilean groups such as Inti-Illimani, based in Rome, and Quilapayún, located in Paris, were significant in both entertaining and sustaining 'expatriates' culture and spirit of resistance' and contributing to the profile of the Chilean struggle abroad (Wright and Oñate, 2007: 38). The Chilean political singer Carlos Arredondo, exiled in Scotland, played many benefits across Scotland and was hugely active in solidarity work there. He was voted the best interpreter of Victor Jara songs at a festival in honour of Jara in London in 1980.[19] Victor Figueroa recalls bringing groups to play in Newcastle 'from El Salvador, from Nicaragua, from Cuba, from Bolivia and Chile, and also musicians who were in exile as well, like the group "Karaxu"' (Figueroa, 1990: 68).

The circulation of the music of *Nueva Canción* singers, particularly of Victor Jara, shaped transnational solidarities with Chilean struggles. Adrian Mitchell's tribute to Victor Jara, set to music by Arlo Guthrie, was part of the repertoire of the Scottish singers Dick Gaughan and Alistair Hulett; it was more recently recorded by the Irish singer Christy Moore.[21] The Clash memorialized him in the song 'Washington Bullets' on their album *Sandinista*. On 'Clampdown', released a year earlier, Joe Strummer sang of 'these days of evil Presidentés' (Gray, 2011: 273).

Jara's memory was directly invoked in campaigns to protest at the Scottish Football Association's (SFA) decision to arrange for the Scottish national team not only to play a fixture in Chile, but to do so at the infamous national stadium, where so many Chileans had been tortured and murdered. The SFA resisted a strong campaign and significant pressure from government ministers to go ahead with the match. The SFA opined in a letter to the STUC of 10 January 1977 that were 'Scotland to play only in those countries whose politics were acceptable to everyone in this country, it would not play many international matches'.[21] The Scottish folk singer and folklorist Adam McNaughtan wrote his song 'Blood upon the Grass' as part of this campaign. Mc-Naughtan's song mobilizes anger towards the SFA and its players and evokes an association of shame through their decision to play at the stadium.

The song is driven by a powerful structure of accusation, naming individual players; this sense of accusation being made more insistent by its repetitive structure.

> Will you go there, Alan Rough?
> Will you play there, Tom Forsyth?
> Where so many folk met early
> The Grim Reaper with his scythe
> These people weren't terrorists
> They weren't Party hacks
> But some were maybe goalkeepers
> And some were centre backs
> (McNaughtan, 2000)

The song creates a strong sense of emotional connection between Scotland and those struggling in Chile, forcefully politicizing the tour. By referring to the football positions they might have played, the song strategically circumvents depictions of the Chileans killed and tortured by the Junta as 'distant others'. Such connections continue to have strong resonances. In October 2009 a performance dedicated to the 'Life and Times of Victor Jara' was held in Edinburgh; it included performances from second-generation Chileans living in Scotland. The album *If it Wisnae for the Union*, released to celebrate the centenary of the STUC in 1997, includes a recording by Victor Jara of his powerful elegy to his mother, 'Te Recuerdo Amanda'.[22]

Conclusion

Accounts of Pinochet's neoliberal experiment have rightly focused on how this depended on the massive repression of the Chilean left. What such accounts sometimes miss, however, is the skill of Chilean exiles in shaping opposition to the Pinochet dictatorship through translocal solidarities and organizing.

These solidarities forged diverse linkages and were integral to the reproduction of the Chilean left in exile. Such solidarities were created through diverse trajectories and links, be it with factory workers in East Kilbride or with political militants in other parts of Latin America.

These solidarities were forged across the spatial partitions produced through the Cold War. Political possibilities were constructed through forging geographies of connection that refused to be confined within the divides of the Cold War. The solidarities and the political cultures shaped in opposition to Pinochet emphasize how the neoliberal experiment in Chile was contested through translocal organizing from the outset. Such solidarities ensured that while the neoliberal experiment gained the Junta 'enormous prestige among international financial institutions', this was not uncontested (Valdés, 1995: 2). Rather, this neoliberal agenda and the political violence it depended on were contested through diverse forms of transnational political activity.

CHAPTER 6

'Beyond the barbed wire':
European nuclear disarmament and
non-aligned internationalism

On a scorching hot Sunday in July 1982 the Scandinavian Women's Peace March walked through central Leningrad. For Danielle Grünberg, a participant on the march, this occasion was particularly memorable. She recalls that,

> as we began walking up the central Kirov Street ... the 300 Scandinavians, forming the core of the march, seemed suddenly to disappear into a sea of Russian people ... thronging the width and breadth of the street. Some older women, less inclined to participate, stood watching by the side of the pavement ... crying at the sight of the peace banners, reviving the memory of their dead relatives. 'The people of our country want peace', said a Russian woman, 'but they feel surrounded and threatened by the United States. We only have nuclear weapons to protect ourselves.' (Grünberg, 1982: 15-16)

The Scandinavian Women's Peace March covered '3,000 miles by boat, foot and train' from Stockholm (via Helsinki, Leningrad and Moscow) to Minsk, marching under the slogans 'No to Nuclear Weapons in Europe, East and West!', 'No to Nuclear Weapons in the World!' 'Yes to Disarmament and Peace!' The marchers' appeals for peace drew some powerful emotional responses, as Grünberg's testimony attests.

The march was part of diverse movements to forge solidarities across the divisions of the Cold War in opposition to nuclear proliferation. The march reflects the importance of transnational circuits of feminist political activity in shaping these solidarities. Grünberg was sponsored on the march by the campaign for European Nuclear Disarmament (END) and the Campaign for Nuclear Disarmament (CND) (Stead, 1982: 11). END was an experiment with transnational organizing that emerged in response to the resurgence of Cold War tensions in the late 1970s and early 1980s. The campaign sought to oppose the destructive logic of the Cold War. END brought together peace activists from both the Eastern bloc and Western and Northern Europe to campaign for Europe to be a zone of neutrality where nuclear weapons were not deployed.

This was a particularly urgent task as Europe was to be a 'theatre of war' in the event of any nuclear exchange. It attempted to organize across the differences marked out in crudely spatial terms through the divisions of Europe into two opposing geopolitical camps. This was based on an imaginative refusal of both Soviet-style communism and the neoliberal ascendancy of Thatcher and Reagan, and drew heavily on the intellectual and political projects of the New Left. END sought to reunite Europe through common struggles for peace and democracy.

Solidarity 'beyond the Cold War'

In December 1979 the NATO 'Euromissile' project was launched to locate Cruise and Pershing II missiles in Western Europe. In response to this decision and the associated increase of Cold War tensions, an 'Appeal for European Nuclear Disarmament' was drafted by the English socialist historian E.P. Thompson, author of, among many other works, *The Making of the English Working Class*. A version revised by Ken Coates (of the Bertrand Russell Peace Foundation), Mary Kaldor, Robin Cook and others was released at a press conference in the House of Commons in April 1980. The appeal sought to mobilize a popular movement to campaign for a non-aligned and nuclear-free Europe 'from Poland to Portugal'. The Appeal implored:

> We appeal to our friends in Europe, of every faith and persuasion, to consider urgently the ways in which we can work together for these common objectives. We envisage a European-wide campaign, in which every kind of exchange takes place; in which representatives of different nations and opinions confer and co-ordinate their activities; and in which less formal exchanges, between universities, churches, women's organizations, trade unions, youth organizations, professional groups and individuals, take place with the object of promoting a common object: to free all of Europe from nuclear weapons. (END, 1980: 225)

Central to the declaration was a critique of the polarizing ideological work that the Cold War depended on. This was articulated by key peace movement intellectuals in both East and West as undergirding the antagonisms on which nuclear missiles depended (Thompson, 1982a, 1982b; Köszegi, 1982; Šabata, 1983). This position sought to move debates in the peace movement on from campaigns focused narrowly against nuclear missiles. END sought to contest these antagonistic logics through bringing together diverse activists from both Eastern and Western Europe.

The Appeal was defined by an explicit attempt to construct transnational solidarities in opposition to the Cold War. It sought to mobilize a campaign across civil society which reached out beyond traditional left constituencies. This transnational organizing brought together peace activists from the West and Northern Europe, with dissidents and peace activists from across Eastern Europe and the Soviet Union. The appeal argued that it was necessary to 'act as if a united, neutral and pacific Europe already exists (END, 1980: 225). In this way the appeal sought to create political spaces and conversations which enabled what activists associated with END called 'détente from below'. This process sought to construct 'links between peace, green and human rights groups in East and West; initiating a dialogue between citizens and not just between governments' (Kaldor, 1991a: 1).

The Appeal was signed by 'thousands of influential people in the West but only a handful on "the other side" due to the difficulties of signing a public document which was publically critical of the USSR' (Thompson, 1991: 8). The strategy developed through the END declaration of bringing together activists from East and West was more than about building a bigger movement. These connections and solidarities sought to change the terms on which opposition to the Cold War was constructed. Rather than just contest the deployment of US missiles in Europe, END sought to challenge the whole logic of the Cold War. From the outset END opposed the siting of Cruise and Pershing II missiles from within a 'beyond the Cold War' perspective (Thompson, 1991: 8). This refers to the political position of non-alignment which attempted to construct left alternatives/peace movements which were not defined by loyalties to either of the key antagonists in the Cold War. To forge such solidarities involved significant political skill and involved negotiating significant pressures. The appeal noted: 'We must resist any attempt by the statesmen of East or West to manipulate this movement to their advantage' (END, 1980: 225). The polarizing logic of the conflict meant that if you opposed the nuclear policies of NATO or the Soviet Bloc you were immediately labelled a 'communist sympathiser' or conversely an apologist for the West. I recall from my own late Cold War childhood that to mark something with a CND sign was to invite immediate taunts of 'Commie'. Billy Bragg sang on his first LP released in 1983: 'Just because I dress like this doesn't mean I'm a communist.'[1]

These solidarities were shaped through 'imaginative' maps of grievance. The siting of Cruise missiles at Greenham Common, and other sites, was contested not just through hostility to the USA, but within a critique of the very logic of the Cold War. This generated 'maps of grievance' which saw both 'sides' as implicated in the production and reproduction of Cold War hostilities. These maps of grievance enabled the construction of shared political spaces, solidarities and analysis across Cold War divides. This non-aligned logic created important political possibilities for peace movements in the East.

The formation of independent peace movements in the Eastern Bloc involved a concerted struggle over the very meaning of the term 'peace'. Václav Havel, the influential Czechoslovak dissident, noted in his essay 'Anatomy of a Reticence', which first appeared in the samizdat publication *Obsah*, that for 'thirty-seven years every possible and impossible open space in Czechoslovakia has been decorated with slogans such as "Building up our homeland strengthens peace"' (Havel, 1985: n.pag.). For Havel this official saturation 'with the same weary clichés about peace' explained the reticence of many in Eastern Europe towards the proclamations of the Western peace movement. 'Václav Racek', an anonymous Czech critic, accused Thompson of a very 'dangerous naivety' for his identification of both blocs according to the principle of 'exterminism' and compared CND's activity to the appeasement policy of the 1930s (Racek, 1982: 83; Hauner, 1990: 101).[2]

There were, however, significant struggles within Eastern Europe and the USSR by independent 'unofficial' peace movements to articulate peace in ways which challenged both Cold War blocs. Independent peace movements emerged in Czechoslovakia, allied to Charter 77, in Hungary and in East Germany. An Independent Peace Group was formed in Moscow, which was subject to severe repression. The demands for peace intersected with a range of grievances. In October 1982, for example, several hundred women signed a letter to the GDR leader Erich Honnecker which contested the passing of a new Conscription Law. The letter refused the official gendered discourse that military service for women was 'an expression of their equal rights' (Sandford, 1983: 33, 97). The letter contended that we 'women want to break the circle of violence and to withdraw from our participation in the use of violence as a means of resolving conflicts' (97).

The pan-European platform articulated by END had strong appeal in this regard. The political possibilities opened up by such a political approach were articulated by Ferenc Köszegi of the independent Hungarian peace movement. Noting the difficulties of generating an 'autonomous' peace movement in Hungary outside of the Communist Party apparatus, he argued

> The new peace movement has to stand firmly on a pan-European platform. It must seek counterparts in both the East and the West, which could later be expanded between continents. But the transcontinental course is our only course for the time being. (Köszegi, 1982: 17)

The engagements of independent peace movement activists such as Köszegi were central to shaping, circulating and intensifying the terms of these non-aligned geographies of solidarity. END supported and forged dialogues between dissidents such as Köszegi in the East and intellectuals and activists in the West like E.P. Thompson and Mary Kaldor. Köszegi's article cited here, for example, comes from a pamphlet jointly written by Köszegi and Thompson and published by END (see Köszegi and Thompson, 1982).

Central to this project was the formation of spaces which enabled different political trajectories to come together. This allowed dissidents from Eastern Europe such as Adam Michnik, Rudolf Bahro and Roy Medvedev to exchange and debate ideas with figures from the Peace Movement and the New Left in Western and Northern Europe (see Bahro, 1982; Medvedev and Medvedev, 1982; for a more critical Eastern European perspective see Racek, 1982). This intersected with forms of dissident Marxist opposition, which were articulated most forcefully in Rudolf Bahro's *The Alternative in Eastern Europe* (Bahro, 1978). The exchanges, debates, conflicts and arguments conducted through these spaces produced a transnational political movement. This movement brought together dissidents and peace activists in different countries through common networks and dialogues. Such networks were fashioned through particular sites and places, whether the flats of dissidents in Prague and Budapest where Dorothy and E.P. Thompson met dissident historians and peace activists, or the annual END conventions 'which brought together activists from all over Europe' (Kaldor, 2003: 63; see also Palmer, 1994: 134-5; Thompson, 1991: 10). This was commonly a fractious, contested and difficult process (Kaldor, 2003: 63). It was also a productive one.

These exchanges and connections, rather than just rolling out the agenda signalled through the END appeal, shifted and intensified the political logic and programme envisioned through the appeal. Conversations with movements and dissidents in Eastern Europe had effects in reconfiguring and developing the END agenda. Charter 77 noted the unequal terms of involvement in peace activism and solidarity. They noted that we 'do not have the same opportunity as they have to voice our joint belief in the indivisibility of peace and freedom as loudly as they can' (Charter 77, 1983a: 22-3). Nonetheless the positions and declarations of the unofficial peace movements in Eastern Europe made significant interventions.

The 'Prague Appeal', addressed to the 1985 Amsterdam Peace Congress, was central in this regard. Linked to Charter 77, it was signed by forty Czechoslovak activists. It argued:

> If our aim is European unification, then no one can be denied the right to self-determination; and this applies equally to the Germans. The freedom and dignity of individual citizens are the key to the freedom and self-determination of nations. And only sovereign nations can transform Europe into a community of equal partners which would not pose the threat of a global nuclear war, but instead, serve as an example of real peaceful co-existence.
>
> Perhaps this ideal sounds like a dream. However, we are convinced that it expresses the desire of a majority of Europeans. It is therefore an ideal worth striving for; all the more so, in view of the fact that today's world will hardly surmount its crisis unless Europe also takes the path its citizens desire. We believe that our views will meet with your understandings and we wish you every success in your proceedings. (Charter 77, 1985b: 28)

The Prague Appeal distinctly echoes and intensifies the argument of the END Appeal that it was necessary to act as if a unified

Europe existed. This engagement developed the non-aligned perspective of the END appeal, particularly through touching on the taboo subject of the divided Germany. The appeal argues that self-determination of nations is necessary to develop peaceful forms of coexistence.

The Prague Appeal generated further dialogue and connection. Charter 77 received replies and comments 'from Britain (Labour Party, Liberal Party, CND, END, National Peace Council, and East-West Peace People), Holland (IKV), Denmark (*Nej til Atomvabens*), West Berlin (Group for East-West Dialogue), Norway (*Nei Til Stomvapen*), France (CODENE, Association Initiative pour le Dialogue Est-Ouest), USA (Humanitas International), and the Belgrade *Praxis* group' (Hauner, 1990: 107). The Western peace movement's response was generally positive, 'especially from among the Social Democrats who were sceptical about the whole Helsinki process and opposed the idea of German reunification' (107). Charter 77 also constructed solidarities with the emergent independent peace movements in East Germany. A 'Call to the peace movement in the German Democratic Republic' welcomed the emergence of that country's unofficial peace movement (Charter 77, 1983b: 25).

Central to Charter 77's approach was a distinction between political and technical disarmament. By this distinction they drew attention to the need to 'tackle the sources of the Cold War, not just the symptoms' (Kaldor, 1991: 1). This account of political disarmament linked struggles for peace to struggles for human rights in ways which extended and deepened the terms of the END appeal. This analysis dislocated the language of peace from links to the official discourses of Soviet/state socialism with which, as Havel argued, it had become saturated. This position became central to the terms on which non-aligned solidarities were constructed. Before engaging in depth with the conduct of non-aligned solidarities, it is useful to situate END in relation to histories and geographies of attempts to forge non-aligned political positions.

END and the spatial politics of non-alignment

The political imaginary of the campaign for European Nuclear Disarmament was decisively shaped by a distinctive articulation of left democratic internationalisms. This was a significant intervention. As Perry Anderson notes, for much of the twentieth century 'the doctrine of "socialism in one country" nourished practices of left internationalism based around an unconditional loyalty to the Soviet Union' (Anderson, 2002: 21). END involved a direct contestation of the terms through which internationalism was constructed. The collective experiment with non-aligned solidarities which marked END, however, did not take place in isolation. It was part of a tradition of diverse engagements with 'non-aligned' internationalism, especially associated with the New Left of the 1950s and 1960s. These political trajectories shaped the imaginaries and connections that were central to the forms of internationalism shaped through END.

To understand the forms of non-aligned internationalism constructed by END it is essential to interrogate the emergence of the 'New Left'. The genealogy of the term 'New Left' offered by Stuart Hall, the first editor of *New Left Review*, foregrounds the relations and geographies of non-alignment. He notes that

> The term 'New Left' is commonly associated these days with '1968', but to the '1956' New Left generation '1968' was already a second, even perhaps a third, 'mutation'. We had borrowed the phrase in the 1950s from the movement known as the 'nouvelle *gauche*', an independent tendency in French politics associated with the weekly newspaper *France Observateur* and its editor Claude Bourdet. Bourdet, a leading figure in the French Resistance, personified the attempt, after the war, to open a 'third way' in European politics, independent of the two dominant left positions of Stalinism and social democracy, 'beyond' the military power blocs of NATO and the Warsaw pact, and opposed to both the American and the Soviet presences in Europe. This 'third position' paralleled the political aspirations of many of the people who came to form the early British New Left. (Hall, 1989: 14-15)

This genealogy of the New Left foregrounds the centrality of the formation of a political project which refused either 'Stalinism' or 'social democracy'. It signals the presence of left internationalisms constituted through opposition to both camps throughout the Cold War period. Hall recalls that the Cold War dominated 'the political horizon, positioning everyone and polarizing every topic by its remorseless binary logic' (Hall, 1989: 17).

These histories and geographies shaped the political positions adopted by END. END also drew on the political resources and connections generated through the construction of earlier 'non-aligned' solidarities. This signals the significant ways that past histories and geographies shape the terrain on which solidarities are constructed. Hall's account of the New Left foregrounds the importance of Claude Bourdet. Bourdet was a leader of the French Resistance and opposed French colonialism, denouncing torture and repression in Algeria and Madagascar (Johnson, 1996). Hall and other figures of the 'British New Left' first met Claude Bourdet in Paris, at a conference called to consider 'setting up an International Socialist Society, across the divisions between Western and Eastern Europe' (Hall, 1989: 15). Dorothy Thompson attended the conference of the French new left party Parti d'Union de la Gauche Socialiste in 1958 as a representative of *The New Reasoner*. Afterwards she stayed with Claude Bourdet in Paris and met 'many of the leading communist dissidents inside and outside the French Communist Party' (Thompson, 1996: 97).

Bourdet made a key contribution to shaping a non-aligned New Left discourse. This is vividly set out in his essay 'The Way to European Independence'. Bourdet's essay contended that the importance of 'a disengaged nation or group of nations depends specifically not on its own potential, but on the equilibrium between the two blocs.'

> In such a situation there is a neutralisation, a real cancelling out so long as peace lasts of these two enormous accumulations of power. Not only do the strength and scope for action of the small,

independent nations then become quite appreciable, but additional factors not involved in the material balance of forces also become politically essential – diplomatic skill, gaining the ear of world opinion, and even the simple objective situation of independence which makes one sought after as a mediator by the more power-ful. It is quite apparent that India and Yugoslavia have over the past few years exercised an influence out of all proportion to their material power (the size of India's population is irrelevant, as India is financially, economically and militarily a small nation); and the same situation is probably beginning to apply to the United Arab Republic. (Bourdet, 1958: 17)

Bourdet's agenda for a non-aligned left democratic Europe was to have significant legacies. James Hinton has described the essay as like reading a first draft of the END appeal of 1980 (Hinton, 1989: 235 n19). This 'neutralist' position also attracted concerted and vehement opposition. Bourdet notes that 'The Communists violently accused us of failing to recognise the differences between "the camp of peace" and "the camp of war", and therefore of playing the game of the latter. The anti-Communists and pro-Americans treated us as disguised agents of international Communism' (Bourdet, 1958: 12).

A translation of 'The Way to European Independence' was carried by the summer issue of *The New Reasoner* of 1958. *The New Reasoner* was a key conduit of 'non-aligned' opposition. It was edited by E.P. Thompson and John Saville, a fellow member of the Communist Party Historians' Group. Published first as *The Reasoner*, the journal became the hub of a democratic opposition within and around the Communist Party of Great Britain (CPGB) in the wake of the revelations about the scale of Stalin's crimes in the Khrushchev speech and the 1956 Soviet invasion of Hungary. On Saville's and Thompson's expulsion from the CPGB it was renamed the *The New Reasoner* and later merged with *Universities and Left Review* to become *New Left Review* (see Thompson, 2007). From its base in Yorkshire[3] *The New Reasoner* became a key nexus through which dissident Communist and New Left dialogues circulated. The intellectual positions and exchanges developed in *The New Reasoner*, and beyond, were to shape powerfully the terrain on which later non-aligned solidarities were to be constructed.

Thompson made this lineage explicit in many of his writings and speeches for END. He offers the following account of the way his involvement in the post-1956 debates shaped the positions adopted in the 1980s:

> In 1956 we took a leading part in the autocritque which swept the world Communist movement, forming an opposition journal within the British Communist Party, which resulted in our departure from the Party after the suppression of the Hungarian insurrection. From that time forward we developed in little journals, and then with the first British New Left – in association with friends in Western Europe and C. Wright Mills in the USA – a new strategy of 'active neutrality' and a third way of peace and human rights. We converted the mass British peace movement (CND) to some of these positions and then, after 1980, converted it again. We reached out, after 1956, to voices in Gomulka's Poland (Adam Wazyk, Leszek Kolakowski) and in the thawing USSR. In 1968 we suffered the agony of witnessing the worst Brezhnevite repression of the Prague Spring. Since 1980 we have steadily advanced and developed in every way our former strategies, which have come to command a vast spectrum of non-aligned opinion. (Thompson, 1991: 21)

What is significant here is not just the continuity in relation to a commitment of a democratic, principled left internationalism. It is also the way that the spatial practices of solidarities generated through the post-1956 conjuncture shaped possibilities. Thus, as Thompson notes, after 1956 they had reached out to dissident figures such as Wazyk and Kolakowski. These histories and geographies of political activity shaped possibilities for how forms of solidarity were constructed and negotiated.

Dissident left and democratic communist activists in Eastern Europe had faced severe repression in the late 1940s and early 1950s (Eley, 2002: 310-11; James, 2010). Purges of the Czechoslovakian Communist Party between 1949 and 1954, for example, targeted 'the old communists, those who had been in the Spanish Civil War, those who had been in the resistance movement abroad, people of Jewish origin who had been exiled in the West, the best economists, in short, all the people who were able to think for themselves' (Pelikán, 1972: 12). It appeared shocking 'that the number of the victims of repression should be highest in Czechoslovakia despite all our democratic traditions' (16). Pelikán himself was involved in the 'bureaucratic purges of Czech universities in the later forties', something of which he was later to declare himself 'ashamed' (Mulhern, 2011: 28).

The New Reasoner published material from left dissidents in Eastern Europe. It published Adam Wazyk's poem 'Critique of the Poem for Adults', introduced as his protest against the 'degradation of socialist ideals' (Wazyk, 1957: 51). In 1958 it published Stevan Dedijer's paper on 'Freedom and Scientific Research', which on its earlier publication in the *American Bulletin of Atomic Scientists* had led to his dismissal from a research post with the Institute of Nuclear Science in Belgrade (Dedijer, 1958). The generation of such connections was significant and had effects. This positions the END appeal in relation to ongoing histories and geographies of connection, rather than just as a one-way dialogue. For Peter Worsley the 'extraordinarily difficult task of trying to build a common front against nuclear war, despite the division of Europe, began in the very first issues of *The New Reasoner*' (Worsley, 1989: 89).

Worsley notes, however, that while the interventions around *The New Reasoner* were significant, 'resistance to nuclearism was, at the time, far more widespread outside Europe' (Worsley, 1989: 89). This raises a set of questions about the geographies of non-aligned internationalism. Worsley notes how 'we'

> aligned ourselves squarely with these new movements for national liberation: John Rex attended one conference in Ghana on behalf of CND, while I went for the New Left, and Stuart Hall went later. Tom Mboya, Kenneth Kaunda and Kanyama Chiume wrote for the *New Reasoner*.[4] Both John Rex and I regularly appeared on anti-colonial platforms in this country, as did Doris Lessing. (Worsley, 1989: 90; see also Barratt Brown, 1989: 84)

The significance of the emergent, independent 'Third World' nations to Non-Alignment suggests that there were multiple and contested geographies of non-alignment. While Thompson et al. frequently acknowledged the importance of 'Third World' nations, the spatial politics of non-alignment that emerged through END was a resolutely European-centred version of internationalism (Thompson, 1982a). This was to efface the significant contributions of non-European political leaders and movements to political articulations of non-alignment. As Worsley argues, these shaped New Left imaginaries in decisive ways.

The Ghana conferences that Worsley mentions are particularly significant here. Kwame Nkrumah, the first post-independence leader of Ghana, in 1957, was a vocal proponent of non-alignment, though his position shifted over time (see Das Gupta and Shahid, 1981). For Nkrumah non-alignment was central to the formation of an independent Africa in the post-colonial period. He argued that the 'unity of Africa and the strength it would gather for continental integration, supported by a united policy of the non-aligned, could have a most powerful effect for world peace' (cited by Das Gupta and Shahid, 1981: 406). Nkrumah elaborated a 'neutral, nonaligned Pan-Africanism', exemplified by his advocacy of the neutralist All Africa Trade Union Federation (Von Eschen, 1997: 182).

The Accra assembly held in 1962 sought to develop a stronger non-aligned peace movement, drawing partly on connections and networks forged though opposition to French nuclear tests in the Sahara in February 1960. The *Ghana Evening News* compared the tests to Mussolini's invasion of Ethiopia, exclaiming that 'There is only one incident in living memory, that compares in magnitude with the ephemeral, almost agonizing, triumph of Might over Right at Reggan last week – Mussolini's rape of Abyssinia with the gas bombs and mass slaughter that eventually sounded the death-knell of the League of Nations' (cited by Allman, 2008: 93). The Ghanaian government broke off diplomatic relations with France, and pan-African political networks shaped significant transnational organizing against the tests

(Allman, 2008: 93). This organizing, however, mobilized a more radical programme than the Accra Assembly in 1962, which through its narrow focus on the nuclear arms race closed down a 'radical transformative agenda' (97).

The tensions of this 'third-worldist' opposition to nuclearism are noted by Vijay Prashad. He observes that at the founding Non-Aligned Movement conference in Belgrade in 1961 'one leader after another of the darker nations spoke against the logic of nuclearism. But their bombast recognized that they had little leverage on the four nuclear powers (who stood poised against each other on two sides, the Atlantic versus Moscow)' (Prashad, 2007: 95; see also Bidwai and Vanaik, 2000). Many emergent Non-Aligned Movement leaders were subjected to 'political assassination' (Prashad, 2007). The British peace activist Peggy Duff, who attended the Accra Assembly, noted that with Nkrumah's ousting by a coup led by dissident military officers, and allegedly supported by the CIA, 'the Accra Assembly died' (Duff, 1971: 236–7). She lamented that except 'for one week in June 1962 it had never really lived'.

These traditions of anti-imperial non-alignment were signalled in E.P. Thompson's essay 'Notes on Exterminism, the Last Stage of Civilisation', one of his most influential contributions to the intellectual terms of peace activism in the early 1980s. He argued that END should 'forge alliances with existing anti-imperialist and national liberation movements in every part of the world. At the same time, by strengthening the politics of non-alignment, it will develop a counter-force to the increasing militarization in Africa and Asia, of post-revolutionary states' (Thompson, 1982a: 28–9). The spatial imaginary of non-alignment articulated by Thompson, however, remains resolutely European-centred. Thompson argued that the preoccupation of the New Left with 'anti-imperialist movements in Africa, Asia and Latin America' had left 'western socialists' as mere 'observers and analysts of that external confrontation' (Thompson, 1982a: 26). Attempts to understand the Cold War solely within analytic frameworks of imperialism and anti-imperialism, he contended, had led the New Left to ignore the 'central fracture' of East-West confrontation (3).

This European-centred imaginary of non-alignment became the subject of criticism through the debates around END. The Czech dissident Jaroslav Šabata argued, in an influential open letter to Thompson, that the 'gradual integration of Europe through an ever deeper and all-embracing process of demo-cratic and autonomous development "inwards and outwards"' had a chance 'only if it gains influential allies in the camp of both "superpowers" and in the Third World, China included' (Šabata, 1983: 64). Saburo Kugai averred that Thompson's focus on the 'European theatre of the re-emergent Cold War' risked marginalizing the Asian and Pacific dimension of the 'perilous international situation', which had 'historically been as signifi-cant as the European and Atlantic dimension' (Kugai, 1982: 185). The American leftist Mike Davis made particularly trenchant criticisms of Thompson's position. Davis argues that

> Thompson's passionate call to protest and survive should not be deflected by radical platitudes or appeals to Marxist orthodoxy. But it can be sharpened by a more acute attention to the interlinkages of the actual struggles unfolding across five continents. ... The new movements for peace must mobilize the deepest levels of human solidarity, rather than pine nostalgically for the restoration of a lost European or Northern civilization. (Davis, 1982: 64)

The linkages made through Davis's arguments with struggles in Central America suggest that different potential ways of en-visioning solidarity were at stake in these different non-aligned maps of grievance of the Cold War. This also emphasizes the importance of solidarities forged between those in radically different geographical locations in relation to Cold War fissures and divisions.

If END maintained a contested European-centred logic it still made a decisive break with certain powerful geographical imaginaries that shaped twentieth-century peace movements. The END strategy was a key challenge to the discourse of unilateralism that had shaped the post-war British peace movement. Unilateral disarmament was the strategy that Britain should unconditionally disarm itself of its nuclear capability in the hope that this would lead international opinion. This demand developed 'particular specific and limited meanings' in 1950s' Britain as at that time it was 'the only nuclear weapons state other than the superpowers, so that on the one hand unilateral British renunciation could be argued as the first necessary practical step to prevent the proliferation of nuclear-weapons states and on the other hand as a moral example to all states including the superpowers' (Williams, 1982: 75-6). This strategy became hegemonic within the post-war peace movement and had a significant impact, at various times, on Labour Party policy, notably as a central (and notorious) demand of the party's manifesto for the 1983 election.[5] However, this strategy could be associated with a rather hubristic tendency within the peace movement which saw Britain as setting an example to the world (see Hinton, 1989). It could also be associated with rather isolationist left geographical imaginaries. James Hinton argues that one of the key attractions for 'many END supporters' was that it offered 'an escape from CND's traditional fixation on Britain leading the world' (Hinton, 1989: 187).

This analysis was made central to Raymond Williams's contribution to the internationalist dialogues prompted by E.P. Thompson's 'Exterminism' essay. He noted how the END campaign productively challenged the terms of 'unilateralism'. He argued that

> Campaigns against Cruise and Trident need not, in these critical years, involve and often be politically limited by, the full unilateralist case. For to refuse the siting of Cruise missiles on our territories, as part of a process of demanding multilateral European negotiations for the removal of all such missiles and the related bombers and submarine bases from the territories of 'Europe from Poland to Portugal', is not, in any ordinary sense 'unilateralism'. It is the

exercise of independence and sovereignty at a stage in a negotiating process for which there is still (just) time. (Williams, 1982: 77)

For Williams, then, the spatial imaginary of the END campaign was a decisive advance on the traditional unilateralist position. Invoking the 'spatial symbolism' of the END appeal of a Europe free of nuclear weapons from 'Poland to Portugal', Williams noted how this generated the possibility and necessity of alliances which stretched beyond narrowly conceived national left movements.

He allied this argument with a critique of the articulation of the British left with inward-looking versions of British nationalism. Williams contended that an interlocking strategy of 'unilateralism' shaped the terms of debate of the 'Labour Left' in this period. This effected the framing of 'economic, political, and peace campaigns'. The demands for unilateral disarmament were allied with proposals to withdraw from the European Community and for a 'siege or near-siege economy, protected by the strongest version of import controls' (Williams, 1982: 78). There were, Williams noted, strong arguments in favour of each of these positions, but he argued that the

> decisive common factors seem to be a radical overestimation of Britain's capacity and effect in independent action, and a radical underestimate of the degree of actual penetration of British economy and society by both international capitalism and the military–political alliance that exists to defend it. (Williams, 1982: 78).

The implications of this were the need to unsettle the 'British-centred' imaginaries of the left and peace movement. The position Williams outlined strongly advocated the importance of the geographies of solidarity and connection that were at the centre of the END project. He argued that these struggles, and 'especially in the struggle against the polarized hegemonism of the nuclear alliances, only combined action, on a European scale (of course based on what are also nationally conducted and to some extent uneven and differently inflected campaigns) has any realistic chance of success. Thus we must consistently advance *European* rather than British unilateralist arguments and objectives' (Williams, 1982: 79, emphasis in original). The generation of European-wide solidarities were not something that merely 'up-scaled' campaigns in particular 'national' peace movements. Rather, they could reconfigure, perhaps necessitated the reconfiguring, of the political imaginaries and horizons of peace movements.

Constructing non-aligned solidarities

Writing in 1982, Ferenc Köszegi argued that the most pressing problem facing the new peace movement in Hungrary was 'the problem of cooption and manipulation' (Köszegi, 1982: 13). He declared that

> There are three important forces which would want to coopt and manipulate the new peace movement. The first is the official Hungarian nation-wide Peace Council. Although this organisation has been relatively successful in the past, it has recently lost influence among the young. When the new wave of peace concern crossed the Hungarian border, the Peace Council was quite bewildered. Their confusion was quickly seen by the youth. It was very disillusioning for the youth representatives when they pressed to organise peace rallies that the Council could not answer until it had consulted with the Communist Party. This crippled the Council's credibility in the eyes of the young. (Köszegi, 1982: 13)

Köszegi's analysis here suggests how non-alignment was generated through particular spatial strategies and tactics. These tactics weren't incidental to the formation of such a non-aligned political project, but were integral to its identities and the spaces of solidarities it generated. The diverse forces of Cold War reaction, however, exerted considerable pressure on the formation of such alliances. The creation of non-aligned political spaces became, in itself, a key contribution and achievement of END.

The formation of contacts between peace activists in the East and West had to negotiate formidable political and material divisions. The pressures on constructing relations across such divides can be usefully illustrated by the conduct of the Scandinavian women's peace march, which opened the chapter. The account of the march by Jean Stead, then assistant editor of the *Guardian*, writing in an END published pamphlet on the Independent Moscow Peace Group, gives a sense both of some of the possibilities opened up by such exchanges, and also of their tensions and difficulties. From the start of the march in Stockholm five of the leading members of the official Soviet Peace Committee, including Grigory Lokshyn, the organizing secretary, joined it.

Stead notes that the 'Russians found it difficult at first to deal with the women' (Stead, 1982: 9). The non-hierarchical participatory ethos shaped by feminist organizing practices was a significant challenge to their conception of politics. (It was also to prove challenging to some of those involved in END!) There were tensions between the bureaucratic approach of the Soviet Peace Committee and feminist/peace movement activists 'who insisted on democratic participation and lengthy meetings on every detail of the pre-planning and on an inquest into every occasion when the Soviets appeared to break the agreements they had made on how the march should be conducted.' The Danish contingent on the march 'refused to have a leader, so that there was no one for Lokshyn to negotiate with' (Stead, 1982: 9). There was, however, a productive aspect to these solidarities. Stead argues that during 'the hot, thirsty marches, the long train rides, and the nights on the bare school floors in Finland', 'an uneasy sort of trust began to form between the Russians and the Scandinavians' (9).

This emphasizes the way that trust and solidarity can be forged through political activity, rather than pre-existing it, even through what were undeniably difficult and fraught circumstances. The difficulties of constructing non-aligned solidarities, however, were made clear when the march reached Moscow. The marchers decided not to meet with the representatives of the unofficial peace movement in the city after pressure from the

Soviet Peace Committee (Stead, 1982: 11). Two 'distinguished professors' who were part of the Moscow Independent Peace Group, including the geographer Professor Yuri Medvedkov, were sent to a detention centre for 'alcoholics and hooligans' for fifteen days while the marchers were in town.

The Moscow Independent Peace Group had come to global prominence with its appeal to the governments and publics of the USSR and the USA launched on 4 June 1982. This argued for friendship and solidarity to emerge between the peoples of the USSR and the USA through circumventing their governments. They argued that it was through the 'people' that durable ties for peace would be forged (Moscow Independent Peace Group, 1982). The group noted that it was drawn from 'various strata' of Soviet society, including 'scientists and workers, artists and writers, clergy and laity, Russians, Jews and other ethnic minorities etc.' (Moscow Independent Peace Group, 1982: 5). They warned that pressure would be mobilized to prevent them meeting with the marchers, urging that vigilance was needed 'regarding our fate during the Moscow phase of the "Peace-82" march' (5).

Only one of the marchers, Danielle Grünberg, was to visit the dissidents, in the company of Jean Stead of the *Guardian* and the Dutch journalist Cees van der Val. They met under the intimidating presence of ten KGB men waiting in cars outside. Grünberg's notes of the meeting record the routinized persecution and intimidation visited on the group. She observes that when Olga Medvedkov 'went down to buy some food' she 'was followed by 8 men to the shop' (Grünberg, 1982: 17). Grünberg also gives a strong sense of the way the group sought to position itself. The group, like the independent peace groups in Eastern Europe, 'did not join the "Soviet Peace Committee" as it was organised by the government and is not independent'. They contended that peace and trust 'cannot only be on a political and government level' but must 'be discussed amongst ordinary people' (18).

Constructing solidarities with activists from the Moscow group was a difficult process. Ann Pettit, of the Welsh group

Women for Life on Earth, whose march from Cardiff to Green-ham Common led to the founding of the peace camp in 1981, visited the Medvedkovs in 1983 (Pettit, 2006: 197-8). Her account emphasizes the extraordinary difficulties involved in meeting them. Their phones had been cut off and the front access door to the flats where they stayed firmly locked, so there was no means of attracting the attention of a resident. Somebody had 'thoughtfully provided a solution to this dilemma by breaking out the large pane of glass in the window to the side of the door, and neatly clearing the waist-high exposed edge of razor-sharp glass debris' (197-8). She recalls the atmosphere of meetings with the group in vivid terms:

> All our meetings with people in the Trust group over the next eight days would have contradictory elements: we would sit around tables drinking black tea, eating black bread, cheese and pickled cucumbers, and discussing the pros and cons of high rise buildings, or sharing our information about the arms race, and hearing about how, despite the known risks, more and more people were wanting to sign the Trust group's document, or were forming their own groups, in other towns and cities. People would seem remarkably up-beat and positive. Then, inevitably talk of 'the repressions' would surface and someone would talk about the latest arrest, and the latest rumoured arrest. (Pettit, 2006: 199)

The accounts of Pettit and Grünberg suggest the importance of struggles over spaces of association to forging non-aligned solidarities. Pettit evokes the omnipresent fear of arrest and discussion of rumours of repression. There were diverse struggles to generate such spaces of association and exchange under these conditions.

One of the key ways dialogues and exchange took place under such conditions was in samizdat form, typescript texts which circulated clandestinely (Merlin Press, 1977: v). This drew on specific genres and cultures of samizdat that were central to the forms of political culture shaped by dissidents. Samizdat texts sought to mimic but rework official discourses and were characterized by 'a disjuncture "between the dissidents" (subordinate)

social location and the type of (authoritative) discourse they borrowed and tried to master' (Oushakine, 2001: 204). Oushakine
positions samizdat journals as a component of national dissident
cultures. Samizdat texts were also central to the formation of
solidarities and transnational exchanges. Key articles and letters
that were central to these dialogues circulated in samizdat form.
E.P. Thompson's pamphlet 'Beyond the Cold War', for example,
was circulated in a Hungarian samizdat version.

That key texts had to be circulated in samizdat form underlines
the difficult conditions through which such exchanges took place.
Thompson had struggles in both the UK and in Eastern Europe
to forge political spaces for the articulation of a 'Beyond the
Cold War' perspective. During a visit to Budapest in 1981 he was
invited by the independent Peace Group for Dialogue 'to give a
public lecture while in Budapest, and (somewhat to my surprise)
it was suggested that I might take up themes from "Beyond the
Cold War"' (Thompson, 1982d: 6-7). On his arrival in Budapest,
however, it transpired that there were difficulties in 'obtaining
a public place for the lecture'. Officials and members of the
National Peace Council invited him to give the lecture but on
their premises before a closed audience. Thompson refused to
give the lecture under such restricted conditions. In the event
he delivered it in the apartment of the novelist George Konrad
(Thompson, 1982e). Despite 'the somewhat short notice (only two
hours) some eighty attended the lecture – mainly young people
– which was in any case as many as could occupy the floor space
of our generous hosts' (Thompson, 1982d: 6-7).

It wasn't only in the Eastern Bloc, however, where the intellectual positions of the non-aligned peace movement were
uncomfortable enough to invite state censorship. In the summer
of 1981 Thompson was invited to give the prestigious Dimbleby
Lecture. His proposal for a lecture on the theme of 'Beyond the
Cold War' was approved by Features and by the BBC managing
director Alasdair Milne. The lecture, however, was pulled by the
director general of the BBC Ian Trethowan, who 'insisted that
Thompson must not be allowed to deliver the lecture'. Trethowan

was sure that Thompson would get his message of disarmament across 'unmistakably', and 'was equally sure that the government would be furious' (Leapman, 1986: 184–5). The lecture was eventually published as a pamphlet, *Beyond the Cold War*, by Merlin Press, the left publisher that played a key role in making samizdat publications available in English (Thompson, 1982f).

The formation of political spaces that cut across such entrenched and aggressively policed divisions were not a by-product of the organizing of END. Rather, they were integral to the political organizing and a key achievement. The formation and maintenance of such spaces and connections were integral to the construction of non-aligned forms of internationalism. The solidarities fashioned through such political spaces opened up important political possibilities. They articulated presents and futures which refused to be confined within Cold War divisions. This was a condition for imagining, and enacting, alternative futures 'Beyond the Cold War'.

Conclusion

On 4 July 2011 a statue of Ronald Reagan was unveiled in Grovesnor Square in London by the United States embassy. Margaret Thatcher's accolade that 'Ronald Reagan won the Cold War without a shot being fired' is inscribed on the plinth. Such extraordinary and lingering triumphalism has shaped dominant narratives about the Cold War ever since the fall of the Soviet Union. This narrative ignores those who were killed during the many Cold War-related conflicts. It also depends on a pervasive silencing of the popular mobilizations and solidarities that opposed the two dominant Cold War positions.

In 1991 E.P. Thompson targeted such triumphalism, writing in typically coruscating terms of 'prestigious persons in Washington who rabbit on about the "end of history"' (Thompson, 1991: 20). In opposition to Francis Fukuyama's notorious argument that the fall of the Cold War necessitated the triumph of Western liberal democracy, he contended that the 'non-aligned peace movements made a large contribution to the end of the Cold War and is one of the only traditions to emerge from it with any honour' (23). Thompson's key concern was to ensure that the political alternatives nourished through the non-aligned peace movement would shape the politics of a post-Cold War Europe. He also had a keen sense of the importance of struggles over how the end of the Cold War was to be understood. He was vigilant of the dangers of triumphalist narratives in producing neoliberalism as hegemonic.

If in 1991 there were still powerful counter-voices to the emergence of such a triumphalism, it seems now that such a narrative is almost uncontested. The role of the independent peace movement in opposing the logic of the Cold War has been profoundly marginalized. Despite the pressures exerted on the formation of non-aligned solidarities, however, it is clear that they had significant effects. They generated dialogues and movements which refused the binary logics of the Cold War. These were never smooth or consensual; nor would it have been desirable if they had been. These fraught processes and alliances, however, were significant in shaping political spaces that decisively challenged the terms on which the Cold War was produced and reproduced. They were also significant in bringing the conflict to an end.

PART IV

Solidarity in the shadow of neoliberalism

CHAPTER 7

'Our resistance is as transnational as capital': the counter-globalization movement and prefigurative solidarity

In early 2003 the Indian *Economic and Political Weekly* carried a report on the Asian Social Forum (ASF) by Devaki Jain. The ASF took place in Hyderabad and was one of many regional spin-offs from the World Social Forum (WSF), the influential hub of different social and political movements opposed to globalization. Jain situated the WSF as belonging to an important independent internationalist tradition that included the Non-Aligned Movement (Jain, 2003). Her report discussed tensions that were raised at the Forum, centring on criticisms of the diversity of political positions it brought together. The report, however, notes:

> To a criticism that all these alternatives do not add up to a unity, and that a mere celebration of identities in such diverse contexts and approaches cannot provide the basis for a challenge to the exterminator, a feminist, once a member of the CPML,[1] retorted that it was good to be free of a unifying political theory. Belonging to such formal ideologies had been suffocating, as it quelled difference of opinion, debate and transformation. Confusion was good, as it gave the space to form new alliances, shape new formulations, design new approaches, and maybe even new theories to underpin all the alternatives. Unity can be forged, but not forced as was happening

before the diverse groups got a shared space to understand their differences and shape their commonality. (Jain, 2003: 100)

As Jain notes, feminist positions have opened up spaces of political possibility that have often been closed down by sectarian left positions and affiliations. The analysis she recounts here suggests the importance of feminist positions in asserting that commonality and unity can be forged from diverse perspectives rather than imposed by particular political lines.

Jain's account speaks to productive tensions within the political analysis and forms generated by the networked movements against neoliberal globalization. She highlights the influence of transnational feminism on the organizing practices and political imaginaries articulated by the counter-globalization movement. The alternatives have sought to shape a 'prefigurative' ethics of solidarity; that is, a commitment that organizing practices should bring into being the alternative worlds they seek to create. This chapter explores the terms on which such solidarities have been both constructed and contested.

Making prefigurative solidarities

The dominant political narratives of the late 1990s assumed the superiority of a specific form of neoliberal globalization. Mainstream politicians, including those from the centre-left, bought into a political consensus which assumed that this form of globalization was inevitable. This approach, which came to be known as the 'Washington Consensus', depended on a passive construction of politics. It denied citizens any role or agency in negotiating, shaping or engaging with the terms on which globalization was fashioned. Neoliberal globalization, however, proved not to be politically omnipotent. It was brought into contestation by diverse overlapping political networks mobilized against key sites, conferences and meetings associated with neoliberal institutions such as the World Trade Organization and the G8 (Routledge and Cumbers, 2009).

These movements were in part catalysed by the Zapatistas' uprising in San Cristobal, Chiapas, on 1 January 1994. The Zapatistas' insurgency against a North American Free Trade Agreement that included Mexico's indigenous populations 'only as disposable waste' did much to circulate and intensify oppositional movements that were explicitly against neoliberalism (Marcos, 1995: 73). The Zapatistas hailed the transnational support networks that emerged in solidarity as part of the same movement and the same anti-neoliberal struggles (Khasnabish, 2010; Olesen, 2005). They developed an innovative approach to these transnational solidarities by convening two large international gatherings, the Encuentros 'for humanity and against neoliberalism'. These events took place in Mexico in 1996 and in Spain in 1997 (see De Angelis, 1998). They shaped the terms of internationalist opposition to globalization. The events were generative of unofficial alliances, friendships and meetings that crossed between different activist groupings and cultures. One of the outcomes of these meetings was the formation of the network People's Global Action Against Free Trade (PGA), which was central in shaping the terms of the counter-globalization movement.

The Zapatistas have shaped a distinctive approach to left politics. Rather than attempting, in Leninist fashion, to take control of the state, they sought to open up 'autonomous' political spaces (Rabasa, 2010). They have 'introduced a new language of political struggle, identity and possibility. Instead of the bureaucratic language and rigid style used so often by insurgent and revolutionary groups the political discourse of the Zapatistas is one alive with poetry, myth, wit and hope' (Khasnabish, 2010: 192). Their political activity has been informed by a commitment to producing different worlds through the logic of their organizing, including in a number of autonomous communities in Chiapas. This is captured by Subcomandante Marcos's dictum that 'We need not conquer the world. It is enough to build it anew' (cited by Maeckelbergh, 2011: 1). That is to say, alternative political futures are not just the end points of political movements. Rather, their organizational practices are integral to the political alternatives they generate.

A central claim of counter-globalization movements has been that their organizing practices are 'actually existing' alternatives to neoliberalized social relations. David Graeber contends that such prefigurative forms of direct-action politics are a central political innovation of the movements against neoliberal globalization. He argues that

> The very notion of direct action, with its rejection of a politics which appeals to governments to modify their behaviour, in favour of physical intervention against state power in a form that itself prefigures an alternative – all of this emerges directly from the libertarian tradition. Anarchism is the heart of the movement, its soul; the source of most of what's new and hopeful about it. (Graeber, 2002: 62)

For Graeber, then, rather than lacking a coherent ideology these forms of direct action are the means through which actually existing alternatives are made. This is positioned as a key break from hierarchical political practices based around the capture of state power by a vanguard that seeks to represent the interests of others (see also Holloway, 2002). Graeber argues that these movements have generated a diversity of organizational practices, 'all aimed at creating forms of democratic process that allow initiatives to rise from below and attain maximum effective solidarity, without stifling dissenting voices [or] creating leadership positions' (Graeber, 2002: 71).

One of the key forms of political innovation that has characterized the alter-globalization movement has been its experiments with alternative forms of organizing. The use of affinity groups and hubs and spokes councils was central to the organizing practices adopted at Seattle by activist groups such as the Direct Action Network. An affinity group is a 'small group of people united by friendship, a history of political work together, a common issue or identity, or a shared adoption of a particular tactic.' (Ross, 2003: 284). The term is a translation of the

Spanish *grupo de affinidad* and was pioneered by the Iberian Anarchist Federation (FAI) in the pre-Franco era (Bookchin, 1971: 221). The use of affinity groups as a key mode of organizing is a direct challenge to more hierarchical and controlled forms of left practice. This also breaks with the traditional pattern of a march with a pre-planned route followed by speeches, which characterized the political activity of organized labour and mainstream environmental movements at Seattle (Wainwright et al., 2000).

For the veteran American anarchist Murray Bookchin affinity groups are intended to function 'as catalysts within popular movements not as 'vanguards'' (Bookchin, 1971: 221). Affinity groups are linked together to generate joint actions through 'spokes councils' 'in which information is shared, tactical, strategic, or organizational issues are discussed, and decisions are made' (Ross, 2003: 285). The 'selection of delegates', according to Graeber, 'is not as delicate a matter as it might be because spokes are not, technically, empowered to make decisions for the group. They're not really representatives. They are basically conduits for information: they explain what their group is intending to do, bring proposals and convey information and proposals back to the group for it to consider collectively' (Graeber, 2009: 37).

Diverse movements have drawn on, and shaped, such non-hierarchical organizing logics. Barbara Epstein notes that the 'affinity group structure and consensus process were attractive to both Christians and feminists' involved in the Pledge of Resistance, the organizational hub of the peace movement in Boston in the 1970s and 1980s (Epstein, 1991: 188). For Kate Hoffman, a coordinator of the Pledge within a background in the lesbian feminist community, both groups shared a concern 'with building community, and emphasis on personal experience, and the search for a politics that avoids hard rhetorical stances' (cited by Epstein, 1991: 188).

Diverse feminist interventions have decisively shaped the terms of prefigurative politics. As Jain's account of the Asian

Social Forum emphasizes, feminist critiques of vanguardist and hierarchical left organizing practices have been central to articulating prefigurative politics. There are important histories of struggle over the terms on which feminist struggles have intersected with and challenged dominant left political cultures. The lineages of such contestation are captured by Doreen Massey. Reflecting on how her involvement in the women's movement of the 1970s shaped her political trajectories, she insists that the 'feminism of my generation wasn't just about gender it was about much more general liberation. It was, to some extent, a response to the 60s, which were very male dominated, but it was part of that real challenge to hierarchies' (Massey, 2013). She argues that feminism in this period was about more than problematizing unequal gender relations and involved a thoroughgoing critique of the unequal power relations of left politics.

Raya Dunayevskaya, who pioneered a distinctive feminist, anti-Stalinist, Marxism in the mid-twentieth century,[2] similarly insisted on the importance of the creation of 'new relations' in political struggle rather than merely contesting 'what is' (Dunayevskaya, 1985: 51). In her essay on 'The Black Dimension in Women's Liberation' she cites Doris Wright's contention that

> I'm not thoroughly convinced that Black Liberation, the way it's being spelled out, will really and truly mean my liberation. I'm not sure that when it comes time to 'put down my gun', that I won't have a broom shoved in my hands, as so many of my Cuban sisters have. (Wright cited by Dunayevskaya, 1985: 51)

Dunayevskaya elucidates the significance of Wright's position. She asserts that Wright 'was not putting the question down as a condition – "I will not make a revolution unless you promise"'. Rather, she was 'posing the question of what happens after. That is what we have to answer before, in the practice of our own organisations, our own thought and our own activity' (Dunayevskaya, 1985: 51).

Dunayevskaya's engagement with Wright emphasizes the diverse political trajectories through which feminisms have been articulated. Here there is contestation of both a male-centred black liberation movement, but also of a women's liberation movement that marginalized the experiences of oppression of 'women of colour' (Pulido, 2006). Post-colonial feminist writers such as Chandra Talpade Mohanty and Carole Boyce Davies have emphasized the importance of articulating feminist solidarities which transcend the Western-centred notions of 'sisterhood' that shaped some versions of second-wave feminism (Mohanty, 2003: 17-84; Davies, 2008). Mohanty argues instead that 'transnational feminist practice depends on building feminist solidarities across the divisions of place, identity, class, work, belief, and so on' (Mohanty, 2003: 250).

This has important resonances with attempts to construct transnational and non-hierarchical solidarities in opposition to neoliberal globalization. The diverse influences of feminism on the forms of these struggles have, however, often been rather overlooked (Eschle, 2005; Lindell, 2011). Mohanty has argued that there has been an 'implicit masculinization of the discourses of antiglobalization movements' (Mohanty, 2003: 250). Despite this she contends that 'many of the democratic practices and process-oriented aspects of feminism appear to be institutionalized into the decision-making processes of some of these movements. Thus the principles of non-hierarchy, democratic participation, and the notion of the personal being political all emerge in various ways in this antiglobal politics' (250). She argues that such feminist lineages, practices and agendas should be made explicit.

This raises a set of challenges for thinking about the 'spatial politics' of organizing and political activism. What kinds of solidarities might a prefigurative politics imagine and envision? How might solidarities be generated as an integral part of a prefigurative politics? Further, what kind of tensions and struggles emerge over how prefigurative politics is conducted and practised?

Interrogating the diverse forms of solidarities shaped through counter-globalization struggles involves considering the relations between prefigurative politics and the spatial practices of activist politics (Featherstone, 2010). Particular uses of space can shape, and be shaped by, the relations produced through activist politics. Tom Goyens's account of the political cultures of German-speaking anarchists in the United States at the turn of the nineteenth century notes how the ways in which 'anarchists conceived of specific places, such as beer halls and even picnic grounds' shaped the alternative political imaginaries they fostered (Goyens, 2009: 449). Such spatial relations, then, are not a fixed backdrop to activist practices. The terms on which they are shaped and constructed can be central to different ways of envisioning prefigurative politics.

Following the way activist connections are shaped and generated is important for engaging with tensions that emerge through political activity. The terms on which solidarities are constructed through counter-globalization movements have been brought into contestation (Featherstone, 2003; Routledge and Cumbers, 2009). This has involved problematizing the relations and forms of political organization shaped through such movements. The terms on which solidarities are constructed and the linkages they make between diverse struggles can be central to engaging with the political alternatives they shape. As Juris argues, 'micro-level struggles over political vision, strategy and tactics' are integral to these forms of political activity and the alternative futures they seek to make (Juris, 2008: 97). Feminist accounts of power have been important here in drawing attention to the importance of such micro-political relations (Vargas, 2002).

In this regard counter-globalization movements have experimented with alternative ways of generating globalization through their organizing practices. They have sought to challenge and rework existing geographies of power. The formation of solidarities between different struggles and connections between overlapping networks of resistance has been a productive outcome of such organizing. This has shaped articulations of the terms of an internationalist opposition to globalization. The terms on which such relations have been forged and the improvisation of new relations have been productive and contested (Graeber, 2009: 38).

Engaging with these productive and generative solidarities asserts the inventive character of the political movements. The construction of solidarities between diverse actors was a central and inventive achievement of counter-global organizing. This enabled the formation of political spaces that were shaped through alternative logics of connection to the exploitative unequal relations that are central to neoliberal globalization. The construction of such political spaces and connections was not a by product of these movements. It was integral to their attempts to create and shape different worlds.

The 'Battle of Seattle', whiteness and contested organizing practices

On 30 November 1999, a public uprising shut down the World Trade Organization and took over downtown Seattle, transforming it into a festival of resistance. Tens of thousands of people joined the non-violent direct action blockade which encircled the WTO conference site, keeping the most powerful institution on earth shut down from dawn until dusk, despite an army of federal, state and local police shooting tear gas, pepper spray, rubber, plastic and wooden bullets, concussion grenades and deploying armoured vehicles. The Washington National Guard's 81st Infantry Brigade, 1-303 Armor Battalion and the 898th Combat Engineer Battalion were deployed. People continued to resist throughout the week despite a clampdown that included nearly 600 arrests and the declaration of a 'state of emergency' and suspension of basic civil liberties in downtown Seattle. Longshore workers shut down every West Coast port from Alaska to Los Angeles. Large numbers of Seattle taxi drivers went on strike. All week the fire fighters' union refused authorities' requests to turn their fire hoses on people. Tens of thousands of working people and students skipped or walked out of work or school.

People across the globe took action in solidarity. In India, thousands of farmers in Karnataka marched to Bangalore, and over a thousand villagers from Anjar in Narmada Valley held a procession. Thousands took to the streets in the Philippines, Portugal, Pakistan, Turkey, Korea, and across Europe, the United States and Canada. 75,000 people marched in 80 different French cities and 800 miners clashed with Police. In Italy, the headquarters of the National Committee for Bio-Safety was occupied. In the period leading up to the WTO Ministerial resistance increased; an occupation of the WTO world headquarters in Geneva; Turkish peasants, trade unionists and environmentalists marched on the capital of Ankara; a street party shut down traffic in New York City's Times Square; activists took over US Trade Representative Charlene Barshefsky's offices; and workers and students rallied in Seoul, Korea. (Solnit, 2009: 10-11)

The Seattle protests dramatically brought the terms of neoliberal globalization into contestation. They took the World Trade Organization, a 'boring', 'faceless' and relatively unknown institution, and made it, and its role in formatting and shaping globalization on neoliberal terms, centre-stage. David Solnit's account stresses the diverse forms of solidarity that were integral to the protests. This makes an important contribution to understanding these events. The account makes clear that the 'rising' was not something that came from nowhere. It wasn't, as sometimes has been suggested, a 'spontaneous' set of events. Rather, it was part of sustained practices of transnational organizing which had emerged through the mid-1990s. These forms of organizing brought together diverse groups protesting against neoliberal globalization in different places. These included projects like the Inter-Continental Caravan, sponsored by People's Global Action. This brought 400 activists from Indian farmers' movements to Western Europe in May and June of 1999 and shaped alliances defined by shared opposition to transnational capital and agribusiness (Featherstone, 2003).

Solnit's account makes clear that this was not just a US-centred resistance to neoliberalism. Some of the movements at Seattle did frame contestation of the WTO in chauvinistic

US-centred terms. The Seattle chapter of the Sierra Club, the rather elite US environmental group, for example, used a postcard which featured 'three colonial era men marching defiantly, one brandishing an American flag' and the slogan 'No globalization without representation' (Wong, 2002: 219). These images were seen as deeply alienating by 'activists of colour' and were part of a populist nationalist framing of anti-WTO sentiment. The resistances, however, were also formed through diverse geographies of connection. Thus labour leaders from 'Mexico, the Caribbean, South Africa, Malaysia, India, and China spoke alongside with every major U.S. union leader' (Martinez, 2000: n.pag.). Solidarity events were held across the globe. This made the 'protests' not just a US-centred event but one which was part of, and also inspired, a vibrant transnational movement.

The protests were characterized by alliances between activist constituencies that had often been held apart or been mutually suspicious, encapsulated in the famous slogan 'Teamsters and Turtles together at last'. US Earth First! activists joined with steel workers in the Alliance for Sustainable Jobs and the Environment 'to build a partnership fighting for the protection of both people and planet' (Brecher et al., 2000: 50). These alliances were one of the most powerful and innovative aspects of the actions against the World Trade Organization in Seattle in 1999 (Cockburn and St Clair, 2000: 17). These solidarities were formed through intense political activity under conditions of severe repression (Juris, 2008). The protests were hailed as a dramatic example of prefigurative, alternative politics in action. 'This is what democracy looks like' was a key chant.

The events in Seattle have acquired the status of a 'political myth'. A.K. Thompson argues that the 'mythic dimensions' of the 'Battle of Seattle and the Black Bloc actions that took place there' are 'indebted to the event's disclosure of an unrealized future' (Thompson, 2010: 153). This myth, he contends, has three key dimensions: 'that people can work together across difference', that 'the state's might is nothing when compared to the strength of dissident refusal' and that 'catastrophe and solidarity share a profound co-implication' (153). These elements of the Seattle 'protests' have inspired alternative political futures.

There have, however, been tensions over the terms on which this political myth is constructed. David Solnit reflects on this in his essay 'The Battle of the Story of the Battle of Seattle'. Solnit was involved with the Direct Action Network in 1999. The essay recounts his attempts to engage critically with the process of production of the feature film the *Battle in Seattle*. Through a long, tortuous and ultimately unsuccessful dialogue he attempted to persuade Stuart Townsend, the director of the film, to give more accurate depictions of activist political cultures. Solnit concluded, however, that 'what was really lacking was for people and organizations to tell our own story, to tell it compellingly to amplify it (Solnit, 2009: 53).

Solnit's aim to forge space for activists to tell their own stories about the protests is significant. His account, however, envisions a singular activist story about the 'rising'. This silences some of the key movement debates that shaped the contested organizing practices prior to Seattle and that erupted in the aftermath of the protests. These debates were in part catalysed by an influential and widely circulated article by Elizabeth Martinez querying why the resistance in Seattle was so white. She estimated that 'the overall turnout of color from the U.S. remained around five percent of the total' (Martinez, 2000: n.pag.). Martinez affirmed the significance of the protests. She argued, however, that it was necessary to understand the reasons why there were so few activists of colour present and to relate this to activist organizing practices.

She suggested that activist subcultures were shaped by cultures of assumed whiteness. Martinez contended that, rather than opening up spaces of organizing, such practices could reproduce exclusionary activist subcultures.

In personal interviews, activists from the Bay Area and the Southwest gave me several reasons for this. Some mentioned concern about the likelihood of brutal police repression. Other obstacles: lack of funds for the trip, inability to be absent from work during the week, and problems in finding child care. ... Others were more openly apprehensive. For example, Carlos ('Los' for short) Windham of Company of Prophets told me, 'I think even Bay Area activists of color who understood the linkage didn't want to go to a protest dominated by 50,000 white hippies.' (Martinez, 2000: n.pag.)

This account emphasizes how organizing practices led to the protest being associated with activist subcultures that were defined by unspoken forms of whiteness. For Martinez these tensions were exacerbated through use of the Internet to mobilize for the protests. This failed to broaden the constituency involved in the protests given the unequal access to the Internet, particularly among poor black and Hispanic communities in the USA (Martinez, 2000). Further, she contended that activists failed to make connections between local and transnational issues.

This analysis resonated with, and was echoed by, other activists. Yutaka Dirks, for example, argued that the sites of contestation and organizing of the movement needed to be broadened beyond set-piece confrontations at summits. She noted that 'many radical activists of colour and feminists' had challenged the 'overwhelmingly white and also overly male' 'make-up of the large protests against capitalist globalization'. She also drew attention to 'the privilege that summit hopping demands, privilege that is afforded to white people in a white supremacist society, and men in a patriarchical society' (Dirks, 2002: n.pag.). In a provocative argument centred on the role of the Black Bloc in Seattle and other protests, A.K. Thompson argues that such accounts ignore the fact that these were hugely significant and transformative events for the largely white middle-class activists involved (Thompson, 2010).

Solnit's account does not engage with, or even mention, criticisms of the whiteness of the protests. This silence is remarkable given Robin Kelley's claim that the 'lack of people of colour' involved in the protests in Seattle and in the demonstrations against the IMF and World Bank in Washington in 2000 constituted 'a crisis' (cited by Hsiao, 2002: 344). Chris Dixon, who was involved with the Direct Action Network in Seattle, argues that 'we didn't think carefully enough about laying the foundations for a resilient movement grounded in diverse communities. Many of us were satisfied to stay within our limited activist networks and comfortable social scenes' (Dixon, 2009: 108).

These tensions relate strongly to the issues raised by critics of the conduct and operation of activist subcultures. Thus Stephanie Ross has argued that affinity groups can sometimes serve to reproduce and intensify small 'cliques' of activists, rather than act to generate connections between different groups. She contends that the 'affinity group model can thus be seen as reproducing a debilitating sectarian tradition: smaller and smaller groups are formed by those who already agree with one another' (Ross, 2003: 291). At stake in challenges to these organizing practices were also different ways of articulating opposition to neoliberal globalization.

Colin Rajah, for example, wrote a follow-up piece to Martinez's article, entitled 'Where Was the Color in A16?' This referred to the demonstrations against the annual International Monetary Fund and World Bank meetings that took place in Washington DC in April 2000. Irene Tung, a member of the Young Communist League who helped organize a Brown University contingent to the protests in Washington, noted that

> There was definitely an insider's culture at A16, especially at the convergence spaces. There was a vocabulary and behaviour, an assumed cultural commonality, that was somewhat eerie. It seems that the ideals of absence of leadership and 'facilitated chaos' – as they say – function best in a homogenous group. (Rajah, 2002: 239)

Assumptions that 'horizontal' forms of politics were already being enacted also closed down space for the negotiation of differences and tensions. Eric Tang from 'The Third World Within' contingent complained of 'being constantly "greeted with white paternalism"'.

> The best they could say was 'Yes! This is what democracy looks like!' Given how white-dominated the scene was, this was deeply insulting to all of us, as if the Third World people in our group were some sort of mere add-on to a struggle being waged by radical white college kids and the environmental movement. (Rajah, 2002: 238)

Assertions that movements are creating alternative power relations can, then, paradoxically serve to reproduce uneven geographies of power.

These relations of power are not just about the inclusion/exclusion of particular groups of activists. They had consequences for the forms of solidarity and political analysis that were generated through events like the A16 mobilizations. Kristine Wong describes some of the pressure exerted on her attempts to connect local and transnational struggles. Wong was involved as a print journalist for the Indymedia Center in both the Seattle and the A16 protests. She contributed to *Blind Spot*, a daily paper produced 'for distribution on the streets of Seattle'. She recalls finding the 'atmosphere chaotic and not very welcoming to people of color' (Wong, 2002: 222–3).

During the A16 protests Wong 'focused on stories about people of color that made the local connections to globalization' (Wong, 2002: 223). Her analysis was making precisely the kinds of connections that Martinez argued were marginalized through the Seattle protests. Wong wrote a story for *Blind Spot* about

> the Columbia Heights evictions/anti-gentrification rally on April 15 and turning it in that night. Earlier, I also sent them my interview with a Malaysian-born activist from JustACT, the San Francisco-based group who had brought a number of youth activists of color to the protests. The interview had an international perspective about the repression of Asian/Pacific Islander student activists and linked US youth of color's struggle against police brutality and the prison system with globalization and privatization. (Wong, 2002: 223)

Wong's account focuses on making diverse solidarities between different groups struggling against neoliberal globalization. This constructs particular maps of grievance informed by antagonisms against racism in the USA, and makes creative linkages between antagonisms over police brutality and incarceration and contestation of privatization. It also reflects the construction of solidarities informed by diverse political trajectories.

Wong's articles, however, were not published, despite her being told they were slated for publication in the 16 April edition. This was not an isolated incident. Rather, it was part of a broader lack of engagement with 'anti-racist' and anti-colonial analysis of globalization. As Wong comments, 'The content that did involve stories mentioning the struggles of people of color failed as substantive analyses of the issues. ... The lack of analysis could have been avoided had people of color with an understanding of and experience with these issues have been part of the editorial team' (Wong, 2002: 223). Her internationalist opposition to globalization sought to make articulations between political trajectories that were actively marginalized through exclusionary organizing practices. This challenge to Anglo-centred articulations of counter-global politics generated and envisioned alternative solidarities and connections.

The activist and scholar Amory Starr has implied that such challenges to the whiteness of 'anti-globalization' protest have amounted to a form of sectarianism (Starr, 2003: 273). She concedes the need to 'deal with specific incidents of racism, sexism, homophobia' (276). She ignores, however, the challenges posed by activists such as Dirks and Martinez to broader organizing logics and practices. As a result Starr positions such challenges as undermining the attempts of alter-globalization movements to practise pre-figurative solidarities. An alternative reading is to view such feminist and anti-racist critiques as part of, not antithetical to, these political cultures. They shaped attempts to experiment with different logics of organizing and to articulate the terms of internationalist opposition to globalization.

These challenges sought to extend and deepen the terms on which prefigurative solidarities and organizing cultures are shaped. Through contesting the terms on which solidarities were constructed they contributed to articulations of an internationalist opposition to globalization. As Dirks argues, 'We need to analyze the way that we organize, to make our actions and movements accessible and radical. We need to commit to do the hard work of helping to build an anti-racist, anti-imperialist, multiracial, feminist, queer liberationist, and anti-authoritarian movement against global capitalism.' (Dirks, 2002: n.pag.). Such ways of deepening and extending the terms on which such prefigurative solidarities are fashioned have often arisen through challenges to the conduct of existing organizing practices.

The harassment of women and of non-Indian participants by a small minority of Indian activists involved in the Inter-Continental Caravan, for example, led to contestation of the founding principles of People's Global Action. These principles became the site of contestation and negotiation at the second global meeting of PGA held in Bangalore in the aftermath of the Caravan (see PGA, 1999). As a result PGA adopted a new hallmark, one of 'the basic points of consensus ... on which the network is built'. This hallmark proclaims that 'We reject all forms and systems of domination and discrimination including, but not limited to, patriarchy, racism and religious fundamentalism of all creeds. We embrace the full dignity of all human beings.'

Projects like the Caravan were not an end result, then, but part of a longer process of organizing against neoliberal globalization. Some of the terms and power relations of internationalist counter-globalization politics were contested and negotiated through this process. A participant at the meeting noted, however, that despite these 'beautiful words' and inclusion of a commitment to 'fighting patriarchy' there was 'male domination' in 'both numbers and atmosphere' (Anon., 1999: n.pag.). Further, there were few women present from Indian movements, and women's groups from Karnataka were only present at one of the gender discussions (Anon., 1999: n.pag.).

This emphasizes that transnational organizing practices have brought together activists from markedly different political traditions and trajectories. Such trajectories have not produced smooth articulations, but rather have often been articulated on profoundly unequal terms. The World Social Forum has emerged as one of the most iconic associational spaces through which these different trajectories of opposition and alternative political identities/practices are networked. It is a 'meeting place' which 'is open to pluralism and to the diversity of activities and ways of engaging with the organisations and movements that decide to participate in it, as well as the diversity of genders, races, ethnicities and cultures' (Vargas, 2004: 229). Hardt and Negri argue that it has already become 'one of those positive myths that define our political compass'. They argue that it represents 'a new democratic cosmopolitanism, a new anti-capitalist transnationalism, a new intellectual nomadism, a great movement of the multitude' (Hardt and Negri, 2003: xvi).

Transnational feminism and the World Social Forum

In a trenchant analysis of the fifth World Social Forum held in 2005 in Pôrto Alegre, Brazil, Ana Elena Obando posed a set of challenges about the alternatives being constructed through the event. She argued that within this process 'hopeful groups and individuals came face to face with both the long term and short term limitations and contradiction that have plagued larger movement building' (Obando, 2005: n.pag.). The context for Obando's intervention was serious instances of violence against women, including two rapes in the youth camp of the 2005 World Social Forum. This violence was not treated seriously by organizers of the WSF, who ignored calls for an inquiry into these events (Koopman, 2007). Obando relates this gender-based violence to the whole political analysis of globalization shaped through the WSF. She argues that a 'common denominator amongst the resistance movements' at the WSF 'was their general opposition to neoliberal capitalism, militarization, war and the destruction of the environment and their lack of opposition to one of the expressions of patriarchy that is intertwined with those above: fundamentalisms, particularly religious fundamentalisms' (Obando, 2005: n.pag.).

Obando contends that feminist movements, particularly those from Latin America, had been key to putting the relations between globalization, patriarchy and fundamentalism on the 'analytical terrain of the forum'. Thus she notes that 'feminists from Latin America'

> introduced the issue of fundamentalisms at the World Social Forum (WSF) through the Articulación Feminista Marcosur (Marcosur Feminist Organization) Campaign; this issue is not part of the structure of the political discussion at the forum, in spite of the threat it represents to democracy and the principles of equality and diversity of identities and beliefs. People are also subjugated by alliances between political, economic and ideological-religious fundamentalist groups. The fundamentalist discourse wielded by the right in the United States to win votes during the last elections is contrary to the most basic human rights principles[:] it calls for control over the bodies and the sexuality of LGTBI people. It also perpetuates values that keep women in their traditional roles. (Obando, 2005: n.p.)

This analysis signals how feminist interventions have both challenged and shaped the political understandings of globalization and alternatives forged through the WSF. Obando's account emphasizes that engaging with the gendered and racialized character of globalization opens up political antagonisms which can be marginalized by masculinist analyses of processes of globalization.

Articulación Feminista Marcosur (AFM) has been a key feminist presence at the WSF. It has been shaped by significant histories of transnational feminist organizing in Latin America. Particularly significant here are the feminist *Encuentros* which have brought together women from 'different backgrounds and identities to discuss the issues at stake' (Lopreite, 2010: 136).

Sonia Alvarez describes these as being seen by feminist activists as 'crucial sites in which to re-view and refine their feminist discourses and practices, in dialogue with others in the region' (Alvarez, 2000: 35). These feminist discourses emerged in opposition to the repressive gender politics of military regimes of the 1970s and 1980s. Débora Lopreite argues that 'democratic transitions and women's activism in Latin America were accompanied by demands for democracy, rights and citizenship' (Lopreite, 2010: 135). There have been significant struggles and campaigns over gendered forms of violence, which have been particularly prevalent in post-conflict societies such as El Salvador (Hume, 2009).

Feminist presence in the forum has included marches such as '"a noisy carnival-like rally for the decriminalisation of abortion in Latin America and the Caribbean"' at the second WSF (Eschle and Maiguashca, 2010: 29). Hilary Wainwright has characterized the WSF as 'not so much a stand-alone global organisation but a new kind of convergence of located actors whose activities and strategies are distributed and interconnected, co-ordinated to varying degrees but not through a single centre' (Wainwright, 2013). The WSF is a site of intersection, and intensification of many different campaigning networks, though there are also exclusions. The fact that the Zapatistas are armed has 'made them unwelcome at the World Social Forum' in a process which, as Kolya Abramsky observes, 'seems highly oblivious of the debt the global movement owes to the Zapatistas' (Abramsky, 2006: n.pag.).

In this regard the political trajectories of movements like Articulación Feminista Marcosur have shaped the convergences articulated through the WSF in significant ways. This can shift the very terms of debate on which globalization is contested. Feminist interventions have challenged populist/ nationalist articulations of resistance to globalization (Eschle and Maiguashca, 2010). Opposition to contemporary forms of globalization have often served to reinforce rather than challenge dominant patriarchal gender relations. The resistance to the holding of the Miss World pageant in Bangalore in 1996 is a case in point here. Opposition comprised diverse groups including 'students, farmers, unions, the Hindu Right and a number of women's organizations that formed a loosely defined progressive coalition' (Oza, 2006: 89). The left mobilized a strong critique of the linkages between the state and global and domestic capital through the pageant. It did not, however, contest the conservative narrative of the Hindu right, which counterposed globalization with a "threatened Indian culture" (Oza 2006: 91). Rupal Oza contends that 'local opposition was spatially manifested as preserving the nation against the larger forces of globalization' (Oza 2001: 1068). Here existing gender relations were reproduced rather than challenged through the opposition to the pageant.

By contesting such nationalist articulations of resistance to globalization transnational feminist interventions have shaped different solidarities and internationalist political cultures. The presence of feminist movements in the World Social Forum such as the World March of Women/Articulación Feminista Marcosur campaign has shaped the organizational cultures of the WSF. As the World March of Women emphasize, this has been something which has been a site of struggle and contestation:

> The 2003 edition of the Forum illustrated the impact of our work in that there were definitely more women, particularly feminists, on the panels. We nevertheless saw that women's presence remains marginal and is only 'politely tolerated.' We are still a long way from achieving genuine dialogue on the role of women and feminism in the construction of another world. The struggle against capitalism is still considered to be the primary struggle in the minds of many. The tendency to centralize power in the hands of a few 'enlightened' or 'more capable' individuals remains strong. The WSF continues to be largely characterized by one-dimensional discussion structures like expert panels. Participation of people in the room is limited to asking questions. We must invent new practices for discussion and debate that reflect our non-hierarchical principles and allow individual and collective thinking to advance further. (World March of Women, 2004: 234)

This analysis of the 2003 forum emphasizes how feminist politics has sought to rework the dominant left organizational cultures at the WSF. There is the sense of the critique of top-down discussion structures and a commitment to forging 'new practices for discussion and debate' drawing on non-hierarchical principles. This emphasizes the ways in which feminist engagements can rework the conduct as well as the content of alternative politics in productive ways. At stake here, then, are attempts to create democratic cultures and spaces that prefigure different relations and solidarities.

The concerns of the World March of Women were echoed through other critiques of the 2003 forum. At the root of this was a key tension, as they point out, between an attempt to construct democratic open spaces and a less-than-open form of decision-making. As a political alternative that is very explicit about its radical democratic principles, the WSF has often been remarkably opaque about its own structure and decision-making practices. Peter Waterman argued of the 2003 Forum that it 'is too big; it is lacking in openness, transparency and accountability' and 'thus, it reproduces the traditional politics of party and "bingo" (big international non-governmental organisation) alike' (Waterman, 2003: n.pag.; see also Klein, 2003). Waterman suggests, however, that the mushrooming of the WSF produced creative possibilities. He contends that the 'centre (its initiators) can no longer control the process they themselves invented and developed, now that the idea of social forums is out of the bottle and subject to numerous and varied, local or specific ... claims, forms and inflections' (Waterman, 2003: n.pag.).

Thus, as well as being a space that has been contested by transnational feminist politics, the WSF has been a key site through which diverse feminist trajectories have been articulated. This has been a productive, if often contested, process. Feminists at the WSF, for example, have nourished 'processes that integrate gender justice with economic justice, while recovering cultural subversion and subjectivity as a longer-term strategy for transformation' (Vargas, 2002: n.pag.). Movements against neoliberal globalization have at times challenged the narrow terms of projects where '"giving rights to women" has been conscripted to spread a particular economic agenda founded on the primacy of individual private property rights' (Patel, 2011: 194). Raj Patel argues that a conception of women's rights that is about more than private property has shaped the commitment of the small farmer and peasant international Vía Campesina to campaign for 'access to land' rather than 'ownership of land'.

This integration of economic and gender injustices speaks to the productive engagements between feminist struggles from diverse places and backgrounds. There is a 'plurality of trans-national feminisms active in and over the WSF, emerging from different world regions, expressing distinct political histories and feminist politics, but appearing broadly convergent' (Conway, 2010). This has shaped articulations of transnational feminisms which challenge the terms on which feminism has been institu-tionalized through the UN after the Beijing World Conference on Women in 1995 (Conway, 2010: 153; Dufour et al., 2010: 18). Vargas asks for 'feminisms of these times – as a discursive, expansive, heterogenous panorama, generating polycentric fields of actions that spread over a range of civil-society organizations and are not constrained to women's affairs, although women undoubtedly maintain them in many ways' (cited in de Sousa Santos, 2006: 119–20).

The connections forged between different feminist trajectories through the WSF have, however, been contested. Conway argues that two of the most influential feminist-inspired alliances active at the WSF, Feminist Dialogues, linked to AFM, and the World March of Women, offer radically contrasting views of the politics of transnational feminist practice. She argues, in reference to the 2007 forum in Nairobi, that Feminist Dialogues construct 'more abstract, academic, and often, placeless discourses', which 'clearly resonate with educated women inculturated in the transnational discursive and organizational circuits of feminist advocacy' (Conway, 2010: 162). She directly contrasts the political stance and style of Feminist Dialogues with that of the World

March of Women. She contends that 'The March is more inclined to get its hands dirty through coalition work on concrete issues involving a fuller range of activist partners and practices in which it is a strong feminist partner, but does not set the rules of engagement' (162).

This suggests the existence of entrenched differences in the styles, approach and analyses of these two transnational feminist networks. There have also been more productive engagements between different feminist movements and activists at the WSF. Eschle and Maiguashca recount, for example, a 'Dialogue Between Four Movements' organized by feminist groups including AFM and the Indian National Network of Autonomous Women's Groups at the 6th WSF in Mumbai in 2004 (Eschle and Maiguashca, 2010: 44-5). This sought to create a 'genuine exchange between representatives of women's, lesbian/gay/trans-sexual, Dalit/racial justice, and labour movements'. This demonstrates how the WSF has been used to open up spaces for the articulation of multiple feminist trajectories and is illustrative of 'the remarkable heterogeneity of feminist anti-globalization activism' (53).

Different forms of feminist political agency, then, have been significant in shaping the terms of emerging resistances to globalization and the solidarities they generate. Feminist interventions have both shaped and reshaped the organizational logics and forms of the Forum and shifted the terms on which globalization has been contested. This also emphasizes that there can be radically different feminist articulations of what transnational prefigurative solidarities might look like.

Prefigurative geographies of connection

At the 2005 World Social Forum in Pôrto Alegre a packed workshop brought together resistance against Coca-Cola. Convened by the International Campaign to Hold Coca-Cola Accountable, over 500 activists attended the workshop (International Action Center, 2005). The speakers included Nandlal Master, a community leader from Mehdiganj in India, and Edgar Paez, the international affairs director of Sinaltrainal in Colombia. There was also representation from the National Alliance of People's Movements in India and from Puerto Rico. The three-hour session was translated into English, Hindi, Portuguese and Spanish (International Action Center, 2005). The 2004 World Social Forum in Mumbai also declared its support for the opposition to Coca-Cola associated with the Plachimada movement in Kerala (Raman, 2010: 261).

An iconic global brand, Coca-Cola has long been the subject of global contestation. It is one of a number of multinational corporations, also including Ford, Del Monte and Mercedes-Benz, that have been 'accused in recent years of working closely with Latin American death squads – responsible for the hundreds of thousands of killings throughout the hemisphere in the 1970s and 1980s – to counter labor organizing' (Grandin, 2006: 14). These histories and geographies of Coca-Cola's links with Latin America suggest how there are important intersections between Cold War politics and emergent articulations of neoliberalism. These shape how neoliberal globalization is both experienced and contested.

There are key continuities between Coca-Cola's alleged links to death squads in Guatemala in the 1970s and 1980s and the campaign of repression against trade unionists in bottling plants in Colombia in the 1990s and 2000s. Sinaltrainal, the Colombian food and drink workers' union represented at the WSF workshop, has been at the forefront of international campaigns against Coca-Cola's alleged involvement in the assassinations of trade unionists in the country. The context for the repression of Sinaltrainal activists has been the collusion between right-wing paramilitaries and the Colombian government, resulting in state-sponsored terror against trade unionists. Colombia has become a 'counterinsurgent terror state' built by 'civilian politicians who delegated repression to the military' (Hylton, 2006: 131). This state terror has made being a trade unionist in Colombia 'one of the most dangerous occupations in the world'. Some 4,000 members of the Central Unitaria de Trabajadores, the country's largest trade-union confederation, were killed between 1986 and 2004 (Gill, 2004: 1).

Violent repression has had a devastating impact on Sinaltrainal's attempts to organize bottling plants used by Coca-Cola in the country. Nine unionized workers from Coca-Cola plants in Colombia were murdered during the 1990s and 2000s (Higginbottom, 2007: 279). The most notorious of these was the assassination of Isidro Segundo Gil. Gil was the leader of the local branch union at a Coca-Cola bottling plant in Carepa in Antioquia in north-western Colombia. He was killed inside the plant on 5 December 1996, a week after tabling 'the union's demands in the annual negotiation round with the bottling company'.

> The plant manager declared he wanted to 'sweep away the trade union'. Shortly afterwards rightwing paramilitaries burnt out the local union office and shot Gil inside the plant, the fourth union member they had assassinated. Two days later the paramilitaries re-entered the plant, called the workers together and made them sign prepared letters resigning from the union. The letters had been printed on company machines and were collected by management. The union branch was decimated. Subsequently, after a four year battle to get justice for her murdered partner, Isidro's wife Alcira del Carmen Herera Perez was murdered in front of their daughters. (Higginbottom, 2007: 279)

Coca-Cola has been accused of complicity with the assassinations of trade unionists such as Gil. In this case there were clear links between paramilitaries and the management of the plant. Given the contested character of private property rights in much of Colombia, it is 'not surprising that foreign corporations paid protection money to paramilitaries as a "capitalist insurance policy"' (Hylton, 2006: 91).

In 2003, Sinaltrainal, the International Labor Rights Fund (ILRF) and the United Steelworkers of America filed a lawsuit in the USA alleging the complicity of Coca-Cola with the assassination of Gil. They asserted 'that the Coke bottlers "contracted with or otherwise directed paramilitary security forces that utilized extreme violence and murdered, tortured, unlawfully detained or otherwise silenced trade union leaders"' (United Steel Workers Union and the International Labor Rights Fund, 2001). These links between Sinaltrainal and the international labour movement demonstrate the important transnational solidarities constructed in opposition to human rights abuses in Colombia associated with Coca-Cola bottling plants. The union has engaged with diverse international strategies. In 2003 Sinaltrainal initiated calls for a boycott of Coca-Cola. This boycott is one of the key ways in which the union's leadership has 'internationalized its conflict with the Coca-Cola Company' in response to the violent repression of organization (Gill, 2007: 238).

An earlier boycott of Coca-Cola was central to solidarity actions with Guatemalan workers during the 1980s. This was due to the alleged complicity of Coca-Cola in the violent repression of trade unionists working at the Embotelladora Guatemalteca S.A. (EGSA) bottling plant in Guatemala City. In the 1970s and 1980s workers at the plant were at the forefront of struggles to maintain and reproduce a trade-union movement in the face of severe repression by successive military dictatorships (Dunkerley, 1988: 471-2). The immediate post-war period had seen a massive upsurge of trade unionism in Guatemala. Whereas trade unionism 'barely existed' in 1944, by 1954 'three hundred thousand members filled the ranks of nearly two thousand rural and urban unions' (Grandin, 2004: 51). The coup against Arbenz in 1954 ushered in decades of repression, which drove the labour movement in Guatamela underground. After the coup the existing union in the EGSA plant was crushed (LAB, 1987: 6).

Workers in the Coca-Cola franchise bottling plant in the capital were central to resistance to this repression, especially during the 1970s and 1980s. Coca-Cola franchise owner John Trotter was a 'hysterical anti-communist' with 'close ties with the right-wing movement for National liberation and with army intelligence' (Levenson-Estrada, 1994: 176). STEGAC, the Coca-

Cola Bottling Company Workers' Union, 'suffered more violent attacks in the 1970s than any other single union. Because of this, by 1978 the union had gained potent support from international labour and human rights groups that allowed it to survive in the late 1970s and to persist under military rule in the early 1980s' (Levenson-Estrada, 1994: 176). Assassinations continued in the 1980s. On 18 February 1984, after a decision to close the factory, the Coke workers occupied the plant (LAB, 1987).

STEGAC leader Rodolfo Robles explained that 'the outcome of this battle would have a profound influence on the whole future of trade unionism in the country'. He argued that

> The Coca-Cola workers' trade union is a vital component of the trade union movement in Guatemala. By closing down this plant, the employers were automatically destroying the union. A few months later, we reckoned, they would be using the same procedure to close down other factories where there are trade unions. (Robles cited by LAB, 1987: 5)

The international trade-union response was led by the International Union of Food Workers (IUF). The IUF had 'written to all affiliates calling for protests to Coke Atlanta' within two weeks of the occupation (LAB, 1987: 25).

The response of affiliated unions was immediate. Boycott action spread rapidly.

> On 7 May production stopped at 13 different Coke bottling and canning plants in Norway. In Italy several short stoppages occurred at Coca-Cola plants while workers met to hear reports on the situation in Guatemala. Austrian unions wrote to the local Coca-Cola management threatening action. In Mexico, ten different bottling plants held solidarity strikes for three days each on a rotating basis, while in Sweden all five IUF affiliates staged a full production and sales stoppage for three days. (LAB, 1987: 31)

This international support was central to the survival and eventual success of the occupation.

The boycott of Coca-Cola called by Sinaltrainal also had a transnational impact. It gained a high profile on US university campuses, where Coca-Cola held lucrative contracts. Michigan State University passed a motion that called on MSU to 'desist from renewing their contract with the Coca-Cola Company'. A similar motion passed at the University of Michigan lost Coca-Cola the lucrative contract for supplying soft drinks to the University of Michigan campus, which was estimated to be worth $1.27 million (Hardikar, 2006). These boycotts were important in shaping a multifaceted opposition to Coca-Cola. Like the workshop at the WSF, they brought together different movements contesting Coca-Cola for different reasons.

These articulations between different struggles have not just been about creating a bigger, more effective movement. They have also brought together movements which have contested Coca-Cola for different reasons, articulating concerns frequently held apart, such as environmentalism, inequality and labour rights. Different tensions have emerged through the formation of such transnational forms of organizing. Ashwini Hardikar's analysis of the process of coalition-building against Coca-Cola in the University of Michigan suggests that despite the coalition looking representative, linkages between mobilizing against Coca-Cola and anti-racism were closed down (Hardikar, 2006). She suggests that even when coalitions look 'representative', pressure can still be exerted on the practices through which maps of grievance are shaped and defined. Thus Hardikar argues that the coalition didn't make anti-racism central to the contestation of Coca-Cola, and that there was a disjuncture between the anti-racist and anti-globalization aspects of the coalition. Unequal gender relations have also at times been reproduced through such organizing, as has also been noted. Thus Gill argues that Sinaltrainal has had 'little to say about the particular vulnerabilities of working-class women' (Gill, 2007: 238).

The WSF linked activists from Sinaltrainal with activists from struggles in India where Coca-Cola has been contested primarily for its poor environmental record. There have been major campaigns against the role of Coca-Cola plants in exacerbating water shortages. The most high-profile of these has been the ongoing campaign in Plachimada, a tiny hamlet in the state of Kerala. Here a diverse coalition has campaigned against the effect of the company's plants on water supplies. The multinational has been accused of 'creating severe water shortage, of polluting its groundwater and soil, and also of distributing toxic waste as fertiliser to farmers in the area' (Raman, 2005: 2481; see also Bijoy, 2006). Organizing in Plachimada brought together subaltern groups such as adivasis and dalits with human rights and left activists.

The Coca-Cola Virudha Janakeeya Samara Smithi (Anti-Coca-Cola People's Strike Committee) was formed comprising the diverse constituencies involved in contesting Coca-Cola in Plachimada. It included Gandhian, moderate-radical groups such as the SUCI, and the Maoist groups Pottoram and Ayyankali Pada, 'in addition to the subalterns whose livelihood had come under direct threat' (Raman, 2008: 85). The Plachimada struggle is one of many struggles that have brought the increasing inequalities and social and environmental associated with neoliberalization in India into contestation (Oza, 2010).

In both Colombia and India, then, marginal and precarious communities have been impacted on by the terms in which Coca-Cola draws them into global connections and flows. Transnational solidarities and mobilizing against Coca-Cola have had an effect on how these grievances are imagined. Plachimada's struggle against Coca-Cola has 'raised serious issues about the role of transnational corporations and globalization in India' (Aiyer 2007: 652). The campaign also had an inspirational effect. Aiyer argues that it is now 'firmly tied in the hearts and minds of many activists to the struggles against the Coca-Cola Company in Colombia ... or the victory against Bechtel in Cochabamba, Bolivia'. The struggle has generated opposition to the 'Coca-Cola Company and PepsiCo in other rural communities in India' (652)

These solidarities have productively shaped the terms on which Coca-Cola has been contested. Contesting Coca-Cola, then, is not just about holding to account the actions of one of the world's richest and most globally recognizable transnational companies. It is also about assembling connections between actors and movements in different parts of the world. These solidarities have been forged across uneven terrain of neoliberal globalization. This has not been a smooth or even process. These relations and organizing practices, however, prefigure logics on which globalizations might be generated different to the exploitative neoliberalism practised by the Coca-Cola Company.

Conclusion

Writing in the winter of 2011, Mike Davis argued that for the moment 'the survival of the new social movements – the occupiers, the *indignados*, the small European anti-capitalist parties and the Arab new left – demands that they sink deeper roots in mass resistance to the global economic catastrophe which in turn presupposes – let's be honest – that the current temper for "horizontality" can eventually accommodate enough disciplined "verticality" to debate and enact organizing strategies' (Davis, 2011: 5). Davis's account captures a certain dismissive attitude to the forms of organization adopted by the movements against neoliberal globalization which is influential in parts of the intellectual left. This emphasizes the ways in which attempts to create prefigurative left politics can still be seen as undermining left strategies. It also suggests some of the importance of the political trajectories of the counter-globalization politics in shaping the ground for ongoing contestation of neoliberalism.

Forms of non-hierarchical protest have been central to the emergent movements associated with the transnational Occupy movement and to many of the movements associated with what has been termed the 'Arab Spring'. This helps to position the current conjuncture in relation to ongoing contestation of neoliberalism, rather than as an isolated crisis moment where neoliberalism has suddenly become challenged. This opens up political possibilities, as the concluding chapter notes. It also decisively shaped the ways in which climate politics was constructed and challenged during the Copenhagen round of climate talks in 2009.

CHAPTER 8

'If the climate were a bank it would be bailed out': solidarity and the making of climate justice

On 14 December 2010 I attended a small demonstration outside the Bella Centre Copenhagen where the COP15 round of UN Framework on Climate Changes negotiations were taking place. Billed as 'Climate Reparations' and organized by Jubilee South, we chanted slogans at delegates as they entered and left the convention centre. Speakers from activist groups based in the Philippines, Senegal, India, Brazil and beyond insisted that climate change be understood in relation to the unequal histories of colonialism and continuing global inequalities. This shaped vociferous demands for 'climate justice'. Sited under the tram station that served the Bella Centre, this felt like an inauspicious space for a picket. It became more so when the Danish police started erecting a wire fence to separate us from the delegates. In a rather surreal turn of events, they then helped us to pin up stickers on the fence. The actions of the police led to chants of 'Fence the corporations not the people'.

This was a small demonstration. It didn't attract much press attention. It was far less dramatic than the events that were to happen outside the Bella Centre a couple of days after. On 16 December the major action of the COP attempted to shut down the centre through an alliance of protestors from the outside with dissenting delegates from the inside. This was met with severe police repression, including widespread use of tear gas and pepper spray.[1] The speakers at the 'climate reparations' demonstration, however, shaped a distinctive approach to the politics of climate change. In contrast to the official negotiations, concerns of social and environmental justice were made central. There was an insistence on linking climate change to histories of unequal relations between North and South. This was defined by attempts to politicize the relations of 'place beyond place' (Massey, 2007: 188-209). Such interventions have the potential to reconfigure the terms of climate change politics. This chapter explores how emerging articulations of climate justice have been shaped by the solidarities produced between different climate struggles.

Contested maps of grievance

The demonstration at the Bella Centre mobilized a set of ideas around climate justice which have become increasingly influential. Discourses of climate justice have been shaped by different political trajectories. One of the most significant contributions was protests organized in 2007 at the COP13 negotiations in Bali, Indonesia. During the UN climate summit 'peoples from social organizations and movements from across the globe brought the fight for social, ecological and gender justice into the negotiating rooms and onto the streets' (Climate Justice Now, 2007). Both 'inside and outside the convention centre, activists demanded alternative policies and practices that protect livelihoods and the environment'. They sought to make challenging the injustices that structure the production and impact of climate change central to climate politics. These mobilizations led to the founding of the Climate Justice Network (Bond, 2010).

The terms of such organizing was powerfully shaped by the Bali Climate Justice principles. This platform for an 'international movement of all peoples for Climate Justice' were developed by the International Climate Justice Network in June 2002 at preparatory negotiations in Bali ahead of the Earth Summit in Johannesburg. The International Climate Justice Network included big transnational NGOs such as Friends of the Earth International and Greenpeace alongside more popular movements and alliances such as the Indian National Alliance of People's Movements, Third World Network and National Fishworkers' Forum. The Bali Principles articulate a set of key elements of climate justice based on the insistence that 'communities have the right to be free from climate change, its related impacts and other forms of ecological destruction' (International Climate Justice Network, 2002: n.pag.). The Principles articulated an analysis of climate politics which contested market-based mechanisms as solutions to climate change.

The Principles also contested the differentiated effects of climate change. They drew attention to the way 'the impacts will be most devastating to the vast majority of the people in the South, as well as the "South" within the North'. Central to the Bali Principles is a set of interventions around 'ecological debt'. The document argues for 'the recognition of a principle of ecological debt that industrialized governments and trans-national corporations owe the rest of the world as a result of their appropriation of the planet's capacity to absorb greenhouse gases'. This principle of ecological debt positions the impacts of climate change in relation to histories and geographies of unequal relations between the global North and South; as was made clear through the climate reparations demonstration that I noted at the start of the chapter.

This position around the importance of foregrounding justice in relation to climate politics was itself directly influenced by the 'Environmental Justice Principles' developed at the 1991 People of Color Environmental Justice Leadership Summit in Washington DC. These Principles were used 'as a blueprint' for the Bali declaration. This locates the articulation of climate justice in relation to ongoing attempts to politicize environmental inequalities. The Environmental Justice Principles were a key distillation of the influential environmental justice movement in the USA. This movement rose to prominence in the 1980s when diverse movements contested the disproportionate siting of hazardous dumps and waste facilities in poor black and Hispanic communities in the USA (see Bullard, 1990; Pulido, 2000). In doing so they not only contested these unequal, unjust practices. They also challenged the limits of a US environment movement which would not recognise 'hazardous waste, air quality, and land use' as adequately 'environmental' (Di Chiro, 1996: 298–9). The translation of environmental terminology beyond the USA has shaped the adoption of the term 'climate justice' (Walker and Bulkeley, 2006; see also Patel, 2006).

This has important implications for the ways in which climate change politics is understood. Erik Swyngedouw has argued that climate change has been constructed as a consensual, post-political issue (Swyngedouw, 2007). The term 'post-political' has been used to signal the disavowal of conflict and the distinction between left and right in many mainstream forms of political debate characterized by consensus. Swyngedouw contends that 'the mobilization of environmental issues is one of the key arenas through which this post-political consensus becomes constructed' (Swyngedouw, 2007: 22). This fits into long histories of left critiques of environmentalism for ignoring relations of power (Enzensberger, 1974). Swyngedouw usefully draws attention to the ways in which climate change has been actively depoliticized. He also suggests the ways in which antagonistic constructions of climate change politics have been marginalized.

There are, however, important tensions in this argument. First, it shares with other work that adopts a post-political turn a rather limited engagement with actually existing forms of contestation. There are key attempts to depoliticize key issues such as climate change. To imply that these are the only ways that such politics is being articulated, however, is reductive. It is also to ignore interventions like those at COP13, which have sought to actively politicize and contest the terms of climate politics. Second, this work has tended to adopt a rather nation-centred account of the political (Mouffe, 2005; Žižek, 1999, 2005). Swyngedouw fails to engage with the ways in which contestation to climate change, such as the organizing in advance of COP15 and the alliances configured through the protests, exceed, unsettle and undermine attempts to contain contestation within the nation. He ignores the contestation of how climate politics is constructed, which is central to movements around climate justice. This suggests that climate politics is the product of much more generative political trajectories of contestation.

Established commentators on the left have marginalized the importance of the ongoing contestation of neoliberalism in relation to debates around the economic crisis (Blackburn, 2008; Panitch and Gindin, 2010). Thus dominant left accounts and analysis have concentrated on mapping, delineating and analysing the financial practices and capital flows through which the economic crisis unfolded (e.g. Harvey, 2010; Peck, 2010). This work is, of course, important and necessary. However, it risks ignoring a broader set of questions about how contestation is generated and enacted in the current conjuncture.

These capital-centred accounts marginalize an engagement about the significance of the ongoing movements that have brought the terms of neoliberal globalization into contestation. This deals with contestation in an impoverished way, viewing oppositional politics as merely a set of responses to neoliberalization and the crisis, rather than something which more actively shapes the terrain of political debate. By focusing primarily on issues of capital and dominant economic practice, the tone of left debate has also led to a rather narrow set of alternative proposals around financial regulation (Blackburn, 2008; Gowan, 2009). Diverse struggles have made links between the economic crisis and climate politics. The protests of workers at the Vestas plant in Newport on the Isle of Wight in the UK are a case in point here.

In the summer of 2009 workers at the Vestas plant, which made wind turbines, occupied the factory for eighteen days after mass redundancies. Vestas, a profitable Danish multinational, was seeking to move the work to Colorado and to close both its British factories with the loss of more than 600 green jobs, citing 'lack of demand' and opposition to onshore wind farms in the UK (Milne, 2009). The workers demanded that the government demonstrate its 'commitment to a green economy by taking over the plant and restarting production under new management' (Milne, 2009: n.pag.). There was a culture of management bullying at the plant. Workers involved in the occupation, for example, were sent their redundancy notices in pizza boxes. During the occupation food had to be smuggled, or thrown, into the plant as the management refused to let adequate supplies in.

Red–Green alliances developed around the dispute, which linked climate change politics to an innovative attempt to politicize the economic crisis – a crisis that continues to be rather successfully depoliticized. The occupation made clear the distance between the rhetoric of an economic recovery being led by 'green jobs' and a situation where workers making wind turbines were being laid off. The conditions and actions of Vestas workers suggest that 'green jobs' can frequently be more precarious than rhetoric about the 'green economy' sometimes suggests (Green New Deal Group, 2008). Greenpeace hailed the Vestas dispute as promising 'a historic change from a situation where the labour movement and environment activists have found themselves on different sides of the fence' (MacAlister, 2009: n.pag.). The way that these red–green alliances were hailed as innovative, however, would seem to underline the extent to which 'red' and 'green' politics are still frequently held apart, rather than to be particular evidence of their convergence. The Greenpeace statement, while welcome, ignores long-standing connections between environment and labour politics/justice issues which have shaped different ways of understanding what counts as environmental politics. This suggests that the terms on which social and environmental forms of justice are articulated through emerging solidarities demands scrutiny.

There are, as Swyngedouw emphasizes, plenty of ways in which climate change politics is mobilized in ways which close down contestation and actively depoliticize issues. This also draws on important ways in which environmental politics has been mobilized and framed. However, it is unhelpful to extrapolate from this that all climate change politics is necessarily depoliticizing. There are important ways in which dominant responses to climate change are being brought into contestation. These practices of contestation can be productive of translocal alliances and of different ways of envisioning alternatives to neoliberalism. Tracing the contested maps of grievance shaped through these practices shows how different forms of climate change politics can emerge through bringing dominant geographies of power into question.

Climate justice and the formation of solidarities

The terms of climate justice politics have been shaped through ongoing struggles over social and environmental injustices. Central here has been transnational organizing around the politics of oil. Such injustices were brought into contestation through a set of public hearings around the operation of the oil industry in Colombia. This was set up by the People's Permanent Tribunal (PPT), a non-governmental tribunal set up to investigate and challenge the role of multinationals in Colombia. The PPT uses 'exemplary cases' 'to show how the Colombian state has facilitated and contributed to the exploitation of [the country's] natural resources by these companies, by committing crimes and permanently violating the rights of the individual citizens and their organizations' (PPT, 2007). In 2007 the PPT held a public hearing in Bogotá in relation to the oil industry. There were also seven preliminary public hearings. There were hearings in Colombia in Saravena, Barrancabermeja, El Tarra in Northern Santander, and Cartagena. Preliminary hearings were also held in the USA, Spain and the UK, the home countries of the three biggest oil corporations with major operations in Colombia: Occidental, Repsol and BP (Colombia Solidarity Campaign, 2007). The evidence presented at these preliminary hearings fed into a formal public hearing on the policies of the three oil corporations in Bogotá in August 2007. These events produced a networked opposition constructed through connections between activists in different places and through bringing together different groups mobilizing around oil politics and the political situation in Colombia.[2]

Through interrogating the power relations of the global oil industry, this process directly linked the politics of climate change to contestation of the violence and inequalities that structure neoliberalization. Thus, in the event held in Glasgow in June 2007 activists from trade unions and social movements in Colombia presented evidence of British Petroleum's 'corporate crimes'. They gave testimonies of BP's poor environmental record in Colombia, particularly in Casanare. They also argued that there had been at the very least complicity between BP and assassinations of leaders and activists of the Colombian Oilworkers' Union USO. Since 1988 USO has suffered

> 105 assassinations of its members, 2 members 'disappeared', 6 kidnapped, 35 wounded in assassination attempts, 400 internal refugees, 4 members in exile, 300 members have experienced death threats, 30 have been detained, 900 are undergoing criminal proceedings and 55 have been subject to 'mobbing'.[2]

The Colombian speakers related this to the broader context of assassination and intimidation of trade unionists and to the impunity of multinationals in Colombia. The financial support of 'Occidental and BP-Amaco, the two largest players in the Colombian oil market', for the military and paramilitaries has been documented (Hylton, 2006: 91). The Glasgow organizing committee itself included a Colombian exile. Through directly linking the politics of climate change to the violence and unequal social and environmental relations involved in the production of oil in Colombia and elsewhere, this event suggested the importance of framing climate change politics in antagonistic ways. A politics that doesn't challenge the unequal power relations related to climate change risks being redundant.

This process also produced a set of innovative alliances and exchanges between different groups and activists based in different parts of the world. Thus Scotland was chosen as the site to host the public hearing related to BP because of its importance for oil production within the UK. Links were made with community groups that had campaigned against oil refineries in Grangemouth and other environmental groups in Scotland. Nonetheless, the event also raised significant questions about how these links between environmental concerns and more traditional left concerns around labour and human rights are negotiated. The dominant framing of this politics was through a concern with BP's violations of labour and human rights in ways which sometimes edged out engagements with environmental injustices. This raises questions about the necessity of challenging unequal social and environmental relations in ways that allow them both to be made central. It also emphasizes that there can be discontinuities and tensions in the ways that these relations are articulated through solidarities.

The PPT process demonstrates, however, the way that such internationalist organizing can open up a contested politics of climate change. It emphasizes that the political trajectories that movements and activists bring to understanding the politics of climate change matter. The political trajectories of diverse movements have also been important in generating actually existing alternatives to neoliberalized ways of producing globalization. One of the key ways in which they have done this is through experiments with localization. Thus significant movements in the global South, such as Movimento dos Trabalhadores Rurais Sem Terra (MST), the movement of the landless in Brazil, have sought to produce alternatives to neoliberal forms of agriculture. After initially mimicking intensive agriculture on the land gained through their occupations, the MST has begun to experiment with alternative forms of agriculture and has produced the first organic seeds in Latin America (Branford and Rocha, 2002: 211-39; MST, 2005). Allies of the MST in the global North, such as the Confédération Paysanne, have backed alternative proposals for rural development based around 'solidaristic agriculture', related to radical non-agricultural actors in rural communities (Herman and Kuper, 2002: 106–7).

There are, however, key differences over ways in which practices of localization are envisioned. Arguably, some versions of localization being produced through responses such as the transition town movement constitute what might be termed a 'new parochialism'. These movements have had significant effects in shaping low-carbon alternatives. They have also been significant in drawing in people to political engagement who have traditionally not been engaged with activist subcultures. The particular practices of localization they adopt, however, are limited in key ways. They have generally been rather silent about the relations of power that shape these practices. Further, they have tended to generate the practices in isolationist rather than solidaristic ways.

A different and more politically productive approach to localization has emerged through some aspects of the opposition to dominant responses to climate change. That is, strategies of localization that are envisioned and practised directly as part of solidaristic alternatives (see also North and Featherstone, 2012). These strategies do not produce localization in bounded or isolationist ways. Rather, they envision localization as part of strategies to 'trans-localize' (Chatterton et al., forthcoming). This can be exemplified by the political strategies adopted by Via Campesina, the transnational network of small farmers and peasants. Via Campesina's opposition to dominant responses to climate change has combined a commitment to the importance of localized forms of agriculture as an alternative to carbon-intensive agribusiness. This has been developed through a focus on translocal circuits of opposition to neoliberalization. Thus one of their statements prior to the Copenhagen meetings argues:

> La Via Campesina believe we must implement new initiatives aiming at changing the model of production. Local production and people- based protection of resources should be encouraged because it uses less fossil energy and it maintains livelihoods

and local communities. Small farmers around the world defend food sovereignty as a way to overcome the climate crisis. It is the people's right to define their own food policies, with a priority to local food production and sustainable small-scale agriculture. (Via Campesina, 2009a)

It is clear that this articulation of the local is one which is challenging the unequal geographies of power that shape places. The translocal geographies of connection that shape the movement, drawing together alliances from across the global South and links with movements like Confédération Paysanne in the global North, challenge the association of localization with chauvinism or isolationism.

This is a significant alternative to the ways in which localization is mobilized as part of the 'new parochialisms' associated with the Transition Town movement (see Trapese Collective, 2009). This emphasizes how the distinctive political trajectories of oppositional movements have shaped the terms of climate justice politics. Thus Via Campesina was one of the movements that was central to the translocal solidarities forged through counter-globalization movements (Desmarais, 2007). It has brought these forms of political mobilizing and analysis to climate justice politics. The importance of these connections was made clear through the mobilizations in Copenhagen.

'System change not climate change'

One set of climate change politics constituted through COP15 was about the inexorable rise of market-led solutions to climate change. Carbon trading was promoted as a key solution to the crisis. This approach depends on isolating carbon from social and environmental relations and transforming it into a commodity. Through enrolling carbon into marketized relations, the dominant approach sought to deepen and extend neoliberal relations and logics. Though, as Patrick Bond points out, 'the global climate governance elites simply could not generate the consensus required for a renewed carbon market initiative'

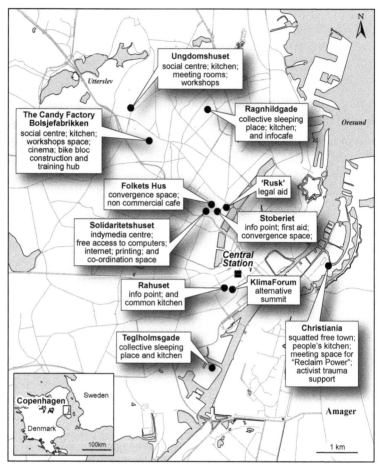

Map showing the activist spaces during COP15 at Copenhagen

(Bond, 2011: 11). This attempt to deal with 'dangerous climate change' through the fetishization and reproduction of market mechanisms was contested through protests and organizing. Thus the mobilizations were not simply about arguing for lower emissions targets. Rather, they contested the very logic on which the official negotiations were conducted.

This opposition was crafted through various sites. There was an alternative climate summit, the Klimaforum, held near the centre of Copenhagen. There were numerous actions and protests on the streets of the city. The map opposite depicts some of the key spaces through which the mobilizations were organized. Some delegates in the COP15 negotiations – from NGOs, political organizations and country delegations – contested the dominant terms through which climate politics were framed. These protests made unequal and destructive environmental relations 'matters of concern' (Latour, 2004: 25). They constructed solidarities across divides. Solidarities were made with those who were facing immediate threats from climate change in different parts of the world and with future generations. These solidarities were forged through attempts to construct different and more just social and environmental relations. These solidarities also linked human and diverse non-human others.

The protests were shaped by translocal activist networks that were influential in the alter-globalization movements. The Climate Justice Action (CJA) network, for example, drew on forms of political analysis and modes of organizing that were shaped by earlier engagements/movements against corporate globalization (CJA, 2010: 1). These connections were made explicit through the 'Trade to Climate Caravan' which travelled from protests at the 7th Ministerial of the World Trade Organization in Geneva to the Climate Summit in Copenhagen. This involved forty-four representatives from the social movements of the 'Global South', who explained 'the connections between world trade and climate change with speeches and actions' (Trade to Climate Caravan, 2009). The Caravan was organized by People's Global Action, one of the key networking movements that shaped the counter-globalization movement.

The Caravan comprised sixty participants 'from around the world from the worst of environmental and social situations to demand and claim a better world and save our planet from those that wish to profit out of the death of the biosphere' (Trade to Climate Caravan, 2009; see also Burton, 2011). The project was

articulated as being about 'more than a friendship but born of
political solidarity, labour and land ownership, climate justice,
the exploitation of the south by the north, even knowing that
you can find pockets of the south in the north and the north
in the south'. Participants from a diverse range of struggles
and organizations were involved. This included activists from
the Bangladesh Krishok Federation, a peasant movement that
'has been successful in helping landless farmers to gain access
to fallow land in areas along the coast, which is related to the
achieving of food sovereignty'.

This project was structured to demonstrate and contest connections between the WTO and the climate change negotiations.
This underlines the way that at least some of the mobilizations
at COP15 were not in any straightforward way about pressuring
the process to adopt more stringent targets. Rather, as in Bali,
there was a direct contestation of the way that the COP15 process
was using the climate negotiations as an opportunity to deepen
processes of marketization (Bond, 2011). There was strong dissent at the use of mechanisms such as carbon trading. For the
Caravanistas, drawing together the two events brought the direct
linkages between climate change and neoliberal globalization
into contestation.

The Caravan included members of Via Campesina. Via
Campesina had a significant, 150-strong presence in Copenhagen,
marked out by their distinctive green flags. They mobilized both
distinctive actions and solutions. Via Campesina's opposition to
dominant responses to climate change has combined a commitment to the importance of localized forms of agriculture as an
alternative to carbon-intensive agribusiness (Via Campesina,
2009b). During COP15 Via Campesina was involved in two key
actions against the Danish meat industry and in relation to
bio-fuels. The targeting of these sought to politicize the links
between agribusiness and climate change (Levidow and Paul,
2010).

Via Campesina activists argued that small-scale producer-
owned and -led agriculture could be a form of low-carbon

alternative to such forms of agribusiness. They argued that '[l]ocal production and people based protection of resources should be encouraged because it uses less fossil energy and it maintains livelihoods and local communities. Small farmers around the world defend food sovereignty as a way to overcome the climate crisis' (Via Campesina, 2009a). Like other oppositional movements, Via Campesina positioned climate change politics in relation to the economic crisis. Josie Riffaud, one of the leaders of Via Campesina, argued that 'Money and market solutions will not resolve the current crisis. We need instead a radical change in the way we produce and we consume, and this is what was not discussed in Copenhagen' (Via Campesina, 2009c).

One of the defining slogans of the protests was that 'If the climate was a bank it would be saved!' This slogan was invoked by Hugo Chávez in his address to the summit. Among the many inventive puppets and banners in the street demonstrations, my favourite was a giant puppet of Karl Marx imploring that 'It's the economy, stupid'. These slogans and interventions had a double effect. First, they sought to position the climate negotiations in the context of the failure of the aggressive forms of neoliberalism, even on their own terms, to provide financial growth and stability. This deepened antagonisms against the neoliberal tenor of the climate negotiations. Second, they sought to open up political spaces and possibilities by drawing attention to the failure of neoliberalism. This was an attempt to challenge the closing down of political horizons and alternatives through neoliberal politics.

The coming together of different political trajectories in Copenhagen was productive, but there were tensions. Many potential alliances were rather fraught and characterized by different styles of politics talking past each other. A panel at the Klimaforum on Danish trade-union responses to climate change, for example, was dull and technocratic. Of the few who turned up for the panel, many swiftly left. The trade unionists made a serious attempt to think about the possibilities of green jobs. Asked about the possibilities for contestation of neoliberalism in the current conjuncture by myself and another participant in the workshop, one of the trade unionists responded that he had given up on socialism twenty years ago![4] This contrasted with the imaginative green-left politics that characterized other sessions. At a debate on left alternatives, speakers from parties such as Die Linke offered a convincing and passionate left articulation of climate change politics. Trade-union federations such as the International Transport Workers' Federation have also sought to construct more imaginative engagements with climate politics (International Transport Workers' Federation, 2010).

Tensions that have long dogged alter-globalization politics recurred. Tadzio Mueller, of the Climate Justice Action network, and Naomi Klein were barracked at a rally of several thousand activists in Christiania, the long-standing 'autonomous area' in Copenhagen, for arguing for a non-violent approach to the 'mass action' at the Bella Centre on 16 December 2009. This mass action was seen as the centrepiece of direct action and was planned to involve both activists on the outside together with a walkout of militant delegates from the inside. Klein and Mueller's defence of non-violence depended, though, on a rather troubling mobilization of activists from the 'global South'. They argued that non-violent strategies were necessary to 'protect' more vulnerable activists from the 'global South' with visa privileges or juridical status. This spoke in significant ways to the terms in which solidarities and connections were constituted.

This position acknowledged the differential conditions activists from 'the global South' face in terms of unequal visa privileges. This is something about which activists from 'the global North' have not always been particularly aware when engaging in the construction of translocal solidarities (Featherstone, 2008: 167). But it positioned such activists in paternalistic and unitary ways. 'They' became 'represented' in these debates rather than being allowed to shape the terms of discussion. Such geographical imaginaries of solidarity rework rather than challenge unequal geographies of power (Sundberg, 2007). It suggests, however, that in important ways, for leading figures in 'counter-globalization' movements, there is still a tendency to represent figures from the 'global South' in unitary and rather passive ways. This serves to reinforce a set of divisions between activists in the global North and South, closing down the emergence of more productive and nuanced ways of negotiating activists' different positions in relation to global geographies of power. This intersects with wider practices of representation. The European green movement continues to have issues with orientalism. An NGO activist from São Paulo I spoke to, for example, was fed up with people assuming that because he was Brazilian he came from 'the rainforest'.

The context for the angry exchanges in Christiania was concerted with violent police repression of peaceful demonstrations and actions. At the first major demonstration on 12 December 2009, when over 100,000 marched on the Bella Centre, the police made 900 arrests. This was during an overwhelmingly peaceful march. The arrests were said to be 'pre-emptive'. Of the 900 arrested only three were brought to trial. Police held protesters in wire cages, joking that they were 'mini-Guantánamos'. There were persistent allegations that police had used pepper spray on protesters held in cages. On 20 October 2010 these 'pre-emptive' arrests were ruled illegal by the City Court of Copenhagen. Knud Foldschack, who represented some of those arrested, commented that the 'verdict is a clear signal to the Danish Parliament that they should stop degrading legal rights in Denmark, in order to comply with international conventions such as the European Convention on Human Rights'.[5]

This police repression, however, cannot be dismissed as a 'legitimate' reaction to a few violent protesters. It was systematic and state sanctioned. The Danish parliament voted through legislation, days before COP15, effectively to criminalize peaceful protest. These new powers enabled Danish police to detain for up to twelve hours people who they suspected 'might break the law in the near future' and to jail protesters for forty days. This legislation is consistent with a broader 'authoritarian populist' political culture in Denmark (see Hall, 1988: 123–49). This political culture has been allied with 'neo-nationalist' narratives that have demonized immigrants (Haldrup et al., 2006). This is also part of the circulation of techniques of policing and containment of protest among different sites, such as the G20 protests in London and Toronto in 2009 and 2010. There was widespread use of 'kettling' in response to student protests in November 2010 (Solomon, 2011). These police tactics sought to close down vibrant forms of political protest. Significant pressure was exerted to prevent activists travelling to Copenhagen. Buses of activists were stopped and searched in operations which drew on cross-border cooperation between the Danish and German police.

These actions put significant pressures on the terms of exchanges and connections through which solidarities were forged. Solidarities also shaped different positions on the terms on which climate justice was mobilized. A key tension that emerged during and after the mobilizations was around different constructions of climate justice and debt. Mark Lynas, a prominent green activist and writer in the UK, has argued that climate change is such an urgent problem that struggles for equity need to take second place (Lynas, 2004, 2010; for critical discussion see Blagojevic, 2010). These disputes bear strongly on the relation between the construction of solidarity and the politics of time. In the debates at the Klimaforum and in many demonstrations and actions, issues of justice were not deferred, but were made central to climate change politics.

The terms on which 'climate justice' is defined and articulated have been disputed. Simons and Tonak, in a blistering critique of the oppositional climate politics at COP15, argue against notions of climate justice and debt. They declare that conceptions of 'climate debt' perpetuate 'a system that assigns economic and financial value to the biosphere, ecosystems' and 'infects relations between the Global North and South' with 'the logic of commodification' that is central to carbon markets (Simons and Tonak, 2010: n.pag.). Simons and Tonak are right to caution about the potential dangers of deepening monetized logics of connection. This is particularly crucial given the way the COP15 negotiations were so dominated by monetized and market-led solutions.

There are, however, key tensions in their critique of discourses of climate debt and justice. It ignores how climate debt and reparations were articulated in ways which sought to situate climate politics in relation to the unequal histories and geographies of connection between North and South. This was crucial in attempting to forge solidarities that constructed different logics of connection between movements in the North and South. This cannot be reduced to a sense of monetized linkages. Rather, it is about an attempt to challenge the ongoing inequalities being reproduced through climate politics. As Patrick Bond argues, 'Climate Debt is about reparations to people who are suffering damages by the actions of Northern overconsumption of environmental space – damages that can be proven even in courts', pointing to the way the Alien Tort Claims Act in the USA has proven useful for some of the Niger Delta plaintiffs against Shell (Bond, 2010: n.pag.). This emphasizes how notions of climate debt and climate justice can forge solidarities through contesting exploitative relations and institutions. At the demonstration on climate reparations, with which I started this chapter, discourses of climate debt were linked to a direct critique of the role of international financial institutions in climate negotiations. We chanted 'World Bank and IMF out of climate now.'

In the debates at the Klimaforum and in many demonstrations and actions, then, issues of justice were not deferred, but were made central to climate change politics. There was a strong insistence on questions of social and environmental justice. This suggests the importance of solidarities forged between activists in different parts of the world in shaping notions of justice and challenging inequalities. This is important. The Copenhagen protests marked the coming together of political trajectories that have constructed climate change politics in antagonistic ways and through confrontational, non-violent direct action.

This has the potential to make a significant intervention in the terms of debate of climate politics.

While discourses of climate justice were generally mobilized through street demonstrations and actions, there were some leaders who took up such language. During the COP15 negotiations, Bolivian president Evo Morales 'called on the world leaders to raise their ambitions radically and hold temperature increases over the next century to just 1 C. He also demanded that rich countries pay climate change reparations and he proposed the establishment of an international climate court of justice to prosecute countries for climate "crimes"' (Vidal, 2009). Morales has been central to shaping a radical climate politics, most notably through convening the World Peoples' Conference on Climate Change and the Rights of Mother Earth (PWCCC) held in Tiquipaya in Bolivia in April 2010 and attended by 33,000 people.

Climate justice and state-led internationalism

Writing in an introductory 'statement' on the World Peoples' Conference on Climate Change and the Rights of Mother Earth, the Indian social movement activist and intellectual Jai Sen argued that 'any government can call for a "People's Conference" (and many do); but few have any legitimacy to do so, and to do something like this. This one does' (Sen, 2010: n.pag.). This demonstrates the recognition that Evo Morales and the Movimiento al Socialismo (MAS) that he leads had within transnational activist networks. This is unusual given their intense suspicion of state-led political activity. Patrick Bond has argued, in similar terms, that the final lesson of Copenhagen was that the only really reliable government in supporting climate justice principles is that of Bolivia (Bond, 2010). Such an ambitious state-led climate justice conference depended on social movements recognizing Morales's legitimacy.

This recognition stems from a number of key sources. First, MAS came to power as part of a coalition of social and political movements which actively sought to decolonize the state. The

Bolivian state had long been marked by deep exclusions in relation to indigenous majorities. Central to Morales's project has been a refiguring of Bolivia as a constitutionally pluri-national, multi-ethnic state. Morales had been a key figure in the meeting of People's Global Action in Cochabamba, which began less than a week after 11 September 2001. He was 'publicly threatened by the US Ambassador ... for having dared to simultaneously condemn the terrorist attack and the state terrorism practised by the USA in Iraq, Colombia' (Building Bridges Collective, 2010: 25). These histories of connections with transnational activist networks shaped Bolivia's ability to mobilize for the CMPCC (25).

Second, contemporary Bolivia has seen an extraordinary intensity of social and political movements. This has happened in the context of a two-decade project of 'implementation of neoliberal markets and liberal democracy' (Kohl, 2006: 304). This implementation of neoliberal policies began with the structural adjustment programme of the mid-1980s. This popular resistance to neoliberalism culminated in the well-publicized disputes over water and gas in the early 2000s (Perrault, 2006). These dramatic confrontations around attempts to privatize key resources, popularly known as the Water and Gas Wars, had massive impacts on the political terrain in Bolivia. Movement intellectuals and leaders like Oscar Olivera, of the Cochabamba Federation of Factory Workers, mobilized around not just the rejection of water privatization but also a critique of existing state-led provision. The mobilizations drew on significant popular forms of organizing. Raul Zibechi notes that for ten or twelve days in October 2003 'residents of El Alto, organized through neighborhood councils and other means, operated as a neighborhood government that supplanted the delegitimized and absent state' (Zibechi, 2010: 13).

Third, there was the high-profile action of Morales's administration in contesting market-led climate politics. Bolivia was one of the very few nations that rejected the agreement reached in Copenhagen. Morales was active in constructing connections between left governments, NGOs and activist constituencies.

Lastly, Morales's reputation was distinctive within the left governments of the 'pink tide' in Latin America. Sen's account contrasts the CMPCC with Hugo Chávez's (typically) ambitious attempt to construct a 'Fifth International'. He contends this is the case on account of both 'its spirit of openness' and its being recognized as a 'process international (or movement international)' rather than a 'new institutional international' (Sen, 2010: n.pag.).

The CMPCC made a significant intervention in trying to shift massively the terms of debate on climate change. Conceived as an alternative to the 'moribund UN process', the CMPCC was shaped by radical articulations of climate justice (Weinberg, 2010). Internationalist connections enabled the way it mobilized questions of climate justice and debt. It was also characterized by innovative attempts to bring 'governments and civil society groups together to work to address climate change' (Weinberg, 2010). The World Peoples' Conference on Climate Change and the Rights of Mother Earth demanded 'that developed countries reduce their domestic greenhouse gas emissions by 50% based on 1990 levels for the second commitment period of the Kyoto Protocol' (World Peoples' Conference on Climate Change and the Rights of Mother Earth, 2010: n.pag.). Morales presented the 'People's Accord' to the UN, arguing that he was 'convinced that the only way to guarantee a positive result' in the COP16 negotiations in Cancún, Mexico, was 'through the broad participation of the world and the ironclad unity of the countries of the G77 + China' (Morales, 2010: n.pag.). The People's accord demanded that an international tribunal on environmental and climate justice be instigated, with its seat in Bolivia, and that developed countries 'should commit to annual financing from public sources in addition to the Official Development Assistance in order to confront climate change in developing countries' (World Peoples' Conference on Climate Change and the Rights of Mother Earth, 2010: n.pag.).

The conference opened up an important space for a prominent articulation of a very different way of constructing climate politics, albeit one that was largely ignored by Western media outlets. This state-led internationalism was the site of coexistence of diverse political trajectories. The CMPCC suggests the significant persistence of state-led internationalism, albeit shaped by the construction of solidarities through movements. There was a dynamic relation here between 'state' political activity and attempts to 'internationalize' the 'political approach and radical discourse' of MAS (Building Bridges Collective, 2010: 57). The CPMCC operated in a context of struggle over the relations between social movements and the state (Zibechi, 2010). An acceptance of the legitimacy and radical credentials of Morales and MAS was a necessary condition of the conference. The form of the state, however, wasn't just a 'given'. Rather, it was contested, reworked, articulated through this process and through connections with international social movement networks.

These entanglements between social movement activity and state-led internationalism pose challenges to ways of thinking about internationalist solidarities. Work on 'global civil society', for example, has frequently counterposed state and civil society (Kaldor, 2003; Edwards and Gaventa, 2001). This obscures diverse and important entanglements between social movement activity and state activity and formation (Dangl, 2010; Zibechi, 2010). The dominant character of social movement engagement with the Bolivian state under Morales has been positive. There have also been allegations of cronyism and of social movements refusing to criticize the government, partly because of the threat posed by the right. Julieta Ojeda Marguay of the feminist-anarchist movement Mujeres Creando, based in La Paz, has criticized social movements for acting as 'functionaries of the MAS and the party's interests' (cited by Dangl, 2010: 23). Oscar Olivera, who refused the position of labour minister in the Morales administration, has also taken a more critical position, arguing that MAS has worked to demobilize and domesticate social movements (25). The politicization of such entanglements between the state and social movements impacted on and shaped the conduct of the CMPCC in important ways.

One of the key ways that the CMPCC process intersected with such tensions over the relations between social movements and the state was through Mesa 18 (Table 18), which focused on 'Collective Rights and the Rights of Mother Earth'. There were seventeen official working groups in the CMPCC. Mesa 8, for example, addressed questions of climate debt. Mesa 18 was organized following a pre-conference meeting convened by CONAMAQ, a national indigenous council. It was set up by 'groups wanting to highlight the contradictions between the Bolivian government's external discourses on capitalism and the rights of Mother Earth, and its ongoing support for domestic megaprojects and reliance on extractive industries' (Building Bridges Collective, 2010: 33). Mesa 18 was barred by organizers from the official summit grounds on the campus of the University del Valle (Univalle). Aymara elders of the National Council of Ayllus and Markas of Cullasuyu (CONAMAQ) and their allies convened the dissident forum in a Brazilian restaurant just off the campus (Weinberg, 2010: n.pag.).

One of the organizers of the Table, Carlos Crespo Flores of the Universidad Mayor de San Simón, Cochabamba, argued that

> What we saw again in Copenhagen is that externally our president is the defender of the mother earth, of nature, but internally he is doing the opposite – we have seen this, this is our experience. And then we realised that they were trying to hide these internal contradictions, and we thought, why don't we do an event, a table, where we make these visible, these internal themes, the contradictions of our president? (Building Bridges Collective, 2010: 33)

Eduardo Gudynas has similarly pointed to a contradiction between the international stance of Morales and his domestic policies (Gudynas, 2010). This demonstrates how challenging such exclusions can produce different connections, networks and solidarities.

The panel was not uniformly hostile to the government. It credited Morales's administration with 'recognizing the collective rights of Bolivia's "original nations," as well as Afro-Bolivians and "inter-cultural communities"' (Weinberg, 2010:

n.pag.). Pablo Regalsky of the Andean Center for Communication and Development (CENDA) stated: 'Here in Bolivia, we are building a new model – in practice, not theory – so we have to discuss the problems that arise in the creation of this new model' (Regalsky cited by Weinberg, 2010: n.pag.). He warned, however, that 'there are some in the Evo Morales government, especially in the Finance Ministry, who seek a "forced march to industrialization".'

He articulated trans-regional solidarities in contesting plans for an 'inter-oceanic transport link through Bolivia, and mineral and gas exploitation on the Guarani indigenous lands of the country's remote east'. Refuting government charges that Mesa 18 was only dealing with internal Bolivian issues, Regalsky said: '"These questions also have implications for Paraguay, Brazil, Chile and Peru. And they have implications for the rights guaranteed by the Bolivian constitution"' (Regalsky cited by Weinberg, 2010: n.pag.). These contradictions between Morales's 'international discourse surrounding climate justice, anti-neoliberalism and indigenous rights' and his domestic policies have become increasingly contested. In 2011 there were massive protests 'demanding the cancellation of the government's planned highway set to cut through the ancestral lands of the lowland indigenous people of the Yuracarés, Mojeños and Tsimanes' (Laing, 2012).

The reaction of the Bolivian government was to dismiss the Mesa 18 and to claim it was sponsored by the right. Attempts to co-opt the Table by rightist representatives, however, were directly resisted. When Norma Pierola, a 'national legislator from Cochabamba with the right-opposition National Convergence party, attempted to enter the restaurant to address Table 18 (on environmental concerns, she said), her way was blocked by attendees who barred the entrance with their bodies, chanting *"¡No pasará!"* (she shall not pass)' (Weinberg, 2010). This is in keeping with the government's attitude to other challenges from social movements that have criticized it. Oscar Olivera has argued that 'those who stand in the MAS government's way, in a critical position on the left, are pushed aside, stigmatized, and labelled as allies of the right' (Dangl, 2010: 25). This also reflects the pressure on the Morales government/MAS from rightist forces. This has included violent assaults on Morales supporters. On 11 September 2008, in the state of Pando, a private militia 'allegedly funded by the opposition governor, Leopoldo Fernandéz, fired on a thousand unarmed pro-Morales men, women and children marching toward the state's capital', leaving numerous people dead and wounded (Dangl, 2010: 27). There was also right-wing violence in the city of Santa Cruz.

The reaction to the 'dissident' Mesa 18 exemplifies some of the policing and exclusion constituted through state-led internationalism. Such processes can exert considerable pressure on how internationalist networks are constituted and configured. The CMPCC, however, provided important spaces through which productive connections were made between social movements and the state. Social movements struggled within the process to articulate distinctive sets of proposals. This became an issue of contention during the final stages of discussions over the 'findings' of working groups. During the final discussions of the working group on 'action strategies', Via Campesina and the MST 'made a formal submission that all references to a top-down initiative of organising movements to be taken out from the final declaration' (Building Bridges Collective, 2010: 32-3). This was partially successful.[6]

The pressure exerted by the MST and Via Campesina exemplifies how 'bottom-up agency' was formed through contesting the process. 'The final text still maintained a less explicit reference to a '"top-down" organisation of movements' (Building Bridges Collective, 2010: 32-3). Nonetheless this suggests important ways through which concerted social movement presence and activity in the CMPCC were able to shift the tenor of the final outcomes. It is notable that such agency was constructed through a direct critique of the outcomes of the process. This emphasizes the existence of tensions and conflicts over different ways of envisioning internationalist climate politics. The actions of MST and Via Campesina suggest that there were potential challenges

and conflicts between social-movement-led and state-led internationalisms and solidarities. Movement agency, in shaping the
terms of internationalist connection, was constituted through
negotiating and contesting the terms of such entanglements.

Conclusion

Political trajectories antagonistic to neoliberal globalization have
decisively shaped alternative ways of articulating climate change
politics. Their forms of political activity challenge reductive accounts of climate change politics as uniformly post-political. The
terms on which solidarities have been shaped between different
climate struggles have shaped the emergence of discourses of
climate justice. These have challenged and reshaped the terms
of debate over climate change. This is missed by debates which
argue for or against the mobilization of terms such as 'climate
justice' (see e.g. Lynas, 2010; Simons and Tonak, 2010). Rather,
it is necessary to engage with the way such terms are being
mobilized and the antagonisms they articulate.

The unruly multiple political trajectories brought together
through the Copenhagen protests were productive. Antagonistic
ways of envisioning climate change politics were certainly in existence before COP15. In Copenhagen these alternatives asserted
a significant presence, articulacy and vitality. Such alternatives
have the potential to reconfigure the terms of debate around
climate change politics in important ways. These solidarities
have politicized the terms of climate politics, demonstrating the
importance of following the construction of antagonisms around
unequal social and environmental relations, even as such protest
is subject to significant repression. The continuing and deepening of such antagonistic constructions of climate change through
the CMPCC in Bolivia are a testament to their significance and
potential. These internationalisms were forged through contested
articulations between state politics and social movement activity. This suggests that both possibilities and tensions can be
constructed through such relations and entanglements.

Solidarity without guarantees

In his book *On the Shores of Politics* Jacques Rancière makes the arresting argument that

> the immigrant is first and foremost a worker who has lost his name, a worker who is no longer perceptible as such. Instead of the worker or proletarian who is the object of an acknowledged wrong and a subject who vents his grievance in struggle and disputation, the immigrant appears as at once the perpetrator of an inexpiable wrong and the cause of a problem. (Rancière, 1995: 105)

Rancière contends that at stake in asserting who has the right to be seen as engaging in struggle and disputation is the limits of what is to be articulated as political. For Rancière the denial of 'immigrants' right to mobilise around grievances prevents their recognition as political subjects (Dikeç, 2012). They are constructed instead as a 'problem'.

This book has mobilized an account of solidarity as a transformative political relation. I have sought to tell stories about forms of internationalism where the diverse connections and linkages that have made up the left are taken seriously. I have asserted the importance of political trajectories and solidarities which have challenged and reconfigured what is counted as left politics. I have sought to challenge and counter ways of constructing histories and geographies of the left where diverse subaltern actors are excluded and denied presence in left internationalisms; where, in Rancière's terms, their presence and agency become 'no longer perceptible'.

Through this approach I have sketched aspects of an alternative genealogy of left politics. This is a genealogy of politics which treats political activity and the spatial practices of left politics as generative, as productive. Central to this approach has been to make perceptible political trajectories and connections that have been silenced, marginalized, ignored. To engage with such connections is never a simple work of recovery, as if such stories were merely waiting to be retrieved and told. Rather, it is a much more active work of asserting the importance of the stories articulating them. This project offers new understandings of what political lefts have been about, are and might be in the future. It challenges dominant accounts of the left that have profoundly marginalized the role of subaltern political activity in shaping internationalist geographies and solidarities.

Solidarity as a world-making process

Positioning solidarity as a transformative relation has been central to asserting the vitality of this political practice. Engaging with the relations through which solidarities are constructed is a condition for asserting the inventive, generative character of solidarity. This positions solidarity as a political relation that is 'without guarantees'. That is to say, it is an open relation that can be articulated and configured in different, potentially conflictual ways. This relational approach is a condition for asserting a politics of solidarity. It shapes different ways of understanding how relations are made political and the terms on which political communities are shaped and constituted.

My use of the term 'solidarity without guarantees' draws on Stuart Hall's project of rethinking left politics in open and productive terms as bearing on generative practices of articulation

(Hall, 1988: 56). This term has two specific resonances here. First, an insistence on the terms of solidarity not being given opens up a sense of the diverse struggles over how solidarities are to be fashioned and constructed. By doing so it politicizes the construction of solidarity, rather than seeing solidarity as something which just binds already formed communities together.

Second, thinking solidarities in relational terms allows an engagement with the diverse relations and connections shaped through solidarities. This asserts a radical openness regarding the terms on which solidarities are shaped. They are unfinished and in process. This is important as it allows solidarities and the political communities they build to be articulated in different ways. This openness asserts that there are to be no guarantees about the end points to which solidarities work. Rather, it suggests that different political futures and relations can be produced through solidaristic practices.

This allows a focus on diverse forms of agency in shaping the construction of solidarity. I have argued that the terms on which such solidarities were crafted have often been brought into contestation. This has sometimes been seen as undermining the effectiveness of left politics. It has been associated with ill-discipline, sometimes dismissed as sectarianism. Drawing on the importance of feminist and anti/post-colonial challenges to dominant left practices, I have argued, however, that such contestation and dispute can be generative. Such challenges can usefully be seen as a productive part of the process of making envisioning world-building practices rather than something which necessarily invalidates solidarities. It is necessary in this regard to see forms of solidarity and contestation as co-constituted.

This stress on the different ways that solidarities are articulated opens up a sense of the heterogeneous, diverse politics of the left. Spatial logics of internationalism are not fixed backdrops to political activity, but are rather brought into contestation through political activity. There can be no guarantees about the terms on which left political projects are replicated, translated or reworked through internationalist political trajectories. In this regard one of the key contributions the book has sought to make is to assert the coexistence of different left political trajectories. I have sought to assert their intersections and coeval relations and the diverse forms of political agency they have constituted.

The book has explored forms of solidarities that shaped and were shaped by many different left political affiliations, including communism, syndicalism, the New Left, anti-colonialism, feminism, anarchism, environmental movements and libertarian socialism. I have interrogated some of the differences between such positions, wary of constructing a Panglossian account which suggests an easy coexistence between these different articulations of left politics. I have, however, refused to delineate obsessively the ways in which different political traditions approach and construct solidarities and internationalisms.

Instead the book has sought to engage with the diverse terms of solidarities from below through which different – and intersecting – left political traditions have sought to construct different worlds. This has involved working across left traditions which have been wary of, sometimes openly hostile to, each other. This necessitates challenging the way that different left political traditions have often been confined within their own literatures, political cultures and specific debates. It suggests the importance of engaging with connections and articulations between different left traditions and refusing to treat them as self-contained, bounded silos.

The book emphasizes the work of different left political movements and activists in shaping solidarities between different places. It has suggested how this has been a key and often neglected achievement of movements and activists. This is a central practice through which very different political movements have shaped world-making processes in more just and equitable ways. I have situated subaltern agency in assembling, making and contesting the terms of connection between places. Such political interventions have reshaped relations between and within places in productive and transformative ways.

In the face of deep stereotypes and caricatures of left politics I have sought to assert the multiple, plural histories and geographies shaped through practices of solidarity from below. This has involved challenging pervasive depictions of left political movements as atavistic, defensive, old, limited, white male movements. This is important and necessary. I have traced and engaged with some of the unequal racialized and gendered practices through which left politics shaped and formatted solidarities. I have, however, insisted on interrogating forms of subaltern cosmopolitanism that have contributed to, and often driven, much internationalist political culture.

Detailing and engaging with the diverse geographies of connection that have shaped, and been shaped through, the activity of left movements is a significant project. Signalling this diversity, situating the left as a product of different relations, flows and circuits of political activity, is not just a project that is about producing a fuller account of political organizing, however. It is not just about adding in hitherto neglected voices or actions. Rather, it is something which can transform understandings of how left politics has worked and what is at stake in the activity and political cultures of different left movements. I have also been alive to the productive, unexpected outcomes that have been shaped through internationalist political cultures. This has implications for how different forms of internationalism are to be recognized and understood.

Geoff Eley has suggested that democratization has been a key achievement of the left in Europe. This argument is echoed by Greg Grandin's contention that left political movements in Latin America have made indispensable contributions to both processes of expansion and the defence of democracy. Eley concedes that socialists' democratic advocacy fell 'woefully short on a series of vital fronts, gender and race primary among them' (Eley, 2002: 504). Eley notes that the 'spread of democracy had a vital transnational dimension. It was shaped to a great extent beyond the frontiers of the nation itself by a series of horizon-expanding pan-European conjunctures between the eighteenth century and the present' (Eley, 2002: 4).

While Eley gestures to the importance of transnational left political cultures, he primarily views the achievements and political cultures of the left in rather limited nation-centred terms. Different ways of recognizing the contributions and significance of left political cultures are enabled by seeing different geographies of connection and solidaristic linkages as significant achievements. This offers different possible ways of valuing left political cultures and agency. Engaging with the trajectories and connections through which solidarities have been forged, for example, can help assert traces of agency in shaping many different processes from below. This book has sought to illuminate the way such solidarities have engaged with, contested and shaped many different processes. Often engaging with such traces of agency involves understanding the impacts of solidarities beyond narrow goal-centred outcomes.

The activity of seafarers' organizers such as Chris Braithwaite and Harry O'Connell are apposite here. Their organizing practices shaped solidarities and internationalist cultures through intervening in the oppressive conditions of black seafarers. They also shaped articulations of anti-colonialism which brought together visions of independence and a concern for labour grievances. Their organizing against the invasion of Ethiopia forged important intersections between anti-colonial and anti-fascist political imaginaries. They also made an important contribution to processes which might best be seen as bearing on the decolonization of the British labour movement (see also Lamming, 2005).

To assert such forms of agency it is necessary to engage with diverse connections and relations between places that were linked on decidedly unequal terms. The forms of agency traced here may not have been, in the final analysis, determinant. They may not have achieved the political goals set by either themselves or others. This does not mean, however, that these are the only ways in which they might be evaluated. Internationalist political cultures shaped from below exerted pressure in ways that limited and contested diverse forms or oppression – and opened up other possibilities and ways of constructing relations. These actions have often had significant and lasting impacts.

Solidarities have been integral to producing ways of connecting places that are antagonistic to those associated with such unequal and divisive formations as colonialism, neoliberal globalization and the Cold War. In this sense, making alternative logics of connection has been a crucial, if often neglected, contribution of left political cultures. The actually existing connections produced between peace movements in East and West Europe were not an incidental part of the activism of ENDS. Rather, the geographies of connection that produced such solidarities, and they in turn shaped, were crucial to the emergence of political spaces and imaginations that refused the 'remorseless binary logics of the Cold War' (Hall, 1989: 17). The production of such solidaristic spaces is an important and necessary political achievement. It is also the product of diverse forms of labour and organizing practices, which are integral to assembling and maintaining such connections.

Solidarities and political possibilities

This book has traced forms of solidarities and internationalisms that have shaped our political presents in significant, albeit frequently ignored, ways. I have contested both miserabilist leftist perspectives and the triumphalist narratives of the political right, which would have us believe that left internationalisms and solidarities have failed to influence the terms of world-making processes. The project articulated particularly in Parts 3 and 4 of the book has been to challenge and complicate accounts of international politics which position the latter half of the twentieth century as an unfettered march towards neoliberal globalization. Contesting such political narratives is of key consequence for opening up different political presents and futures.

Tracing the plural trajectories constituted through solidarities has shaped a concern with the coeval possibilities shaped through internationalisms. The argument of the third part of the book about the importance of solidarities that refused or challenged the spatial demarcations marked out through the Cold War is central here.

This positions the Cold War as not just about East-West conflicts; after Chari and Verdery it asserts the importance of opening up conversations between post-colonial and post-socialist projects. This challenges teleological constructions of the Cold War as an unbridled victory for neoliberalism and the political right and asserts the coexistence of different ways of shaping political alternatives. The case of the Chilean coup is significant here. The coup demonstrates the importance of the Cold War context to the emergence of the aggressive neoliberal political and economic project.

The political skill and solidarities forged through resistance and opposition to the coup assert the importance of seeing such practices of neoliberalism as always already contested. The vibrant forms of transnational solidarity shaped through opposition to the Junta emphasizes the dynamic trajectories of such contestation. It also emphasizes how solidarities forged through opposition to neoliberalization were shaped by Chilean exiles. The involvement of Chileans in the support groups during the 1984-85 miners' strike is a key case in point here. This emphasizes that opposition to neoliberalism was not secondary or localized. Rather, it was the product of internationalist political trajectories which, in this case, were constructed in opposition to political terror. This also signals important ways in which the Cold War shaped the political terrain on which neoliberalism has been both experienced and resisted.

This challenges capital-centred accounts of neoliberalization. It emphasizes that neoliberalization has always been a contested political project. Despite pretensions to consensus, despite assertions of there being no alternative to neoliberalism, it has been assertively opposed by dynamic and spatially stretched political forms of organizing. Key among these has been the transnational solidarities that were central to bringing the terms of neoliberal globalization into contestation. These movements did not only bring neoliberal geographies of power into question; they also sought to shape alternative geographies of connection by doing so. Their contested attempts to produce prefigurative solidarities have articulated different visions of what an internationalist opposition to contemporary forms of globalization might look like. These debates at their best, then, were part of a productive set of processes and engagements that shaped the terrain on which prefigurative practices of solidarity could be constructed.

The practices through which counter-globalization movements brought the terms of neoliberalization into contestation have been systematically ignored in debates over the financial crisis. This has served to close down political possibilities. Thus left political alternatives have frequently been positioned as responding to the crisis. A different set of political narratives can be constructed by positioning the crisis in relation to the ongoing politicization of neoliberalism. This was an important achievement of the mobilizations in Copenhagen during the COP15 negotiations.

Contemporary left discourses in relation to the crisis, however, have frequently been constructed as 'defensive'. Panitch et al. have recently argued in relation to emerging forms of politicization of the crisis that 'every one of these resistances has only served to reveal the continuing impasse of the Left, and its limited strategic and organizational resources.' They caution that 'defensive resistance alone cannot take advantage of the opportunity that the crisis creates' (Panitch et al., 2011: x). This depiction of the resistances as defensive, however, is been created partly by abstracting the crisis from ongoing contestation of neoliberalism.

Some left responses have been technocratic and narrow. They have focused in limited ways on how financial services industries can be regulated. This is partly because the crisis has been treated in narrow financial terms. While this is of course important, it ignores the dynamics through which the crisis is being politicized. It is also because of the extent to which centre-left parties have bought into neoliberal common sense. As Robin Blackburn argues, the 'centre left and centre right were already persuaded that the welfare state was too expensive and bureaucratic, and needed to be handed over to private suppliers' (Blackburn, 2011b: 33). This has been a crisis where the political right has been able to make much of the running in terms of how the response to the crisis is to be 'managed' (Massey, 2010). Witness the ferocity with which regressive discourses of austerity have been rolled out in different contexts in Europe since 2008.

Other responses have gestured to a rather fatalistic economic determinism. David Harvey has suggested that the 'longer the uncertainty and the misery are prolonged, the more the legitimacy of the existing way of doing business will be questioned and the more the demand to build something different will escalate. Radical as opposed to band-aid reforms to patch up the financial system may seem more necessary' (Harvey, 2009: 225). While this might offer hope, it suggests a rather deterministic link between economic immiseration and political responses. It certainly risks underestimating the ways in which the political right has managed to elicit support for its harsh programmes of austerity and attacks on the very notion of a public sector (Featherstone et al., 2012).

Different political stories and narratives emerge if the crisis is understood not as a wholly exceptional event, but as part of ongoing contested politics of neoliberal globalization. This positions the crisis as something which exacerbates, entrenches and intensifies existing inequalities, rather than being fundamentally new. Solidaristic political imaginaries have much potential to refigure the terms of political debate. Emerging solidarities between different contexts can be important in shaping, nourishing and deepening contestation of the crisis in different contexts. Some of the mobilizations in Copenhagen, for example, shaped alternatives which went well beyond appeals for better forms of regulation or financial governance. These alternatives have been shaped by using the crisis as a possibility for posing counter-hegemonic political narratives. They have been deepened by linkages with states, notably Bolivia, which are attempting, albeit in contested and partial ways, to articulate political presents and futures beyond neoliberalism.

The trajectories and internationalist political cultures shaped through these solidarities contradict claims that we are living in post-political times. Politicians of the centre-left and right have created forms of political managerialism where conflict and contestation are eviscerated in diverse contexts. This is a process which is in itself deeply political. This does not mean, however, that forms of antagonistic political cultures and movements are no longer important. In many contexts these forms of political activity are forged, articulated, in ways that exceed the narrow limits of 'organized' politics. The networks, relations and connections they shape also cut across nation-centred notions of the political. The emergent politicization of 'the crisis' through movements like Occupy are just one manifestation of the dynamism of such contestation.

Raymond Williams wrote in the late 1970s of the 'slowly settling loss of any acceptable future' (Williams, 1979: 209). His intervention marked the significant assault on radical political imaginaries associated with the ascendancy of neoliberalism. The resources fashioned through diverse practices of solidarity suggest ways of overcoming such a bleak prognosis. Through attempting to make worlds anew, through constructing forms of internationalism from below, they have forged actually existing alternatives. This attests to the productive force of solidarities in politicizing relations and inventing new ways of relating and being in the world.

Notes

INTRODUCTION

1. See Foner, 1981; Foster, 2000.
2. Chartism, a popular working-class led movement for suffrage and political reform, was a key political force in mid-nineteenth-century Britain.
3. See Blackburn, 2011a for discussion of Marx's writings on the US Civil War. The discussion here was inspired by a talk given by Selma James in Glasgow in 2008.
4. Minutes of the General Council, in First International, n.d.: 54.

CHAPTER 1

1. *Western Mail*, 19 October 1935.
2. Ibid. O'Connell was described as 'the militant leader of the Colonial Workers in Cardiff' in the report of his trial in the *Negro Worker*.
3. Ibid.
4. Mid Glamorgan Record Office, Cardiff, P/S CBO 3/210, Friday 18 October 1935.
5. Schomburg Center for Research in Black Culture, New York, St Clair Drake Papers 62/3, Cardiff Diary and Notes; Sherwood, 1991: 60.
6. For discussion of the contested representations of this multi-ethnic dockside community, see Jordan, 2001.
7. Schomburg Center for Research in Black Culture, New York, St Clair Drake Papers 62/3, Cardiff Diary and Notes.
8. Hull History Centre Archives, National Council of Civil Liberties, Minutes of the British Overseas Sub-Committee, DCL 275/1, notes of meeting on 28 October 1940.
9. *Hansard* Written Answers, 23 January 1941: 332.
10. *Negro Worker*, 5:11, 1935.

11. See also International Trade Union Committee of Negro Workers, 1931.
12. On Huiswood, see James, 1998: 74-5, 156; and Derrick, 2008: 120-21, 304-5.
13. Although, as David Harvey argues, Kant was less than generous in his distribution of potential to all human beings; Harvey, 2009.
14. The UNIA generated black diaspora politics, which were constituted and formatted in part through Garvey's stress on racial homogeneity and purity (Gilroy, 2000; see also Holcomb, 2007; James, 1985, James, 1998). Garvey advocated a translocal imaginary of black men defined by racial purity, for example through anti-Semitic narratives (see Garvey, 1990: 689).
15. Turin, Milan and Genoa were the hub of the movement, but it had a broader geographical reach. As Paolo Spriano records, 'From the great urban centres to the country districts of the Veneto, Liguria, Tuscany, the Marches, wherever there was a factory, a dockyard, a steelworks, a forge, a foundry in which *metalos* worked, there was an occupation' (Spriano, 1975: 60).
16. This account draws on conversations with Kenny and Trish Caird.

CHAPTER 2

1. See Evans, 1980 for a discussion of the Cardiff riots, which were part of a much larger and transnational wave of white supremacist violence, see also Chapter 3 below.
2. 'Account of the 1929 meeting in Cologne', in LAI Press service notes, International Institute of Social History, Amsterdam, League Against Imperialism Papers, ZK 16171.
3. The song 'Dunnes Stores', credited to 'author unknown', is included on the first disc of Moore's box set of unreleased material: Christy Moore, *The Box Set 1964–2004*, Sony, B0001MXPIQ.

CHAPTER 3

1. The National Archives, London, CO 295/606.
2. The union was known as the National Sailors' and Firemen's Union (NSFU) until 1926, when it became known as the National Union of Seamen.
3. Moselle, a leading Cardiff pan-Africanist, had left Philadelphia at the turn of the century and had worked for a while in South Africa before settling in South Wales. He was Paul Robeson's uncle by marriage. According to St Clair Drake he was president of the Cardiff branch of the South Wales Miners' Federation during the 1926 General Strike; Schomburg Center for Research in Black Culture, St Clair Drake Papers, 60/8; see also Adi and Sherwood, 1995: 142; Llwyd, 2005: 119-20.
4. 'Lascars' was a term used predominantly to describe Indian merchant seafarers sailing under 'Asiatic' or 'Lascar' labour contracts (Dabydeen et al., 2007: 251; Visram, 2002: 30). The 1823 Merchant Shipping Act placed lascars 'at the bottom of the racial hierarchy of maritime labour' and ensured that lascar wages remained 'far below those received by British and other colonial seamen' (Visram, 2002: 30).

5. Modern Records Office, University of Warwick, National Union of Seamen's Papers, MSS 175/3/28.
6. Modern Records Office, University of Warwick, National Union of Seamen's Papers, Minutes of Executive Council of NUS, 11 April 1934, MSS 174/1/1/8.
7. Modern Records Office, University of Warwick, National Union of Seamen's Papers, Minutes of Executive Council of NUS, 11 January 1922 MSS 175/1/1/4.
8. Ibid.
9. Tupper's use of the moniker 'Captain' was fraudulent; see Hirson and Vivian, 1992.
10. Modern Records Office, University of Warwick, National Union of Seamen's Papers, Minutes of Executive Council of NUS, 11 January 1922 MSS 175/1/1/4.
11. 'Notes on Seamen', Pankhurst Papers 74, International Institute of Social History, Amsterdam.
12. Ibid.
13. 'Notes on Seamen's Wives', Pankhurst Papers 74, International Institute of Social History, Amsterdam. See Mitchell, 1977 for a sense of some of the contested class politics of suffragette organizing.
14. This was the title of a pamphlet written by George Hardy and published by the International of Seamen and Harbour Workers.
15. *Negro Worker*, 2:6, 1932: 23-5.
16. For Du Bois's critical discussion of the racial politics of the American Federation of Labor, see Du Bois, 1972 [1929]: 228-33.
17. For discussion of Larkin's time in the USA, see O'Riordan, 2006.
18. Chris Jones, 'Seamen's Notes', *International African Opinion*, vol. 1, no. 4, October 1938.
19. Modern Records Office, University of Warwick, National Union of Seamen's Papers, MSS 175/3/28.
20. The National Archives, London, CO 295/606/4.
21. Ibid.
22. The local conditions in Hamburg, where it was produced until the rise of the Nazis, were significant. The city was a useful location for distribution of the newspaper through seamen. The Committee established its headquarters in the waterfront district, at 8 Rotheshoodstrasse, where Communist maritime activity had been organized by the German Communist Albert Walter for some years (Pennybacker, 2009: 70). This organizing received local Communist support. Ernst Thälmann lived in Hamburg and German Communists had good relations with the city administration (see Derrick, 2009: 200).
23. National Archives, MEPO 38/9, 11A.
24. *Negro Worker*, 2:6, 1932: 14.
25. Ibid.: 15.
26. According to newspaper reports, Australian servicemen were involved in the Glasgow riots in 1919 (Griffin, 2011).
27. The National Archives, London, CO 137/733.
28. The National Archives, London, KV2/1102/5c.
29. This description recalls the playwright George Bernard Shaw's notorious comment to Claude McKay that he should have been a pugilist rather than

a poet (see McKay, 1985: 66–72; see also TNA KV2/1102/5c).
30. Schomburg Center for Research in Black Culture, New York, St Clair Drake Papers, 62/2.
31. The National Archives, London, KV2/1102/53a.
32. Schomburg Center for Research in Black Culture, New York, St Clair Drake Papers, 60/8.
33. Schomburg Center for Research in Black Culture, New York, St Clair Drake Papers, 13/6.
34. *Western Mail*, 2 April 1935.
35. *Negro Worker*, 7:2, 1937: 4. On Surat Alley, see Visram, 2002: 239–53.
36. The concerns of Nurse, however, seem pretty marginalized in the keynote address to the Congress by Idris Cox, the Welsh Communist leader.
37. Schomburg Center for Research in Black Culture, St Clair Drake Papers, 62/5.

CHAPTER 4

1. Abraham Lincoln Brigade Archives (ALBA), Tamiment Library and Robert F. Wagner Labor Archives, New York University Library, interview with Salaria Kee O'Neill, ALBA 18/5/8.
2. On Nyabongo, see Makonnen, 1973: 156–8. See *Negro Worker*, May 1937: 2 for discussion of din Josef.
3. George Padmore became a central figure. The IAFA became the International African Service Bureau, which published the journal *International African Opinion*, discussed in Chapter 3.
4. International Institute of Social History, Pankhurst Papers 267, Letters to Editors.
5. See also The National Archives, London, CO 295/599/13.
6. *Negro Worker*, 5:11, 1935: 28.
7. Ibid.: 16.
8. Aime Césaire's searing denunciation of European liberalism in *Discourse on Colonialism* mobilizes a critique of received ways of thinking the geographies of fascism. This is used to powerfully reconfigure dominant understandings of the term. He argues that what the European liberal 'cannot forgive Hitler for is not the crime in itself, the crime against man, it is not the humiliation of man as such'; rather, 'it is the crime against the white man, and the fact that he applied to Europe colonialist procedures which until then had been reserved exclusively for the Arabs of Algeria, the "coolies" of India and the "niggers" of Africa' (Césaire, 2000 [1955]: 36). To Césaire what is significant about fascism of the 1930s is not its novelty per se. Rather, it is its geographical novelty. It is the way that colonialist political technologies were applied in Europe rather than held at a 'safe distance' in 'colonial contexts'; see also Kelley, 2000; Mamdani, 2003.
9. The role of Moroccan soldiers in fighting for Franco was central to Louise Thompson and Langston Hughes's encounters in Spain (see Wright, 1992; Hughes, 1993, 1994).
10. Other volunteers also related what was happening in Spain to their own experiences. Will Lloyd, a miner from Aberdare in South Wales who

volunteered with the International Brigades, commented, for example, that the notorious South Wales mining company 'Powell Duffryn is Fascism' (Francis, 1984: 210; see also Menai Williams, 2004). For an account of the trajectories of Italian anti-fascists involved in the International Brigades, see Ottanelli, 2007.

11. On Robeson's visit to Spain and his support for the Republican cause more generally, see Duberman, 1989: 210-20; Francis, 1984: 249; Robeson, 1978: 118, 123-7. On Hughes, see Hughes, 1993: 321-405. On Thompson, see Wright, 1992.

12. Abraham Lincoln Brigade Archives, New York, ALBA 18/3/9, Interview with Admiral Kilpatrick Cleveland, Ohio, 8 June 1980.

13. It is worth noting that Kilpatrick's interview in 1980 took place in the context of US support for the El Salvador regime against the FMLN and for the Contras in Nicaragua. The VALB were involved in the major solidarity actions in support of the Sandinistas in Nicaragua, donating ambulances (Colow, 1987).

14. '700 Calendar Days' was included in *Heart of Spain: Anthology of a People's Resistance*, edited by Alvah Bessie. It was published in 1952 by the Veterans of the Abraham Lincoln Brigade, as no mainstream publisher would publish it because of its left-wing subject matter.

15. Winston James argues that the experiences of Caribbean troops in the First World War, 'encumbered by their white superiors' racist notions of what black soldiers ought to be allowed to do', led to the radicalization of a significant number of these men (James, 1998: 56).

16. It is likely that Hunter is referring here to the English communist Walter Tapsell.

17. Abraham Lincoln Brigade Archives, New York, Salaria Kee, ALBA, 18/5/8.

18. The National Archives, London, MEPO 38/9.

19. Abraham Lincoln Brigade Archives, New York, Salaria Kee, ALBA, 18/5/8.

20. Radical Elders Oral History Project, interview with Eluard McDaniel, Abraham Lincoln Brigade Archives, ALBA 143 File on Eluard McDaniel.

21. Abraham Lincoln Brigade Archives, New York, ALBA 143, p. 20. Hunter recalled that 'he came up to Jarama with a pretty little suit on and he got the hell out of there real quick and he was a real mess for us blacks up there' (Oscar Hunter, ALBA 18/3/7, p. 25).

22. Abraham Lincoln Brigade Archives, New York, ALBA 18/3/9.

CHAPTER 5

1. According to the final report of the Corporación Nacional de Reparación y Reconcilación, 1,823 of the 3,197 accredited deaths and disappearances during Pinochet's 'rule' in Chile took place in the period from September to December 1973 (Collins, 2010: 62).

2. Pelikán continues with the observation that the Soviets 'were afraid that yet another kind of socialism, a Chilean kind, with a human face, would be added to the four already existing (Soviet, Chinese, Yugoslav and

Cuban –not to mention what the Italian or Spanish communists imagine socialism to be).'

3. This drew on plans that had been drawn up in secret before the coup. In late 1972 the economists and ex-naval officers Roberto Kelly and José Radic 'were asked by naval sources to obtain an economic program that would ease the way for the military coup' (Valdés, 1995: 252). 'Before midday on Wednesday, September 12, 1973, the General Officers of the Armed Forces who performed governmental duties had the Plan on their desks. The timing of the Chicago Boys' first program with the bombing of "La Moneda" and the death of the last constitutional president of Chile had thus been perfect' (Valdés, 1995: 252).

4. Scottish Trade Union Congress (STUC) Archives, Glasgow Caledonian University, STUC Box 516: Folder on Scottish Football Team's Proposed visit to Chile, 1977.

5. STUC Box 531, Folder Chile Solidarity Campaign Correspondence 1974-5.

6. Ibid.

7. STUC Archives, Box 531, Folder Chile Solidarity Campaign Correspondence 1974-5: International Solidarity Platform of the Chilean TUC.

8. STUC Archives, Box 516: Folder on Scottish Football Team's Proposed visit to Chile, 1977.

9. Ibid.

10. From the song 'Victor Jara of Chile', words by Adrian Mitchell, music by Arlo Guthrie (Mitchell 1982: 261).

11. *Hansard*, 21 May 1974: 186.

12. Samuel notes that the AEU was 'for some forty years the bedrock of the party's trade union strength' (Samuel, 2006: 189). Milne, like Somerville, was a Communist.

13. Letter from Ted Rowlands, Foreign Minister to Scottish Football Association, STUC Archives, 516 Folder on Scottish Football Team's Proposed visit to Chile, 1977.

14. Red Herring published a book of Maria's recipes before her return to Chile in 1990.

15. Martin Carthy, cited by Vulliamy, 2011.

16. Thanks to Mo Hume and Ana Langer for the translation.

17. Testimonial literature from El Salvador suggests that protest music played a critical role in arousing emotions and lifting morale for individual participants in the liberation movement in a variety of contexts, such as in religious ceremonies, union meetings, prison cells, street protests and liberated zones (Almeida and Urbizágastegui 1999: 16).

18. For discussion of the civil war in El Salvador when the guerrillas of the FMLN opposed a right-wing dictatorship which received huge amounts of US funding and military support, see Dunkerley, 1988: 335-424; Hume, 2009.

19. See the material at Carlos Arreandado's website: www.carlosarredondo. com/solidarity%20gallery.htm; accessed 20 January 2012.

20. Dick Gaughan sings 'Victor Jara of Chile' on his CD *Live in Edinburgh*, 1985, Celtic Music CMCD030. Alistair Hulett recorded the song on his CD *In the Back Streets of Paradise*, Jump Up Records 002, 1994; and

Moore on *This Is the Day*, 2001, Sony B00005NOMS. Gaughan credits Jara's murder with inspiring him to become a political singer. John Barrow, Gaughan's agent, notes that 'Dick was not really doing what he is doing now in the late 1960s. He says it was not until Allende in Chile that he realised what he should be doing. Though he had a short distance to travel' (cited by McVicar, 2010: 275). Gaughan argues that those that say 'music and politics should not be mixed' 'should tell that to the CIA and their thugs who murdered Victor Jara because his repertoire didn't suit their interests' (cited by D'Ambrosio, 2004: 203).

21. STUC Archives, Box 516, Letter to James Milne, 10 January 1977.
22. STUC Centenary album *If It Wisnae for the Union*, 1996, Greentrax CDTRAX5005.

CHAPTER 6

1. Lyric from 'To Have or To Have Not' on Billy Bragg's LP *Life's a Riot with Spy vs Spy*, Go! Discs, UTIL 1, 1983.
2. Hauner argues that from 'the time that the indivisibility of human rights and peace had become the cornerstone of Charter 77 statements, Czechs had maintained their reservations about Thompson's END and similar anti-American groups in the West, accusing them of bias in favour of the Soviet Union' (Hauner, 1990: 101).
3. Thompson was based in the old mill town of Halifax and Saville taught at Hull University.
4. Mboya was to become a key figure in the politics of post-independence Kenya. He was assassinated in 1969. Kaunda was the first president of Zambia from 1964 to 1991; Chiume was a key figure in the struggles for Malawian independence, serving as a minister in the post-independence government before fleeing to exile in Tanzania in 1964.
5. This manifesto, adopted by the then leader Michael Foot, was famously dubbed the 'longest suicide note in history' by Gerald Kaufman, a figure on the right of the party.

CHAPTER 7

1. The CP(ML) is the Communist Party (Marxist–Leninist): the Maoist Indian Communist Party.
2. Dunayevskaya collaborated with Grace Lee Boggs and C.L.R. James in the 1940s and early 1950s in what was known as the Johnson–Forest tendency (see Bogues, 1997; Boggs and Boggs, 1986; Davies, 2008: 58–9).

CHAPTER 8

1. For detailed reports of the different actions and demonstrations, see Danish Indymedia, http://indymedia.dk.
2. See Escobar, 2008 for a detailed discussion of Colombian social movements and the difficulties of organizing in Colombia.

3. From the Public Declaration of the Glasgow event.
4. See Christiansen, 1994 for a useful discussion of the history of the left in Denmark in the twentieth century.
5. http://uk.oneworld.net/article/view/166581/1/7467.
6. http://pwccc.wordpress.com/2010/04/29/final-conclusions-working-group-16-action-strategies/#more-1860.

References

Abramsky, K. (2006) 'The Bamako appeal and the Zapatista 6th declaration: between creating new worlds and reorganizing the old one'. www.cacim. net/bareader/pages/Reactions%20to%20the%20Bamako%20Appeal1.html. Accessed 17 January 2012.

Adi, H. (1998) West Africans in Britain 1900–1960: Nationalism, Pan-Africanism and Communism. London: Lawrence & Wishart.

Adi, H., and Sherwood, M. (1995) The 1945 Manchester Pan-African Congress Re-visited. London: New Beacon Books.

Agamben, G. (1993) The Coming Community. Minneapolis: Minnesota University Press.

Aiyer, A. (2007) 'The Allure of the Transnational: Notes on Some Aspects of the Political Economy of Water in India'. Cultural Anthropology 22: 4, 640-58.

Allman, J. (2008) 'Nuclear Imperialism and the Pan-African Struggle for Peace and Freedom: Ghana, 1959-1962'. Souls 10:2, 83-102.

Almeida, P., and Urbizágastegui, R. (1999) 'Cutumay Camones: Popular Music in El Salvador's National Liberation Movement'. Latin American Perspectives 26:2, 13-42.

Alvarez, S. (2000) 'Translating the Global: Effects of Transnational Organizing on Local Feminist Discourses and Practices in Latin America'. Meridians: Feminism, Race, Transnationalism 1:1, 29-67.

Anderson, B. (2005) Under Three Flags: Anarchism and the Anti-Colonial Imagination. London: Verso.

Anderson, P. (2002) 'Internationalism: A Breviary'. New Left Review 14, 5-25.

Anderson, P. (1976) Considerations on Western Marxism. London: New Left Books.

Andrews, T.G. (2008) Killing for Coal: America's Deadliest Labor War. Cambridge MA: Harvard University Press.

Anon. (1999) 'People's Global Action Conference: 15th-26th of August 1999, an impression'. www.nadir.org/nadir/initiativ/agp/bangalore/report.htm. Accessed 24 January 2012.

Ansell, C.K. (2001) *Schism and Solidarity in Social Movements: The Politics of Labor in the French Third Republic*. Cambridge: Cambridge University Press.

Asante, S.K.B. (1977) *Pan-African Protest: West Africa and the Italo-Ethiopian Crisis, 1934-1941*. London: Longman.

Atkinson, D. (2000) 'Nomadic Strategies and Colonial Governance'. In J. Sharp, R. Routledge, C. Philo and R. Paddison (eds), *Entanglements of Power: Geographies of Domination/Resistance*, 93-121. London: Routledge.

Atté (1977) 'Rivonia'. on *Freedom Come All Ye: The Poems and Songs of Hamish Henderson*. Dublin: Claddagh Records, CCA7.

Bahro, R. (1982) 'A New Approach for the Peace Movement in Germany'. In E.P. Thompson and others, *Exterminism and Cold War*, 87-116. London: Verso.

Bahro, R. (1978) *The Alternative in Eastern Europe*. London: New Left Books.

Baldwin, K. (2002) *Beyond the Color Line and the Iron Curtain: Reading Encounters Between Black and Red, 1922-1963*. Durham NC: Duke University Press.

Balfour, S. (2002) *Deadly Embrace: Morocco and the Road to the Spanish Civil War*. Oxford: Oxford University Press.

Baptiste, F., and Lewis, R. (eds) (2009) *George Padmore: Pan-African Revolutionary*. Kingston: Ian Randle.

Barker, T. (1965) *Tom Barker and the IWW*. Recorded, Edited and with an Introduction by E.C. Fry. Canberra: Australian Society for the Study of Labour History.

Barratt Brown, M. (1989) 'Positive Neutralism Then and Now'. In Oxford University Socialist Discussion Group (eds), *Out of Apathy*, 81-7. London: Verso.

Bauman, Z. (1989) *Modernity and the Holocaust*. Ithaca NY: Cornell University Press.

Baxell, R. (2004) *British Volunteers in the Spanish Civil War: The British Battalion in the International Brigades, 1936-1939*. London: Routledge.

Beckett, A. (2002) *Pinochet in Piccadilly: Britain and Chile's Hidden History*. London: Faber & Faber.

Benn, T. (1995) *The Benn Diaries*. London: Hutchinson.

Bidwai, P., and Vanaik, A. (2000) *New Nukes: India, Pakistan and Global Disarmament*. Oxford: Signal Books.

Bijoy, C.R. (2006) 'Kerala's Plachimada Struggle: A Narrative on Water Governance Rights'. *Economic and Political Weekly*, 14 October, 4332-9.

Bird, S., Georgakas, D., and Shaffer, D. (1987) *Solidarity Forever: The IWW: An Oral History of the Wobblies*. London: Lawrence & Wishart.

Blackburn, R. (2011a) *An Unfinished Revolution: Karl Marx and Abraham Lincoln*. London: Verso.

Blackburn, R. (2011b) 'Crisis 2.0'. *New Left Review* 72, 33-62.

Blackburn, R. (2008) 'The Subprime Crisis'. *New Left Review* 50, 63-106.

Blagojevic, K. (2010) Blog post: China, climate justice and Mark Lynas. www. wdm.org.uk/blog-post-china-climate-justice-and-mark-lynas. Accessed 18 May 2010.

Blizzard, W.C. (2010) *When Miners March* ed. W. Harris. Oakland: PM Press.

Bloomfield, B. (1986) 'Women's Support Group at Maerdy'. In R. Samuel, B. Bloomfield and G. Boanas (ed.) *The Enemy Within: Pit Villages and the Miners' Strike of 1984–5*. London: Routledge & Kegan Paul, 72-85.

Boggs, J., and Boggs, G.L. (1986) 'A Critical Reminiscence'. In P. Buhle (ed.), *C.L.R. James: His Life and Work*, 180-84. London: Allison & Busby.

Bogues, A. (1997) *Caliban's Freedom: The Early Political Thought of C.L.R. James*. London: Pluto Press.

Bond, P. (2011) 'Emissions Trading, New Enclosures and Eco-Social Contestation'. *Antipode.*

Bond, P. (2010) 'Copenhagen Inside Out: Why Climate Justice Did Not Crumble at the Summit'. *Counterpunch.* www.counterpunch.org/2010/01/12/copenhagen-inside-out. Accessed 11 September 2011.

Bookchin, M. (1971) *Post-Scarcity Anarchism.* San Francisco: Ramparts Press.

Bourdet, C. (1958) 'The Way to European Independence'. *New Reasoner,* Summer 1958, 12-17.

Branford, S., and Rocha, J. (2002) *Cutting the Wire: The Story of the Landless Movement in Brazil.* London: Latin America Bureau.

Brecher, J., Costello, T., and Smith, B. (2000) *Globalization from Below: The Power of Solidarity.* Cambridge MA: South End Press.

Brennan, T. (2006) *Wars of Position: The Cultural Politics of Left and Right.* New York: Colombia University Press.

Brennan, T. (2003) 'Cosmopolitanism and Internationalism'. In D. Archibugi (ed.), *Debating Cosmopolitics*, 40-50. London: Verso.

Brennan, T. (1989) 'Cosmopolitans and Celebrities'. *Race and Class* 31:1, 1-19.

Bressey, C. (2011) 'Black Women and Work in England, 1880-1920'. In M. Davis (ed.), *Class and Gender in British Labour History*, 117-32. Pontypool: Merlin Press.

Bright, B. (1980) *Shellback: Reminiscences of Ben Bright, Mariner.* Recorded and edited by Ewan MacColl and Peggy Seeger. London and Oxford: History Workshop.

Brock, L., Kelley, R., and Sotiropoulos, K. (2003) 'Editors Introduction'. *Radical History Review* 87, Special Issue on Transnational Black Studies, 1-3.

Brockway, F. (2010) [1942] *Inside the Left.* Nottingham: Spokesman Books.

Browder, E. (1938a) *The People's Front.* New York: International Publishers.

Browder, E. (1938b) Untitled contribution. In *Writers Take Sides: Letters about the War in Spain from 418 American Authors.* New York: League of American Writers.

Buchan, J. (2003) Untitled contribution. *Chile and Scotland: 30 Years On.* Glasgow Caledonian University: Research Collections Witness Seminar and Open Forum Series, 20-22. www.gcal.ac.uk/archives/witness/chile/documents/chiletranscript.pdf. Accessed 1 September 2011.

Buck-Morss, S. (2009) *Hegel, Haiti and Universal History*. Pittsburgh: University of Pittsburgh Press.

Building Bridges Collective (2010) *Space for Movement? Reflections from Bolivia on Climate Justice, Social Movements and the State*. Leeds: Building Bridges Collective.

Bullard, R. (1990) *Dumping in Dixie: Race, Class and Environmental Quality* Boulder CO: Westview Press.

Bunting. B. (1975) *Moses Kotane: South African Revolutionary*. London: Inkululeko Publications.

Burton, K. (2011) 'Performing Alter-geopolitics: The Trade to Climate Caravan'. Unpublished paper, presented at the Performing Geo-politic Conference, Durham University.

Burton, V. (1999) "Whoring Drinking Sailors': Reflections on Masculinity in Nineteenth-Century British Shipping'. In W. Walsh (ed.), *Working Out Gender: Perspectives From Labour History*, 84-101. Aldershot: Ashgate.

Butler, J. (2000) 'Competing Univeralities'. In J. Butler, E. Laclau and S. Žižek, *Contingency, Hegemony, Universality: Contemporary Dialogues on the Left*, 136-81. London: Verso.

Calhoun, C. (2003) 'The Class Consciousness of Frequent Travellers: Towards a Critique of Actually Existing Cosmopolitanism'. In D. Archibugi (ed.), *Debating Cosmopolitics*, 86-116. London: Verso.

Caprotti, F. (2011) 'Visuality, Hybridity and Colonialism: Imagining Ethiopia through Colonial Aviation, 1935-1940'. *Annals of the Association of American Geographers* 101:2, 380-403.

Cardiff Coloured Seamen's Committee (1935) 'Coloured Seamen's Struggle Against De-Nationalisation Memorandum'. *Negro Worker* 5:9, 10-11, 18.

Castree, N. (2000) 'Geographic Scale and Grass-roots Internationalism: The Liverpool Dock Dispute, 1995-1998', *Economic Geography* 73:3, 272-92.

Césaire, A. (2000) [1955] *Discourse on Colonialism*. New York: Monthly Review Press.

Chakrabarty, D. (2002) *Habitations of Modernity: Essays in the Wake of Subaltern Studies*. Chicago: Chicago University Press.

Chambers, I. (2010) 'Another Map, Another History, Another Modernity. *Californian Italian Studies Journal* 1:1-2, 1-16.

Chari, S. (2012) ' Subalternities that Matter in Times of Crisis'. In J. Peck, T. Barnes and E. Sheppard (eds), *The New Companion to Economic Geography*, 501-14. Chichester: Wiley-Blackwell.

Chari, S., and Verdery, K. (2009) 'Thinking between the Posts: Postcolonialism, Postsocialism, and Ethnography after the Cold War'. *Comparative Studies in History and Society* 51:1, 6-34.

Charter 77 (1985) 'The Prague Appeal'. *East European Reporter* 1:1, 27-8.

Charter 77 (1983a) 'Statement on West European Peace Movements'. In J. Kavan and Z. Tomin (eds), *Voices from Prague: Documents on Czechoslovakia and the Peace Movement*, 22-3. END and Palach Press: London.

Charter 77 (1983b) 'Call to the Peace Movement in the German Democratic Republic'. in J. Kavan and Z. Tomin (eds), *Voices from Prague: Documents on Czechoslovakia and the Peace Movement*, 25. END and Palach Press: London.

Chatterton, P., Featherstone, D.J., and Routledge, P. (forthcoming)

'Articulating Climate Justice in Copenhagen: Antagonism, the Commons and Solidarity'. *Antipode*.

Chisholm, A. (1992) 'Testimonies: Albert Chisholm'. In D.D. Collum (ed.), *African Americans in the Spanish Civil War: 'This Ain't Ethiopia, But It'll Do'*, 145-50. New York: G.K.Hall.

Christiansen, N. (1994) Denmark: End of an Idyll'. In P. Anderson and P. Camiller (eds), *Mapping the West European Left*, 77-101. London: Verso.

Clark, A. (1996) *The Struggle for the Breeches: Gender and the Making of the British Working Class*. Berkeley: University of California Press.

CJA (Climate Justice Action) (2010) 'What does climate justice mean in Europe?' www.climate-justice-action.org/resources/documents/what-does-climate-justice-mean-in-europe/. Accessed 13 September 2011.

Climate Justice Now (2007) 'What's missing from the climate talks? Justice'. www.climate-justice-now.org/category/events/bali. Accessed 12 September 2011.

Cockburn, A., and St.Clair, J. (2000) *Five Days That Shook the World: Seattle and Beyond*. London: Verso.

Cohen, W.B. (1972) 'The Colonial Policy of the Popular Front'. *Society for French Historical Studies* 7:3, 368-93.

Cole, P. (ed.) (2007a) *Ben Fletcher: The Life and Times of a Black Wobbly*. Chicago: Charles H. Kerr.

Cole, P. (2007b) *Wobblies on the Waterfront: Interracial Unionism in Progressive Era Philadelphia*. Chicago: University of Illinois Press.

Collins, C. (2010) *Post-Transitional Justice: Human Rights in Chile and El Salvador*. Pennsylvania: Pennsylvania State University Press.

Collum, D.D. (ed.) (1992) *African Americans in the Spanish Civil War: 'This Ain't Ethiopia, But It'll Do'*. New York: G.K. Hall.

Colombia Solidarity Campaign (2007) 'It's the oil, stupid!: background'. www.colombiasolidarity.org.uk/content/view/115/68/. Accessed 10 July 2007.

Colow, M. (1987) 'Ambulances for Nicaragua'. In *Our Fight: Writings by Veterans of the Abraham Lincoln Brigade SPAIN 1936-1939*. New York: Monthly Review Press, 349-54.

Conway, J. (2010) 'Troubling Transnational Feminism(s) at the World Social Forum'. In P. Dufour, D. Masson and D. Caouette (eds), *Solidarities Beyond Borders: Transnationalizing Women's Movements*, 149-172. Vancouver: University of British Colombia Press.

Cooper, F. (2005) *Colonialism in Question: Theory, Knowledge, History*. Berkeley: University of California Press.

Cooper, M. (2001) *Pinochet and Me: A Chilean Anti-Memoir*. London: Verso.

Crawford, T. (1977) 'Hamish Henderson'. Liner notes on *Freedom Come All Ye: The Poems and Songs of Hamish Henderson*. Dublin: Claddagh Records, CCA7.

Creighton, M.S., and Norling, L. (ed.) (1996) *Iron Men, Wooden Women: Gender and Seafaring in the Atlantic World, 1700-1920*. Baltimore MD: Johns Hopkins University Press.

Cunard, N. (2002) *Essays on Race and Empire*, ed. M. Moynagh. Ormskirk: Broadview Literary Texts.

D'Ambrosio, A. (2004) 'You Can't Have a Revolution without Songs: The

Legacy of Victor Jara and the Political Folk Music of Caetano Veloso, Silvio Rodriguez and Joe Strummer'. In A. D'Ambrosio (ed.), *Let Fury Have the Hour: The Punk Rock Politics of Joe Strummer*, 197-210. New York: Nation Books.

Dabydeen, D., Gilmore, J., and Jones, C. (2007) *The Oxford Companion to Black British History*. Oxford: Oxford University Press.

Dangl. B. (2010) *Dancing with Dynamite: Social Movements and States in Latin America*. Edinburgh: AK Press.

Daniel, P. (2007) 'Is another world possible without the women's perspective?', Open Democracy, 17 January. www.opendemocracy.net/xml/xhtml/articles/4257.html. Accessed 6 June 2007.

Das Gupta, A., and Shahid, A.S. (1981) 'Ghana's Non-alignment under Nkrumah'. *International Studies* 20:1-2, 401-9.

Davies, A.D. (forthcoming) 'Identity and the Assemblages of Protest: The Spatial Politics of the Royal Indian Navy Mutiny, 1946'. *Geoforum*.

Davies, A.D. (2012) 'Assemblage and Social Movements: Tibet Support Groups and the Spatialities of Political Organisation'. *Transactions of the Institute of British Geographers* 37:2, 273-86.

Davies, A.D. (2009) 'Ethnography, Space and Politics: Interrogating the Process of Protest in the Tibetan Freedom Movement'. *Area* 41:1, 19-25.

Davies, C.B. (2008) *Left of Karl Marx: The Political Life of Black Communist Claudia Jones*. Durham NC: Duke University Press.

Davis, C.J. (2002) 'Shape or fight?': New York's Black Longshoremen, 1945-1961'. *International Labor and Working-Class History* 62, 143-63.

Davis, M. (2011) 'Spring Confronts Winter'. *New Left Review* 72, 5-15.

Davis, M. (1986) *Prisoners of the American Dream: Politics and Economy in the History of the US Working Class*. London: Verso.

Davis, M. (1982) 'Nuclear Imperialism and Extended Deterrence'. in E.P. Thompson and others, *Exterminism and Cold War*, 35-64. London: Verso.

De Angelis, M. (1998) 'Second Encounter for Humanity and Against Neo-liberalism, Spain 1997'. *Capital and Class* 65, 135-58.

Dean, J. (1996) *Solidarity of Strangers: Feminism after Identity Politics*. Berkeley: University of California Press.

Dedijer, S. (1958) 'Freedom and Scientific Research'. *New Reasoner* 4, 131-6.

de Laforcade, G. (2010) 'Straddling the Nation and the Working World: Anarchism and Syndicalism on the Docks and Rivers of Argentina'. In S. Hirsch and L. Van Der Walt (eds), *Anarchism and Syndicalism in the Colonial and Post-Colonial World, 1870-1940: The Praxis of National Liberation, Internationalism and Social Revolution*, 321-62. Leiden: Brill.

Derrick, J. (2008) *Africa's 'Agitators': Militant Anti-Colonialism in Africa and the West, 1918-1939*. London: Hurst.

DeShazo, P. (1983) *Urban Workers and Labor Unions in Chile 1902-1927*. Madison: University of Wisconsin Press.

de Sousa Santos, B. (2006) *The Rise of the Global Left: The World Social Forum and Beyond*. London: Zed Books.

de Sousa Santos, B. (2003) 'The World Social Forum: toward a counter-hegemonic globalization'. www.ces.fe.uc.pt/bss/fsm.php. Accessed 7 July 2003.

Desmarais, A. (2007) *La Via Campesina: Globalization and the Power of Peasants*. London: Pluto Press.

Di Chiro, G. (1996) 'Nature as Community: The Convergence of Environment and Social Justice'. In W.W. Cronon (ed.), *Uncommon Ground: Rethinking the Human Place in Nature*, 2nd edn, 298-320. London: W.W. Norton.

Dikeç, M. (2012) 'Beginners and Equals: Political Subjectivity in Arendt and Rancière'. *Transactions of the Institute of British Geographers*.

Dikeç, M. (2007) *The Badlands of the Republic: Space, Politics and Urban Policy*. Oxford: Blackwell.

Dirks, Y. (2002) 'Doing things differently this time: Kananaskis G8 meeting and movement building'. http://news.infoshop.org/article.php?story=02/02/10/3017765. Accessed 20 January 2012.

Distressed Operatives (1863) 'Address of Cotton Operations to the People of the United States'. www.nytimes.com/1863/02/16/news/address-of-cotton-operations-to-the-people-of-the-united-states.html. Accessed 17 September 2011.

Dixon, C. (2009) 'Five Days in Seattle: A View from the Ground'. In D. Solnit and R. Solnit (eds), *The Battle of the Story of the Battle of Seattle*, 73-108. Edinburgh: AK Press.

DN (2001) 'Globalisation of Protest'. *Economic and Political Weekly*, 6 October 2001, 3818-19.

Douglass, F. (1952) [1862] 'The Slave's Appeal to Great Britain'. In P.S. Foner (ed.), *The Life and Writings of Frederick Douglass*, Volume 1: *The Civil War, 1861–1865*, 299-305. New York: International Publishers.

Dodds, K. (2002) *Pink Ice: Britain and the South Atlantic Empire*. London: I.B. Tauris.

Douglass, F. (1979) *The Frederick Douglass Papers: Series One, Speeches, Debates and Interviews*, Volume 1: *1841–46*, ed. J.W. Blassingame. Newhaven CT: Yale University Press.

Drew, G., and Levien, M. (2006) 'The opposition to Coca Cola and water privatization: activists in Medhiganj, India rise up'. www.zmag.org/content/showarticle.cfm?ItemID=10641. Accessed 2 July 2007.

Du Bois, W.E.B. (1996) [1899] *The Philadelphia Negro*. Philadelphia: University of Pennsylvania Press.

Du Bois, W.E.B. (1972) [1929] 'The AF of L and the Negro'. In D. Walden (ed.), *The Crisis Writings*, 228-33. Greenwich CT: Fawcett Publications.

Duberman, M. (1989) *Paul Robeson: A Biography*. New York: New Press.

Duff, P. (1971) *Left Left Left: A Personal Account of Six Protest Campaigns 1945–65*. London: Allison & Busby.

Dufour, P., Masson, D., and Caouette, D. (2010) 'Introduction'. in P. Dufour, D. Masson and D. Caouette (eds), *Solidarities beyond Borders: Transnationalizing Women's Movements*, 1-34. Toronto: University of Toronto Press.

Dunayevskaya, R. (1985) *Women's Liberation and the Dialectics of Revolution: Reaching for the Future*. Atlantic Highlands NJ: Humanities Press International.

Dunkerley, J. (1988) *Power in the Isthmus: A Political History of Modern Central America*. London: Verso.

Durkheim, E. (1991) *The Division of Labour in Society*. London: Macmillan.

Edwards, B.H. (2003) *The Practice of Diaspora: Literature, Translation, and the Rise of Black Internationalism*. Cambridge MA: Harvard University Press.

Edwards, M., and Gaventa, J. (2001) (eds) *Global Citizen Action*. London: Earthscan.

Eley, G. (2002) *Forging Democracy: The History of the Left in Europe, 1850–2000*. Oxford: Oxford University Press.

END (European Nuclear Disarmament) (1980) 'Appeal for European Nuclear Disarmament'. In E.P. Thompson and D. Smith (eds), *Protest and Survive*, 223-6. Harmondsworth: Penguin.

Enzensberger, H.M. (1974) 'A Critique of Political Ecology'. In *Raids and Reconstructions: Essays in Politics, Crime and Culture*, 253-95. London: Pluto Press.

Epstein, B. (1991) *Political Protest and Cultural Revolution: Nonviolent Direct Action in the 1970s and 1980s*. Berkeley: University of California Press.

Escobar A. (2008) *Territories of Difference: Place, Movements, Life, Redes*. Durham NC: Duke University Press.

Eschle, C. (2005) 'Skeleton Woman: Feminism and the Anti-Globalisation Movement'. *Signs* 30:3, 1742-69.

Eschle, C., and Maiguashca, B. (2010) *Making Feminist Sense of the Global Justice Movement,* Lanham MD: Rowman & Littlefield.

Evans, G. (2009) 'It was an Education'. In *Strike!/ Streic! 25 Years, 1984–2009*, 61-2. Blaenavaon: Big Pit, National Coal Museum.

Evans, N. (1980) 'The South Wales Race Riots of 1919'. *Llafur, the Journal of Welsh Labour History* 3:1, 5-29.

Fair, B. (1987) 'On the Waterfronts'. in S. Bird, D. Georgakas and D. Shaffer (eds), *Solidarity Forever: The IWW: An Oral History of the Wobblies*, 181-4. London: Lawrence & Wishart.

Featherstone, D.J. (2010) 'Contested Relationalities of Political Activism: The Democratic Spatial Practices of the London Corresponding Society'. *Cultural Dynamics* 22:2, 87-104.

Featherstone, D.J. (2009) 'Counter-insurgency, Subalternity and Spatial Relations: Interrogating Court Martial Narratives of the Nore Mutiny of 1797'. *South African Historical Journal* 61:4, 765-86.

Featherstone, D.J. (2008) *Resistance, Space and Political Identities: The Making of Counter-Global Networks*. Oxford: Wiley-Blackwell.

Featherstone, D.J. (2003) 'Spatialities of Transnational Resistance to Globalization: The Maps of Grievance of the Inter-Continental Caravan'. *Transaction of the Institute of British Geographers* 28:4, 404-21.

Featherstone, D.J., Ince, A., MacKinnon, D., Strauss, K., and Cumbers, A. (2012) 'Progressive Localism and the Construction of Political Alternatives'. *Transactions of the Institute of British Geographers*, 37:2, 177-82.

Fieldhouse, R. (2004) *Anti-Apartheid: A History of the Movement in Britain*. London: Merlin Press.

Figueroa, M. (1990) *Food Out of Chile: Recipes and Stories From Maria Figueroa*. Newcastle: Earthright Publications.

First International (1864) 'Address of the International Working Men's Association to Abraham Lincoln, President of the United States of America'. www.marxists.org/archive/marx/iwma/documents/1864/lincoln-letter. htm. Accessed 25 January 2012.

First International (n.d.) *Documents of the First International: The General Council of the First International 1864–1866: Minutes.* London: Lawrence & Wishart.

Fletcher, B. (2007) [1915] 'Transport Workers Strike in Philadelphia'. In P. Cole (ed.), *Ben Fletcher: The Life and Times of a Black Wobbly*, 66-7. Chicago: Charles H. Kerr

Foner, P. (1981) *British Labor and the American Civil War.* New York: Holmes & Meier.

Ford, J.W., and Gannes, H. (1935) *War in Africa: Italian Fascism Prepares to Enslave Ethiopia.* New York: New York Workers Library.

Foster, J. (2000) 'Marx and Internationalism'. *Monthly Review* 52:3, 1.

Francis, H. (2009) *History On Our Side: Wales and the 1984/5 Miners' Strike.* Swansea: Parthian Books.

Francis, H. (1984) *Miners against Fascism: Wales and the Spanish Civil War.* London: Lawrence & Wishart.

Freeman, F. (2003) 'Hamish Henderson: A Unifying Vision'. Liner Notes to *Hamish Henderson Tribute Album.* Greentrax, CDTRAX 244

Frost, D. (1999) *Work and Community among West African Migrant Workers since the Nineteenth Century.* Liverpool: Liverpool University Press.

Frost, D., and Phillips, R. (2011) *Liverpool '81: Remembering the Riots.* Liverpool: Liverpool University Press.

Fryer, P. (1984) *Staying Power: The History of Black People in Britain.* London: Pluto Press.

Garvey, M. (1990) [1936] Editorials by Marcus Garvey in *Black Man.* In *The Marcus Garvey and Universal Negro Improvement Association Papers*, Volume VII: *November 1927–August 1940*, ed. R.A. Hill, 686-95. Berkeley: University of California Press.

Giddens, A. (1972) 'Durkheim's Writings in Sociology and Philosophy'. In A. Giddens (ed.), *Emile Durkheim: Selected Writings*, 1-50. Cambridge: Cambridge University Press.

Gidwani, V. (2008) *Capital Interrupted: Agrarian Development and the Politics of Work in India.* Minneapolis: University of Minnesota Press.

Gidwani, V.K. (2006) 'Subaltern Cosmopolitanism as Politics'. *Antipode* 38:1, 7-21.

Gill, L. (2007) '"Right there with you": Coca-Cola, Labor Restructuring and Political Violence in Colombia'. *Critique of Anthropology* 27:3, 235-60.

Gill, L. (2006) 'Fighting for Justice, Dying for Hope: On the Protest Line in Colombia'. *North American Dialogue* 9:2, 9-13.

Gill, L. (2004) 'Labor and Human Rights: "The Real Thing" in Colombia'. http://killercoke.org/reports_gill.php. Accessed 30 April 2012.

Gillan, A. (2004) 'I was always told I was thick. The strike taught me I wasn't'. *Guardian*, 10 May 2004. www.guardian.co.uk/politics/2004/may/10/past.women. Accessed 4 September 2011.

Gilmore, R.W. (2008a) 'Forgotten Places and the Seeds of Grassroots Planning'. in C. Hale (ed.), *Engaging Contradictions: Theory, Politics, and Methods of Activist Scholarship.* GAIA Books, Global, Area, and International Archive, University of California, Berkeley.

Gilmore, R.W. (2008b) *Golden Gulag: Prisons, Surplus, Crisis and Opposition in Globalising California.* Berkeley: University of California Press.

Gilroy, P. (2004) *After Empire*. London: Routledge.

Gilroy, P. (2000) *Against Race: Imagining Political Culture Beyond the Color Line*. Cambridge MA: Harvard University Press.

Gilroy, P. (1993) *The Black Atlantic: Modernity and Double Consciousness*. London: Verso.

Goodall, H. (2008) 'Port Politics: Indian Seamen, Australian Unions and Indonesian Independence, 1945-47'. *Labour History* 94, 43-68.

Gowan, P. (2009) 'Crisis in the Heartland'. *New Left Review* 55, 5-29.

Goyens, T. (2009) 'Social Space and the Practice of Anarchist History'. *Rethinking History* 13:4, 439-57.

Graeber, D. (2009) *Direct Action: An Ethnography*. Edinburgh: AK Press.

Graeber, D. (2002) 'The New Anarchists'. *New Left Review* 13, 61-73.

Gramsci, A. (1995) *Further Selections from the Prison Notebooks*. London: Lawrence & Wishart.

Gramsci, A. (1985) *Selections from Cultural Writings*. London: Lawrence & Wishart.

Gramsci, A. (1978) *Selections from Political Writings, 1921-26*. London: Lawrence & Wishart.

Gramsci, A. (1977) *Selections from Political Writings, 1910-1920*. London: Lawrence & Wishart.

Gramsci, A. (1971) *Selections From the Prison Notebooks*. London: Lawrence & Wishart.

Grandin, G. (2006) *Empire's Workshop: Latin America, the United States and the New Imperialism*. New York: Metropolitan Books.

Grandin, G. (2004) *The Last Colonial Massacre: Latin America in the Cold War*. Chicago: University of Chicago Press.

Gray, M. (2011) *Route 19 Revisited: The Clash and the Making of London Calling*. London: Vintage.

Green New Deal Group (2008) *A Green New Deal*. London: New Economics Foundation.

Griffin, P. (2011) *The Spatial Politics of Red Clydeside*. M.Res. dissertation, University of Glasgow School of Geographical and Earth Sciences.

Grünberg, D. (1982) 'Peace March "82"'. In *END Special Report: Moscow Independent Peace Group*, 15-21. London: END and Merlin Press.

Gudynas, E. (2010) 'A necessary reflection on the climate change meeting in Bolivia'. www.mediacoop.ca/story/3262. Accessed 25 January 2012.

Guha, R. (1982) 'On Some Aspects of the Historiography of Colonial India'. In R. Guha (ed.), *Subaltern Studies* I, 1-7. New Delhi: Oxford University Press.

Haapamaki, M. (2005) Writers in Arms and the Just War: The Spanish Civil War, Literary Activism and Leftist Masculinity. *Left History* 10:2, 33-52.

Hale, A., and Wills, J. (2005) *Threads of Labour: Garment Industry Supply Chains from the Workers' Perspective*. Oxford: Blackwell.

Hall, S. (2003) 'Marx's Notes on Method: A "Reading" of the "1857 Introduction"'. *Cultural Studies* 17:2, 113-49.

Hall, S. (2000) 'Conclusion: The Multi-cultural Question'. In B. Hesse (ed.), *Un/settled Multiculturalisms: Diasporas, Entanglements, Transruptions*, 209-41. London: Zed Books.

Hall, S. (1996) 'On Postmodernism and Articulation'. In D. Morley and K.-H. Chen (eds), *Stuart Hall: Critical Dialogues in Cultural Studies*, 131-50. London: Routledge.

Hall, S. (1992) 'Cultural Studies and Its Theoretical Legacies'. In L. Grossberg, C. Nelson and P. Treichler (eds), *Cultural Studies*, 277-94. London: Routledge.

Hall, S. (1989) 'The "First" New Left: Life and Times'. In Oxford University Socialist Discussion Group (ed.), *Out of Apathy*, 11-38. London: Verso.

Hall, S. (1988) 'The Toad in the Garden: Thatcherism among the Theorists'. In C. Nelson and L. Grossberg (ed.), *Marxism and the Interpretation of Culture*, 35-73. London: Macmillan.

Hall, S. (1980) 'Race, Articulation and Societies Structured in Dominance'. In UNESCO (ed.), *Sociological Theories: Race and Colonialism*, 305-45. Paris: UNESCO.

Hall, S., and James, C.L.R. (1996) 'A Conversation with C.L.R. James'. In G. Farred (ed.), *Rethinking C.L.R. James*, 15-44. Oxford: Blackwell.

Haldrup, M., Koefoed, L., and Simonsen, K. (2006) 'Practical Orientalism – Bodies, Everyday Life and the Construction of Otherness'. *Geografiska Annaler B*, 88:2, 173-84.

Hardikar, A. (2006) 'Declaring (incomplete) victory: the Coke campaign, corporate accountability & people of color movements'. http://criticalmoment.org/issue15/coke. Accessed 15 June 2007.

Hardt, M., and Negri, A. (2009) *Commonwealth*. Cambridge MA: Belknap Press.

Hardt, M., and Negri, A. (2004) *Multitude*. New York: Penguin.

Hardt, M., and Negri, A. (2003) 'Foreword?' In M. Fisher and T. Ponniah (eds), *Another World Is Possible: Popular Alternatives to Globalisation at the World Social Forum*. London: Zed Books.

Hardt, M., and Negri, A. (2001) *Empire*. Cambridge MA: Harvard University Press.

Hardy, G. (1956) *Those Stormy Years: Memories of the Fight for Freedom on Five Continents*. London: Lawrence & Wishart.

Hardy, G. (1931) *A Fighting International of Marine Workers*. Hamburg: International of Seamen and Harbour Workers.

Hardy, G. (1927) *The Struggle of British Seamen*. London: National Minority Movement.

Harris, J.E. (1994) *African American Reactions to War in Ethiopia, 1936–1941*. Baton Rouge: Louisiana State University Press.

Harris, L.A. (2009) '"What's in a Name?" That Which We Call Brilliance by Any Other Name Would Read as Festus Claudius McKay'. *Radical History Review* 103, 236-43.

Harvey, D. (2010) *The Enigma of Capital and the Crises of Capitalism*. London: Profile Books.

Harvey, D. (2009) *Cosmopolitanism and the Geographies of Freedom*. New York: Colombia University Press.

Harvey, D. (2005) *A Brief History of Neoliberalism*. Oxford: Oxford University Press.

Harvey, D. (1996) *Justice, Nature and the Geography of Difference*. Oxford: Blackwell.

Harvey, D. (1989) *The Condition of Post-Modernity.* Oxford: Blackwell.

Haslam, J. (2005) *The Nixon Administration and the Death of Allende's Chile: A Case of Assisted Suicide.* London: Verso.

Hatta, M. (1928) 'The Latest Development in Dutch Imperialist Policy in Indonesia'. *Anti-Imperial Review* 1:1, 31-7.

Hauner, M. (2008) 'Charter 77 and Western Peace Movements (1980-84)'. www. lse.ac.uk/archived/global/PDFs/Peaceconference/Hauner.doc. Accessed 3 September 2011.

Hauner, M. (1990) 'Anti-militarism and the Independent Peace Movement in Czechoslovakia'. In V. Tismaneanu (ed.), *In Search of Civil Society: Independent Peace Movements in the Soviet Bloc*, 88-117. London: Routledge.

Havel, V. (1985) 'The Anatomy of a Reticence'. www.vaclavhavel.cz/showtrans. php?cat=eseje&val=4_aj_eseje.html&typ=HTML. Accessed 3 September 2011.

Haywood, H. (1978) *Black Bolshevik: Autobiography of an Afro-American Communist.* Chicago: Lake View Press.

Headley, J. (1932) 'Let Us Close Ranks'. *Negro Worker* 7:2, 18-19.

Hechter, M. (1990) 'The Attainment of Solidarity in Intentional Communities'. *Rationality and Society* 2:2, 142-55.

Hector, T. (2002) 'Definitive biography of C.L.R. urgently required'. www.candw.ag/~jardinea/ffhtm/ff020621.htm. Accessed 5 September 2009.

Herman, P., and Kuper, R., for the Confédération Paysanne (2002) *Food for Thought: Towards a Future for Farming.* London: Pluto Press.

Herod, A (2001) *Labor Geographies.* London: Guilford Press.

Higginbottom, A. (2007) 'Killer Coke'. in W. Dinan and D. Miller, *Thinker, Faker, Spinner, Spy: Corporate PR and the Assault on Democracy.* London: Pluto Press.

Hill, R.A. (ed.) (1990) *The Marcus Garvey and Universal Negro Improvement Association Papers*, Volume VII: *November 1927–August 1940.* Berkeley: University of California Press.

Hinchliffe, S. (2007) *Geographies of Nature: Societies, Environments, Ecologies.* London: Sage.

Hinton, J. (1989) *Protests and Visions: Peace Politics in Twentieth Century Britain.* London: Hutchinson Radius.

Hinton, J. (1973) *The First Shop Stewards' Movement.* London: Pluto Press.

Hirsch, S., and Van der Walt, L. (2010) 'Rethinking Anarchism and Syndicalism: The Colonial and Post-Colonial Experience'. In S. Hirsch and L. Van der Walt (eds), *Anarchism and Syndicalism in the Colonial and Post-Colonial World, 1870–1940: The Praxis of National Liberation, Internationalism and Social Revolution*, xxxi-lxxiii. Leiden: Brill.

Hirson, B., and Vivian, L. (1992) *Strike Across the Empire.* London: Clio Publications.

Hirson, B., and Williams, G.A. (1995) *The Delegate for Africa: David Ivon Jones, 1883–1924.* London: Clio Publications.

Hobbs, S. (2003) 'Untitled Contribution'. *Chile and Scotland: 30 Years On.* Glasgow Caledonian University: Research Collections Witness Seminar and Open Forum Series, 1-2. www.gcal.ac.uk/archives/witness/chile/documents/chiletranscript.pdf. Accessed 1 September 2011.

Hobsbawm, E. (2007) 'Intellectuals and the Spanish Civil War'. In *Revolutionaries*, 123-36. London: Abacus,

Høgsbjerg, C. (2011) 'Mariner, Renegade and Castaway: Chris Braithwaite, Seamen's Organizer and Pan-Africanist'. *Race and Class* 53, 36-57.

Høgsbjerg, C. (2006) 'C.L.R. James and Italy's Conquest of Abyssinia'. *Socialist History* 28, 17-36.

Holcomb, G.E. (2007) *Claude McKay, Code Name Sasha: Queer Black Marxism and the Harlem Renaissance*. Gainesville: University Press of Florida.

Holloway, J. (2002) *Change the World without Taking Power*. London: Pluto Press.

Hooker, J. (1967) *Black Revolutionary: George Padmore's Path from Communism to Pan-Africanism*. London: Praeger.

Hsiao, A. (2002) 'Color Blind'. In E. Yuen, D. Burton Rose and G. Katsiaficas (eds), *The Battle of Seattle: The New Challenge to Capitalist Globalization*, 343-6. New York: Soft Skull Press.

Hughes, L. (1993) [1956] *I Wonder as I Wander*. New York: Hill & Wang.

Hughes, L. (1992) 'Too Much of Race'. In D.D. Collum (ed.), *African Americans in the Spanish Civil War: 'This Ain't Ethiopia, But It'll Do'*. New York: G.K. Hall.

Huiswood, O. (1931) 'Imperialist Rule in British Guiana'. *Negro Worker* 1:8, 3-5.

Hume, M. (2009) *The Politics of Violence: Gender, Conflict and Community in El Salvador*. Chichester: Wiley-Blackwell.

Hunter, O.H. (1952) '700 Calendar Days'. In A. Bessie (ed.), *The Heart of Spain: Anthology of a People's Resistance*, 286-304. New York: Veterans of the Abraham Lincoln Brigade.

Hylton, F. (2006) *Evil Hour in Colombia*. London: Verso.

Hyslop, J. (2009a) 'Steamship Empire: Asian, African and British Sailors in the Merchant Marine c. 1880-1945'. *Journal of Asian and African Studies*, 44:1, 49-67.

Hyslop, J. (2009b) 'Guns, Drugs and Revolutionary Propaganda: Indian Sailors and Smuggling in the 1920s'. *South African Historical Journal* 61:4, 838-46.

Hyslop, J. (2004) *Notorious Syndicalist: J.T. Bain: A Scottish Rebel in South Africa*. Johannesburg: Jacana Media.

Hyslop, J. (1999) 'The Imperial Working Class Makes Itself "White": White Labourism in Britain, Australia, and South Africa Before the First World War'. *Journal of Historical Sociology* 12:4, 398-421.

Ignatiev, N. (1996) *How the Irish Became White*. London: Routledge.

International Action Center (2005) 'Massive support for Coca-Cola campaign at World Social Forum'. www.iacenter.org/labor/colomb_colao105. Accessed 26 August 2011.

International Climate Justice Network (2002) 'Bali Principles of Climate Justice'. www.indiaresource.org/issues/energycc/2003/baliprinciples.html. Accessed 1 July 2011.

International Trade Union Committee of Negro Workers (1931) 'What Must Be Done in British Guiana: An OpenLetter'. *Negro Worker* 1:8, 9-13.

International Transport Workers' Federation (2010) 'Transport Workers and Climate Change: Towards Low Carbon Mobility'. www.itfcongress2010.

org/files/extranet/2/24239/ITF%20Climate%20Change%20Conference%
20Discussion%20Document%202010.pdf. Accessed 20 October 2011.

Jain, D. (2003) 'The Empire Strikes Back: A Report on the Asian Social Forum'. *Economic and Political Weekly*, 11 January 2003, 99-100.

James, C.L.R. (2010) *A New Notion: Two Works by C.L.R. James.* ed. Noel Ignatiev. Oakland: PM Press.

James, C.L.R. (1994) [1963] *Beyond a Boundary.* London: Serpent's Tail.

James, C.L.R. (1989) [1937] *The Black Jacobins.* London: Allison & Busby.

James, C.L.R. (1985) [1935] *A History of Negro Revolt.* London: Race Today.

James, C.L.R. (1984a) *80th Birthday Lectures.* London: Race Today.

James, C.L.R. (1984b) *At the Rendezvous of Victory.* London: Allison & Busby.

James, C.L.R. (1974) 'Black Intellectuals in Britain'. In B. Parekh (ed.), *Colour, Culture and Consciousness*, 154-166. London: George Allen & Unwin.

James, C.L.R. (1937) 'Preface'. In M. Low and J. Breá, *Red Spanish Notebook: The First Six Months.* London: Secker & Warburg.

James, C.L.R. (1936) 'Abyssinia and the Imperialists'. *The Keys* 3:3, January-March 1936.

James, W. (2003) 'A Race Outcast from an Outcast Class: Claude McKay's Experience and Analysis of Britain'. In B. Schwarz (ed.), *West Indian Intellectuals in Britain*, 71-92. Manchester: Manchester University Press.

James, W. (1998) *Holding Aloft the Banner of Ethiopia: Caribbean Radicalism in Early Twentieth-Century America.* London: Verso.

Jan, B. (1932) 'The Struggle of Seamen and Harbour Workers in British Guiana'. *Negro Worker* 2, 9-10, 27-8.

Jara, J. (1983) *Victor: An Unfinished Song.* London: Jonathan Cape.

Jazeel, T. (2011) 'Spatializing Difference Beyond Cosmopolitanism: Rethinking Planetary Futures'. *Theory Culture and Society* 28:5, 75-97.

Jeffrey, C., and McFarlane, C. (2008) 'Introduction'. *Environment and Planning D: Society and Space*, special issue on performing cosmopolitanism, 26:3, 420-27.

Jenkinson, J. (2008a) 'Black Sailors on Red Clydeside: Rioting, Reactionary Trade Unionism and Conflicting Notions of "Britishness" Following the First World War'. *Twentieth Century British History* 19:1, 29-60.

Jenkinson, J. (2008b) *Black 1919: Riots, Racism and Britain in Imperial Britain.* Liverpool: Liverpool University Press.

Jessop, B. (2005) 'Gramsci as a Spatial Theorist'. *Critical Review of International Social and Political Philosophy* 8:4, 421-37.

Joannou, M. (2004) 'Nancy Cunard's English Journey'. *Feminist Review* 78: 141-63.

Johnson, D. (1996) 'Obituary of Claude Bourdet'. www.independent.co.uk/news/people/obituary-claude-bourdet-1343622.html. Accessed 3 September 2011.

Johnson, R. (2009) 'CD Liner Notes'. *Margaret Thatcher: My Part in Her Downfall.* Irregular Records, IRR 075.

Jones, A. (2007) '"Sindicalistas Australianos": A Case Study of International Trade Unionism'. *Labour History* 93, 197-212.

Jones, C. (1938) 'Seamen's Notes'. *International African Opinion* 1:4, October 1938.

Jordan, G. (2001) *'Down the Bay': Picture Post, Humanist Photography and Images of 1950s Cardiff, photographs by Bert Hardy.* Cardiff: Butetown Arts and History Centre.

Joshi, C. (2003) *Lost Worlds: Indian Labour and Its Forgotten Histories.* London: Anthem Press.

Jubilee South (2009) 'Press release: Reparations for Climate Debt demanded from Highly-Industrialised Countries'. www.jubileedebtcampaign.org. uk/Climate%20Justice%20Press%20Release%20+5293.twl. Accessed 18 May 2010.

Juris, J.S. (2008) *Networking Futures: The Movements against Corporate Globalization.* Durham NC: Duke University Press.

Justice for Colombia (2004) *Trade Union Delegation to Colombia.* www.tuc. org.uk/international/tuc-9082-fo.pdf. Accessed 3 July 2007.

Kaldor, M (2003) *Global Civil Society: An Answer to War.* Cambridge: Polity Press.

Kaldor, M. (1991) 'Editor's Introduction'. In Kaldor, M. (ed.) *Europe from Below: An East–West Dialogue,* 1-6. London: Verso.

Katsiaficas, G. (1987) *The Imagination of the New Left: A Global Analysis of 1968.* Cambridge MA: South End Press.

Kavan, J., and Tomin, Z. (1983) *Voices from Prague: Documents on Czechoslovakia and the Peace Movement.* London: END and Palach Press.

Kelley, R. (2000) 'A Poetics of Anti-colonialism'. Introduction to A. Césaire, *Discourse on Colonialism* [1955], 7-28. New York: Monthly Review Press.

Kelley, R. (1996) *Race Rebels: Culture, Politics and the Black Working Class.* New York: Free Press.

Kelley, R. (1992) 'This Ain't Ethiopia But It'll Do'. In D.D. Collum (ed.), *African Americans in the Spanish Civil War: 'This Ain't Ethiopia, But It'll Do'*, 5-60. New York: G.K. Hall.

Kelley, R. (1990) *Hammer and Hoe: Alabama Communists in the Great Depression.* Chapel Hill: University of North Carolina Press.

Khader, J. (2003) 'Subaltern Cosmopolitanism: Community and Transnational Mobility in Caribbean Postcolonial Feminist Writings'. *Feminist Studies* 29:1, 63-81.

Khasnabish, A. (2010) *Zapatistas: Rebellion from the Grassroots to the Global.* London: Zed Books.

Kipfer, S., and Goonewardena, K. (2007) 'Colonization and the New Imperialism: On the Meaning of Urbicide Today'. *Theory and Event* 10, 1-39.

Klein, N. (2009) 'The Seattle Activists' Coming of Age in Copenhagen Will Be Very Disobedient'. *Guardian*, 12 November 2010. www.guardian.co.uk/ commentisfree/cifamerica/2009/nov/12/seattle-coming-age-disobedient-copenhagen. Accessed 18 May 2010.

Klein, N. (2003) 'Cut the Strings'. *Guardian*, 1 February. www.guardian.co.uk/ comment/story/0,3604,886644,00.html. Accessed 1 February 2003.

Klein, N. (2002a) 'Farewell to "the end of history": Organisation and Vision in Anticorporate Movements'. *Socialist Register 2002*, 1-14. London: Merlin Press.

Klein, N. (2002b) *Fences and Windows.* London: Flamingo.

Kohl, B. (2006) 'Challenges to Neoliberal Hegemony in Bolivia'. *Antipode* 38:2, 304-26.

Koopman, S. (2007) 'A Liberatory Space? Rumors of Rapes at the 5th World Social Forum, Pôrto Alegre, 2005'. *Journal of International Women's Studies* 8:3, 149-63.

Kornbluh, J. (1964) *Rebel Voices: An IWW Anthology*. Ann Arbor: University of Michigan Press.

Köszegi, F. (1982) 'The Making of the New Peace Movement in Hungary'. In F. Köszegi and E.P. Thompson (eds), *The New Hungarian Peace Movement*, 9-19. London: END and Merlin Press.

Köszegi, F., and Thompson, E.P. (eds) (1982) *The New Hungarian Peace Movement*. London: END and Merlin Press.

Kothari, U. (2012) 'Contesting Colonial Rule: Politics of Exile in the Indian Ocean'. *Geoforum* 43:4.

Kouyaté, G. (1931) 'Black and White Seamen Organize for Struggle'. *Negro Worker* 1:12, 19-20.

Kugai, S. (1982) 'The Nuclear Umbrella in East Asia'. in E.P. Thompson and others, *Exterminism and Cold War*, 185-204. London: Verso.

LAB (Latin America Bureau) (1987) *Soft Drink Hard Labour: Guatemalan Workers Take On Coca-Cola*. London: Latin America Bureau.

Laclau, E. (1996) *Emancipation(s)*. London: Verso.

Laclau, E., and Mouffe, C. (1985) *Hegemony and Socialist Strategy*. London: Verso.

Lamming, G. (2005) *The Pleasures of Exile*. London: Pluto Press.

Laing, A. (2012) 'Beyond the *Zeitgeist* of 'Post-neoliberal' Theory in Latin America: The Politics of Anti-colonial Struggles in Bolivia'. *Antipode* 44.

Latour, B. (2004) *Politics of Nature: How to Bring the Sciences into Democracy*. Cambridge MA: Harvard University Press.

Law, J., and Mol, A.M. (2008) 'Globalisation in Practice: On the Politics of Boiling Pigswill'. *Geoforum* 39:1, 133-43.

Leapman, M. (1986) *Last Days of the Beeb*. London: Allen & Unwin.

Lenin, V.I. (1968) *Lenin: Selected Works*. Moscow: Progress Publishers.

Levenson-Estrada, D. (1994) *Trade Unionists Against Terror: Guatemala City 1954-1985*. Durham NC: University of North Carolina Press.

Levidow, L., and Paul, H. (2010) 'Global Agrofuel Crops as Contested Sustainability, Part I: Sustaining What Development?'. *Capitalism Nature Socialism* 21:2, 64-86.

Levy, C. (1999) *Gramsci and the Anarchists*. London: Berg.

Ley, D. (2004) 'Transnational Spaces and Everyday Lives'. *Transactions of the Institute of British Geographers* 29:2, 151-64.

Lindell, I. (2011) 'The Contested Spatialities of Transnational Activism: Gendered Gatekeeping and Gender Struggles in an African Association of Informal Workers'. *Global Networks* 11:2, 222-41.

Linebaugh P. (1988) 'All the Atlantic Mountains Shook'. In G. Eley and W. Hunt (ed.), *Reviving the English Revolution*, 193-219. London: Verso.

Linebaugh, P., and Rediker, M. (2001) *The Many Headed Hydra: Sailors, Slaves and Commoners and the Hidden History of the Revolutionary Atlantic*. London: Verso.

Llwyd, A. (2005) *Cymru Ddu/ Black Wales: A History of Black Welsh People*. Cardiff: Hughes & Son.

Loach, L. (1985) 'We'll be here right to the end ... and after'. in H. Beynon (ed.), *Digging Deeper: Issues in the Miners' Strike*, 169–180. London: Verso.

López Vigil, J.I. (1995) *Rebel Radio: The Story of El Salvador's Radio Vencer-emos*. London: Latin American Bureau.

Lopreite, D. (2010) 'Transnational Activism and the Argentine Women's Movement: Challenging the Gender Regime?'. in P. Dufour, D. Masson and D. Caouette (eds), *Solidarities Beyond Borders: Transnationalizing Women's Movements*, 127–48. Vancouver: University of British Colombia Press.

Lynas, M. (2010) 'Why It's Wrong to Preach "Climate Justice"'. *New Statesman*, 14 January 2010. www.newstatesman.com/blogs/the-staggers/2010/01/lynas-climate-carbon. Accessed 16 May 2010.

Lynas, M. (2004) 'Interview with Mark Lynas'. *Red Pepper*. www.redpepper.org.uk/Interview-with-Mark-Lynas-author. Accessed 16 May 2010.

Lynskey, D. (2010) *33 Revolutions per Minute: A History of Protest Song*. London: Faber & Faber.

MacAlister, T. (2009) 'Vestas Dispute: Red and Green Coalition Forms to Fight Wind Plant Closure'. *Guardian*, 29 July. www.guardian.co.uk/environment/2009/jul/23/vestas-wind-turbine-plant-closure. Accessed 11 September 2011.

McDonel Hall Government (2006) 'Resolution regarding Michigan State University's Contract with the Coca-Cola Company and further concerning allegations leveled against the Coca-Cola Company'. www.killercoke.org/msures0206.htm. Accessed 2 July 2007.

McFarlane, C. (2009) 'Translocal Assemblages: Space, Power and Social Movements'. *Geoforum* 40:4, 271–80.

McGirr, L. (1995) 'Black and White Longshoremen in the IWW: A History of the Philadelphia Marine Transport Workers Industrial Union Local 8'. *Labor History* 36:3, 377–402.

McKay, C. (2000) [1929] *Banjo: A Story without a Plot*. London: Black Classics.

McKay, C. (1985) [1935] *A Long Way from Home: An Autobiography*. London: Pluto Press.

McKay, C. (1973a) 'How Black Sees Green and Red'. In W. Cooper (ed.), *The Passion of Claude McKay: Selected Poetry and Prose 1912–1948*, 58. New York: Schocken Books.

McKay, C. (1973b) 'North Africa and the Spanish Civil War'. In W. Cooper (ed.), *The Passion of Claude McKay: Selected Poetry and Prose 1912–1948*, 285–9. New York: Schocken Books.

McKay, C. (1968) [1940] *Harlem: Negro Metropolis*. New York: Harcourt Brace Jovanovich.

McKay, C. (1928) *Home to Harlem*. New York: Harper.

McNaughtan, A. (2000) 'Blood upon the Grass'. On *Words I Used To Know*. CD. Greentrax, TRAX195D.

McVicar, E. (2010) *The Eskimo Republic: Scots Political Song in Action 1951–1999*. Linlithgow: Gallus Publishing.

Maeckelbergh, M. (2011) 'Doing Is Believing: Prefiguration as Strategic Practice in the Alterglobalization Movement'. *Social Movement Studies* 10:1, 1-20.

Makonnen, R. (1973) *Pan-Africanism from Within*, recorded and edited by K. King. Nairobi: Oxford University Press.

Malouf, M.G. (2009) *Transatlantic Solidarities: Irish Nationalism and Caribbean Poetics*. Charlottesville: University of Virginia Press.

Mamdani, M. (2003) 'Making Sense of Political Violence in Post-Colonial Africa'. *Socialist Register 2003*, 132–51. Pontypool: Merlin Press.

Mannin, E. (1945) *Comrade O Comrade: or, Low-down on the Left*. London: Jarrolds.

Marcos, S. (1995) *Shadows of Tender Fury: The Letters and Communiqués of the Zapatista Army of National Liberation*. New York: Monthly Review Press.

Martin, T. (1973) 'Revolutionary Upheaval in Trinidad, 1919: Views from British and American Sources'. *Journal of Negro History* 58:3, 313–26.

Martinez, E.B. (2000) 'Where was the color in Seattle? Looking for reasons why the Great Battle was so white'. www.arc.org/C_Lines/CLArchive/story3_1_02.html. Accessed 6 June 2002.

Martinez-Alier, J. (2002) *The Environmentalism of the Poor: A Study of Ecological Conflicts and Valuation*. Cheltenham, Edward Elgar.

Martinez-Alier, J., and Temper, L. (2007) 'Oil and Climate Change: Voices from the South'. *Economic and Political Weekly*, 15 December 2007.

Marx, K. (1974) *The First International and After*. Trans. and ed. David Fernbach. London: Penguin.

Marx, K. (1973) *Capital: Volume 1*. London: Penguin.

Marx, K., and Engels, F. (1978) 'Manifesto of the Communist Party'. In R.C. Tucker (ed.), *The Marx–Engels Reader*, 2nd edn, 649–500. London: W.W. Norton.

Marx, K., and Engels, F. (n.d.) *The Civil War in the United States*. London: Lawrence & Wishart.

Mason, P. (2007) *Live Working or Die Fighting: How the Working Class Went Global*. London: Harvill Secker.

Massey, D. (2013) 'Stories So Far: A Conversation with Doreen Massey'. In D. Featherstone and J. Painter (eds), *Spatial Politics: Essays for Doreen Massey*. Chichester: Wiley-Blackwell.

Massey, D. (2010) 'The Political Struggle Ahead'. *Soundings* 45, 6–18.

Massey, D. (2007) *World City*. Cambridge: Polity.

Massey, D. (2006) 'Geographies of Solidarities'. In N. Clark, D. Massey and P. Sarre (eds), *A World in the Making*, 311–362. Milton Keynes: Open University.

Massey, D. (2005) *For Space*. London: Sage.

Massey, D. (1994) 'Double Articulation. A Place in the World'. In A. Bammer (ed.), *Displacement: Cultural Identities in Question*, 110–121. Bloomington: Indiana University Press.

Massey D. (1991) 'A Global Sense of Place'. *Marxism Today*, June, 24–9.

Massey, D., and McDowell, L. (1994) 'A Woman's Place?' In D. Massey, *Space, Place and Gender*, 191–211. Cambridge: Polity Press.

Massey, D., and Wainwright, H. (1985) 'Beyond the Coalfields: The Work of the Miners' Support Groups'. In H. Beynon (ed.), *Digging Deeper: Issues in the Miners' Strike*, 149–68. London: Verso.

Medvedev, R. (1977) (ed.) *Samizdat I: Voices of the Socialist Opposition in the Soviet Union*. London: Merlin Press.

Medvedev, R., and Medvedev, Z. (1982) 'The USSR and the Arms Race'. In E.P. Thompson and others, *Exterminism and Cold War*, 153-74. London: Verso.

Mejía Godoy, C. (1996) [1973] *Cantos a flor de pueblo*. San José, Costa Rica: Mántica-Waid.

Mendoza, O. (2003) 'Untitled Contribution'. *Chile and Scotland: 30 Years On*. Glasgow Caledonian University: Research Collections Witness Seminar and Open Forum Series, 12-15. www.gcal.ac.uk/archives/witness/chile/documents/chiletranscript.pdf. Accessed 1 September 2011.

Merlin Press (1977) 'Publisher's Note'. In R. Medvedev (ed.), *Samizdat I: Voices of the Socialist Opposition in the Soviet Union*, v-vi. London: Merlin Press.

Milne, S., 2009. Even the Isle of Wight Wants Miliband to Buck the Market. *Guardian*, 22 July. www.guardian.co.uk/commentisfree/2009/jul/22/green-jobs-market-vestas-strike. Accessed 20 October 2011.

Mitchell, A. (1982) *For Beauty Douglas: Collected Poems 1953-1979*. London: Allison & Busby.

Mitchell, H. (1977) *The Hard Way Up: The Autobiography of Hannah Mitchell Suffragette and Rebel*. London: Virago.

Mohanty, C.T. (2003) *Feminism without Borders: Decolonizing Theory, Practicing Solidarity*. Durham NC: Duke University Press.

Moore, C. (2004) *The Box Set, 1964-2004*. New York: Colombia-Sony Music.

Morales, E. (2010) 'United, the developing countries can save the world'. http://climateandcapitalism.com/?p=2438. Accessed 19 September 2011.

Morgan, C. (1992) 'Testimonies: Crawford Morgan'. In D.D. Collum (ed.), *African Americans in the Spanish Civil War: 'This Ain't Ethiopia, But It'll Do'*, 175-82. New York: G.K. Hall.

Morice, H. (1936) 'The Marine Workers' Fight against Italian War'. *Negro Worker* 6:2, 24-6.

Morris, N. (1986) 'Canto Porque es Necesario Cantar: The New Song Movement in Chile, 1973-1983'. *Latin American Research Review* 21:2, 117-36.

Moscow Independent Peace Group (1982) 'Letter to American Friends Service Committee'. In *END Special Report: Moscow Independent Peace Group*, 5-6. London: END and Merlin Press.

Mouffe, C. (2010) 'The Importance of Engaging the State'. In J. Pugh (ed.), *What Is Radical Politics Today?*, 230-37. Basingstoke: Palgrave MacMillan.

Mouffe, C. (2005) *On the Political*. London: Routledge.

MST (Movimento dos Trabalhadores Rurais Sem Terra) (2005) 'Agriculture'. www.mstbrazil.org/ag. Accessed 1 March 2005.

Mulhern, F. (ed.) (2011) *Lives on the Left: A Group Portrait*. London: Verso.

Nairn, T. (1997) *Faces of Nationalism*. London: Verso.

Naison, M. (2005) *Communists in Harlem during the Depression*. Chicago: University of Illinois Press.

Neat, T. (2009) *Hamish Henderson A Biography*, Volume 2: *Poetry Becomes People (1952-2002)*. Edinburgh: Polygon.

Nef, J. (1974) 'The Politics of Repression: The Social Pathology of the Chilean Military'. *Latin American Perspectives* 1:2, 58-77.

Negro Committee to Aid Spain (1992) [1938] 'A Negro Nurse in Republican Spain'. In *African Americans in the Spanish Civil War: 'This Ain't Ethiopia, But It'll Do'*, ed. D.D. Collum, 123-34. New York: G.K. Hall.

Nelson, B. (1988) *Workers on the Waterfront: Seamen, Longshoremen and*

Unionism in the 1930s. Chicago: University of Illinois Press.

Nelson, S., Barrett, J.R., and Ruck, B. (1981) *Steve Nelson, American Radical.* Pittsburgh: University of Pittsburgh Press.

North, P., and Featherstone, D. (2012) 'Localisation as Radical Praxis and the New Politics of Climate Change'. In J. Sen and P. Waterman (eds), *The Movement of Movements: Struggles for Other Worlds.* New Delhi: OpenWord.

O'Brien, P. (2003) 'Untitled Contribution'. In *Chile and Scotland: 30 Years On.* Glasgow Caledonian University: Research Collections Witness Seminar and Open Forum Series, 2-4. www.gcal.ac.uk/archives/witness/chile/documents/chiletranscript.pdf. Accessed 1 September 2011.

O'Connell, H. (1933) 'Race Prejudice in England'. *Negro Worker* 3:4-5, 24-5.

O'Riordan, M. (2006) 'Larkin in America: The Road to Sing Sing'. In D. Nevin (ed.), *James Larkin: Lion of the Fold*, 64-73. Dublin: Gill & MacMillan.

Obando, A.E. (2005) 'Sexism in the World Social Forum – Is Another World Possible?' www.iiav.nl/ezines/web/whrnet/2005/february.pdf. Accessed 26 August 2011.

Ogborn, M. (2002) 'Writing Travels: Power, Knowledge and Ritual on the English East India Company's Early Voyages'. *Transactions of the Institute of British Geographers* 27:2, 155-71.

Olesen, T. (2005) *International Zapatismo.* London: Zed Books.

Orwell, G. (2003) [1938] *Homage to Catalonia.* Harmondsworth: Penguin.

Ottanelli, F. (2007) 'Anti-Fascism and the Shaping of National and Ethnic Identity: Italian American Volunteers in the Spanish Civil War'. *Journal of American Ethnic History* 27:1, 9-31.

Ottanelli, F. (1991) *The Communist Party of the United States: From the Depression to World War II.* New Brunswick NJ: Rutgers University Press.

Oushakine, S.A. (2001) 'The Terrifying Mimicry of Samizdat'. *Public Culture* 13:2, 191-214.

Oza, R. (2010) 'Special Economic Zones: Spaces of Exception in Neoliberal India'. In R. Peet, W. Ahmed, A. Kundu (eds), *India's New Economic Policy.* New York: Routledge.

Oza, R. (2006) *The Making of Neo-liberal India: Nationalism, Gender, and the Paradoxes of Globalization.* New York: Routledge.

Oza, R. (2001) 'Showcasing India: Gender, Geography and Globalization'. *Signs: Journal of Women in Culture* 26:4, 1067-95.

Padmore, G. (1956) *Pan-Africanism or Communism: The Struggle for Africa.* London: Dennis Dobson.

Padmore, G. (1947) 'Colonial ... and Colored Unity', report of the 5th Pan-African Congress'. In H. Adi and M. Sherwood (eds), *The 1945 Manchester Pan-African Congress Re-visited*, 51-124. London: New Beacon Books.

Padmore, G. (1938) 'Untitled Contribution'. In *Authors Take Sides on the Spanish War*, n. pag. London: Left Review.

Padmore, G. (1937) *Africa and World Peace.* London: Secker & Warburg.

Padmore, G. (1932) 'World Congress of Seamen'. *Negro Worker* 6:2, 23-5.

Padmore, G. (1931) *The Life and Struggles of Negro Toilers.* London: International Trade Union Committee of Negro Workers.

Page, T. (1987) 'Interview with a Black Anti-Fascist'. In A. Bessie and A. Prago (eds), *Our Fight: Writings by Veterans of the Abraham Lincoln Brigade,*

Spain 1936–1939, 54-6. New York: Monthly Review Press.

Palmer, B.D. (1994) *E.P. Thompson: Objections and Oppositions.* London: Verso.

Paniagua, J. (2007) 'Republicans, Socialists and Anarchists: What Revolution Was That?' In J.A. Piqueras and V.S. Rozalen (eds), *A Social History of Spanish Labour: New Perspectives on Class, Politics and Gender*, 241-57. New York: Berghahn Books.

Panitch, L., Albo, G., and Chibber, V. (2011) 'Preface'. *Socialist Register 2012: The Crisis and the Left*, ix-xii. Pontypool: Merlin Press.

Panitch, L., and Gindin, S. (2010) 'Capitalist Crises and the Crisis This Time'. *Socialist Register 2011*, 1-21. Pontypool: Merlin Press.

Party, D. (2010) 'Beyond "Protest Song": Popular Music in Pinochet's Chile (1973-1990)'. In R. Illiano and M. Sala (ed.), *Music and Dictatorship in Europe and Latin America*, 671-84. Turnhout: Brepols Publishers.

Patel, R. (2011) 'What Does Food Sovereignty Look Like?'. In A. Desmarais, N. Wiebe and H. Wittman (eds), *Food Sovereignty: Reconnecting Food, Nature and Community*, 186-96. Oxford: Pambazuka Press.

Patel, Z. (2006) 'Of Questionable Value: The Role of Practitioners in Building Sustainable Cities'. *Geoforum* 37:5, 682-94.

Peck, J. (2010) *Constructions of Neoliberal Reason.* Oxford: Oxford University Press.

Peck, J., and Tickell, A. (2002) 'Neoliberalizing space'. *Antipode* 34:3, 380-404.

Pelikán, J. (1976) *Socialist Opposition in Eastern Europe: The Czechoslovak Example.* London: Allison & Busby.

Pelikán, J. (1972) 'The Struggle for Socialism in Czechoslovakia'. *New Left Review*, I/71, 3-35.

Pennybacker, S. (2009) *From Scottsboro to Munich: Race and Political Culture in 1930s Britain.* Princeton NJ: Princeton University Press.

People's Permanent Tribunal (2007) 'What is the Colombia PPT oil industry hearing?' www.tppcolombia.info/node/53. Accessed 10 July 2007.

Perhimpoenan Indonesia (1931) 'Indonesia: An Open Letter of the Perhimpoenan Indonesia'. *Anti-Imperialist Review* 1:2, 134-7.

Perkins, W.E. (1990) 'Harry Haywood'. In *Encyclopedia of the American Left*, ed. M.J. Buhle, P. Buhle and D. Georgakas, 297-8. London: St James Press.

Perrault, T. (2006) 'From the *Guerra Del Agua* to the *Guerra Del Gas*: Resource Governance, Neoliberalism and Popular Protest in Bolivia'. *Antipode* 38:1, 150-72.

Pettit, A. (2006) *Walking to Greenham: How the Peace Camp Began and the Cold War Ended.* Aberystwyth: Honno.

PGA (People's Global Action) (1999) 'Report on Second PGA gathering in Bangalore'. www.nadir.org/nadir/initiativ/agp/en/pgainfos/bulletin4.htm. Accessed 15 January 2012.

Phillips, R. (2011) 'Vernacular Anti-Imperialism'. *Annals of the Association of American Geographers* 101:5, 1109-25.

Phillips, R. (2007) 'Histories of Sexuality and Imperialism. What's the Use?', *History Workshop Journal* 63:1, 136-53.

Pickerill, J., and Chatterton, P. (2006) 'Notes Towards Autonomous Geographies: Creation, Resistance and Self-management as Survival Tactics',

Progress in Human Geography 30:5, 1-17.

Plummer, B.G. (1996) *Rising Wind: Black Americans and U.S. Foreign Affairs, 1935–1960*. Chapel Hill: University of North Carolina Press.

Prashad, V. (2007) *The Darker Nations: A People's History of the Third World*. New York: New School Press.

Pratt, G., and the Philippines–Canada Task Force on Human Rights (2008) 'International Accompaniment and Witnessing State Violence in the Philippines'. *Antipode* 40:5, 759-71.

Pratt, G., and Yeoh, B. (2003) 'Transnational (Counter) Topographies'. *Gender, Place and Culture* 10:2, 159-66.

Pulido, L. (2006) *Black Brown Yellow and Left: Radical Activism in Los Angeles*. Berkeley: University of California Press.

Pulido, L. (2000) 'Rethinking Environmental Racism: White Privilege and Urban Development in Southern California'. *Annals of the Association of American Geographers* 90:1, 12-40.

Quest, M. (2009) 'George Padmore's and C.L.R. James's *International African Opinion*'. In *George Padmore: Pan-African Revolutionary,* ed. F. Baptiste and R. Lewis, 105-32. Kingston: Ian Randle Publishers.

Rabasa, J. (2010) *Without History: Subaltern Studies, the Zapatista Insurgency and the Specter of History*. Pittsburgh: University of Pittsburgh Press.

Racek, V. (1982) 'Letter to E.P. Thompson on Human Rights and Disarmament'. In E.P. Thompson, *Zero Option*, 81-5. London: Merlin Press.

Rajah, C. (2002) 'Where Was the Color at A16?' In E. Yuen, D. Burton Rose and G. Katsiaficas (eds), *The Battle of Seattle: The New Challenge to Capitalist Globalization*, 237-40. New York: Soft Skull Press.

Raman, R. (2010) 'Transverse Solidarity: Water, Power and Resistance', *Review of Radical Political Economics*, 42:2, 251-68.

Raman, R. (2008) 'Environmental Ethics, Livelihood and Human Rights: Subaltern-Driven Cosmopolitanism?' *Nature and Culture* 3:1, 82-97.

Raman, R. (2005) 'Corporate Violence, Legal Nuances and Political Ecology: Cola War in Plachimada'. *Economic and Political Weekly*, 18 June, 2481-5.

Ramnath, M. (2011) *Decolonizing Anarchism: an Anti-authoritarian History of India's Liberation Struggle*. Edinburgh: AK Press.

Rancière, J. (1995) *On the Shores of Politics*. London: Verso.

Red Herring Workers' Co-operative (1996) *Cordon Rouge: Vegetarian and Vegan Recipes from the Red Herring*. Newcastle: Earthright Publications.

Reddock, R. (1988) *Elma Francois: The NWCSA and the Workers' Struggle for Change in the Caribbean in the 1930s*. London: New Beacon Books.

Reilly, C. (2009) 'The Dunnes Stores Staff who stood up to Apartheid'. *Metro Éireann*. www.metroeireann.com/article/the-dunnes-stores-staff-who-stood,2019. Accessed 6 September 2011.

Reyes Matta, F. (1988) 'The "New Song" and its Confrontation in Latin America'. In C. Nelson and L. Grossberg (eds), *Marxism and the Interpretation of Culture*, 447-60. London: Macmillan.

Reynolds, R. (1956) *My Life and Crimes*. London: Jarrolds.

Riesco, M. (1999) 'Chile, a Quarter of a Century On'. *New Left Review* I/238, 97-125.

Robeson, P. (1978) *Paul Robeson Speaks: Writings, Speeches, Interviews 1918–1974*, ed. P.S. Foner. New York: Citadel Press.

Robinson, C. (1985) 'The African Diaspora and the Italo-Ethiopian Crisis'. *Race and Class* 27:2, 51-65.

Robinson, C. (1983) *Black Marxism: The Making of the Black Radical Tradition*. London: Zed Books.

Rodney, W. (1981) *A History of the Guyanese Working People, 1881-1905*. Baltimore MD: Johns Hopkins University Press.

Roediger, D. (1999) *Wages of Whiteness*, 2nd edn. London: Verso.

Roediger, D. (1994) *Towards the Abolition of Whiteness: Essays on Race, Politics and Working Class History*. London: Verso.

Rorty, R. (1989) *Contingency, Irony and Solidarity*. Cambridge: Cambridge University Press.

Ross, K. (2002) *May '68 And Its After Lives*. Chicago: Chicago University Press.

Ross, S. (2003) 'Is This What Democracy Looks Like? The Politics of the Anti-globalization Movement in North America'. *Socialist Register 2003*, 281-304. London: Merlin Press.

Routledge, P., and Cumbers, A. (2009) *Global Justice Networks: Geographies of Transnational Solidarity*. Manchester: Manchester University Press.

Roxborough, I., O'Brien, P., and Roddick, J. (1977) *Chile: The State and Revolution*. London: Macmillan.

Šabata, J. (1983) 'Letter to E.P. Thompson'. In J. Kavan and Z. Tomin, *Voices from Prague: Documents on Czechoslovakia and the Peace Movement*, 52-70. London: END and Palach Press.

Saccarelli, E. (2008) *Gramsci and Trotsky in the Shadow of Stalinism*. New York: Routledge.

Samuel, R. (2006) *Lost Worlds of British Communism*. London: Verso.

Sandford, J. (1983) *The Sword and the Ploughshare: Autonomous Peace Initiatives in East Germany*. London: END and Merlin Press.

Schiller, N.G. (2010) 'Old Baggage and Missing Luggage: A Commentary on Beck and Sznaider's "Unpacking Cosmopolitanism for the Social Sciences: a Research Agenda"'. *British Journal of Sociology* 61:1, 413-20.

Schmidt, M. and L. van der Walt (2009) *Black Flame: The Revolutionary Class Politics of Anarchism and Syndicalism*. Edinburgh: AK Press.

Schwarz, B. (2004) 'Not Even Past Yet'. *History Workshop Journal* 57, 101-14.

Schwarz, B. (2003) 'George Padmore'. in B. Schwarz (ed.), *West Indian Intellectuals in Britain*, 132-52. Manchester: Manchester University Press.

Scott, D. (2004) *Conscripts of Modernity: The Tragedy of Colonial Enlightenment*. Durham NC: Duke University Press.

Scott, J. (1992) *Domination and the Arts of Resistance: Hidden Transcripts*. New Haven CT: Yale University Press.

Scott, W. (1993) *Sons of Sheba's Race: African Americans and the Italo-Ethiopian War, 1935-1941*. Bloomington: Indiana University Press.

Scruggs, T.M. (2002) 'Socially Conscious Music Forming the Social Conscience: Nicaraguan Música Testimonial and the Creation of a Revolutionary Movement'. In W.A. Clark (ed.), *From Tejano to Tango: Latin American Popular Music*, 41-69. London: Routledge.

Sen, J., Anand, A., Escobar, A., and Waterman, P. (eds) (2004) *The World Social Forum: Challenging Empires*. New Delhi: Viveka.

Sen, J. (2010) 'An Introduction to and Commentary on the Government of Bolivia's Call for a "Peoples" World Conference on Climate Change and the Rights of Mother Earth'. www.zcommunications.org/be-the-seed-by-jai-sen. Accessed 6 July 2011.

Shaffer, K. (2010) 'Tropical Libertarians: Anarchist Movements and Networks in the Caribbean, Southern United States and Mexico, 1890s-1920s'. In Hirsch, S. and L. van der Walt (eds), *Anarchism and Syndicalism in the Colonial and Post-Colonial World, 1870–1940: The Praxis of National Liberation, Internationalism and Social Revolution*, 273-319. Leiden: Brill.

Sharp, J. (2011) 'Subaltern Geopolitics: Introduction'. *Geoforum* 42:3, 271-3.

Sharp, J. (2000) *Condensing the Cold War: Reader's Digest and American identity*. Minneapolis: University of Minnesota Press.

Sherwood, M. (1997) 'Elder Dempster and West Africa 1891-c. 1940: The Genesis of Under-Development?' *International Journal of African Historical Studies* 30:2, 253-76.

Sherwood, M. (1991) 'Racism and Resistance: Cardiff in the 1930s and 1940s'. *Llafur, the Journal of Welsh Labour History* 5:4, 51-70.

Simons, T., and Tonak, A. (2010) 'The Dead End of Climate Justice: How NGO Bureaucrats and Greenwashed Corporations Are Turning Nature into Investment Capital'. *Counterpunch*. www.counterpunch.org/simons 01082010.html. Accessed 18 July 2010.

Slater, D. (2013) 'Space, Difference and Democracy: For a Post-Colonial Perspective'. In D. Featherstone and J. Painter (eds), *Spatial Politics: Essays for Doreen Massey*. Chichester: Wiley-Blackwell.

Slater, D. (2004) *Geopolitics and the Post-colonial*. Oxford: Blackwell

Smethurst, J. (2009) 'The Red is East: Claude McKay and the New Black Radicalism of the Twentieth Century'. *American Literary History* 21:2, 355-67.

Smith, A. (2002) 'From Subordination to Contestation: The Rise of Labour, 1898-1918'. In A. Smith (ed.), *Red Barcelona: Social Protest and Labour Mobilization in the Twentieth Century*, 17-43. London: Routledge.

Solnit, D. (2009) 'The Battle of the Story of the Battle of Seattle'. In D. Solnit and R. Solnit (eds), *The Battle of the Story of the Battle of Seattle*, 5-56. Edinburgh: AK Press.

Solnit, R. (2009) 'The Myth of Seattle Violence: My Battle with the New York Times'. In D. Solnit and R. Solnit (eds), *The Battle of the Story of the Battle of Seattle*, 57-72. Edinburgh: AK Press.

Solomon, C. (2011) 'We Felt Liberated'. In C. Solomon and T. Palmieri (eds), *Springtime: The New Student Rebellions*, 11-16. London: Verso.

Somerville, R. (2003) Untitled presentation in *Chile and Scotland: 30 Years On*. Glasgow Caledonian University: Research Collections Witness Seminar and Open Forum Series, 9-12. www.gcal.ac.uk/archives/witness/chile/documents/chiletranscript.pdf. Accessed 5 October 2007.

Sparke, M. (2005) *In the Space of Theory: Postfoundational Geographies of the Nation State*. Minneapolis: University of Minnesota Press.

Spivak, G.C. (1985) 'Subaltern Studies: Deconstructing Historiography'. In

Subaltern Studies IV, ed. R. Guha, 330-62. New Delhi: Oxford University Press.

Spriano, P. (1975) *The Occupation of the Factories: Italy, 1920*. Trans and intro. Gwyn A. Williams. London: Pluto Press.

Stead, J. (1987) *Never the Same Again: Women and the Miner's Strike*. London: Women's Press.

Stead, J. (1982) 'The Peace March and the Moscow Independent Group'. In *END Special Report: Moscow Independent Peace Group*, 7-14. London: END and Merlin Press.

Stephens, M. (2005) *Black Empire: The Masculine Global Imaginary of Caribbean Intellectuals in the United States, 1914–1962*. Durham NC: Duke University Press.

Stibbe, M. (2008) *British Civilian Internees in Germany: The Ruhleben Camp, 1914–18*. Manchester: Manchester University Press.

Starr, A. (2003) 'Is the North American Anti-globalization Movement Racist? Critical Reflections', *Socialist Register 2003*, 264-80. London: Merlin Press.

Stoler, A. (2009) *Along the Archival Grain: Epistemic Anxieties and Colonial Common Sense*. Princeton NJ: Princeton University Press.

Sundberg, J. (2007) 'Reconfiguring North-South Solidarity: Critical Reflections on Experiences of Transnational Resistance'. *Antipode* 39:1, 144-66.

Swyngedouw, E. (2007) 'Impossible "Sustainability" and the Post-Political Condition'. In D. Gibbs and R. Krueger (eds), *The Sustainable Development Paradox: Urban Political Economy in the United States and Europe*, 13-40. New York: Guilford Press.

Tabili, L. (2011) *Global Migrants, Local Cultures: Natives and Newcomers in Provincial England, 1841–1939*. Basingstoke: Palgrave Macmillan.

Tabili, L. (1996) '"A Maritime Race": Masculinity and the Racial Division of Labour in British Merchant Ships, 1900–1939'. In M.S. Creighton and L. Norling (eds), *Iron Men, Wooden Women: Gender and Seafaring in the Atlantic World, 1700–1920*, 169-88. Baltimore MD: Johns Hopkins University Press.

Tabili, L. (1994) *We Ask for British Justice: Workers and Racial Difference in Late Imperial Britain*. Ithaca NY: Cornell University Press.

Taffet, J.F. (1997) '"My Guitar Is Not for the Rich": The New Chilean Song Movement and the Politics of Culture'. *Journal of American Culture* 20:2, 91-103.

Tarrow, S. (2005) *The New Transnational Activism*. Cambridge: Cambridge University Press.

Tarrow, S., and McAdam, D. (2005) 'Scale Shift in Transnational Contention'. In D. Della Porta and S. Tarrow (eds), *Transnational Protest and Global Activism*, 121-50. Lanham MD: Rowman & Littlefield.

Taylor, M. (2006) *From Pinochet to the 'Third Way': Neoliberalism and Social Transformation in Chile*. London: Pluto Press.

Thomas, M. (2005) 'Colonial States as Intelligence States: Security Policing and the Limits of Colonial Rule in France's Muslim Territories, 1920-40'. *Journal of Security Studies* 28:6, 1033-60.

Thompson, A.K. (2010) *Black Bloc, White Riot: Anti-Globalization and the Genealogy of Dissent.* Edinburgh: AK Press.

Thompson, D. (2007) *Pessimism of the Intellect: A History of New Left Review* London: Merlin Press.

Thompson, D. (1996) 'On the Trail of the New Left'. *New Left Review* I/215, 93-100.

Thompson, E.P. (1997) *Beyond the Frontier: The Politics of a Failed Mission, 1944.* London: Merlin Press.

Thompson, E.P. (1994) *Persons and Polemics.* London: Merlin Press.

Thompson, E.P. (1991) 'Ends and Histories'. In M. Kaldor (ed.), *Europe from Below: An East–West Dialogue,* 7-26. London: Verso.

Thompson, E.P. (1982a) 'Notes on Exterminism, the Last Stage of Civilization'. In E.P. Thompson and others, *Exterminism and Cold War,* 1-34. London: Verso.

Thompson, E.P. (1982b) 'Europe, the Weak Link in the Cold War'. In E.P. Thompson and others, *Exterminism and Cold War,* 329-50. London: Verso.

Thompson, E.P. (1982c) *Zero Option.* London: Merlin Press.

Thompson, E.P. (1982d) 'Foreword'. In F. Köszegi and E.P. Thompson (eds), *The New Hungarian Peace Movement,* 1-7. London: END and Merlin Press.

Thompson, E.P. (1982e) 'The 'Normalisation' of Europe'. In F. Köszegi and E.P. Thompson (eds), *The New Hungarian Peace Movement,* 35-53. London: END and Merlin Press.

Thompson, E.P. (1982f) *Beyond the Cold War.* London: Merlin Press.

Thompson, E.P. (1980) *Writing by Candlelight.* London: Merlin Press.

Thompson, E.P. (1978) *The Poverty of Theory and Other Essays.* London: Merlin Press.

Thompson, F., and Murfin, P. (1955) *The IWW: its First Fifty Years, 1905-1955.* Chicago: Industrial Workers of the World.

Trade to Climate Caravan (2009) 'Caravan From WTO to COP15'. www. climatecaravan.org. Accessed 30 April 2012.

Trapese Collective (2009) *The Rocky Road to a Real Transition.* http://sparror.cubecinema.com/stuffit/trapese/rocky-road-a5-web.pdf. Accessed 18 July 2010.

Trewhela, P. (1988) 'George Padmore: A Critique. Pan Africanism or Marxism'. *Searchlight South Africa* 1:1, 42-63.

Trouillot, M.R. (1995) *Silencing the Past: Power and the Production of History.* Boston MA: Beacon Press.

Tyner, J. (2004) 'Territoriality, Social Justice and Gendered Revolutions in the Speeches of Malcolm X'. *Transactions of the Institute of British Geographers* 29:3, 330-43.

United Steel Workers Union and the International Labor Rights Fund (2001) 'Coca-Cola (Coke) sued for human rights abuses in Colombia'. www.mindfully.org/Industry/Coca-Cola-Human-Rights2ojul01.htm. Accessed 2 July 2007.

Valdés, J.V. (1995) *Pinochet's Economists: The Chicago School in Chile.* Cambridge: Cambridge University Press.

Valtin, J. (2004) *Out of the Night.* Edinburgh: AK Press.

Vanaik, A. (2004) 'Rendezvous at Mumbai'. *New Left Review* 26, 53-65.

Vargas, V. (2004) 'WSF 3 and Tensions in the Construction of Global Alternative

Thinking'. in J. Sen, A. Anand, A. Escobar and P. Waterman (eds), *The World Social Forum: Challenging Empires*, 228-232. New Delhi: Viveka.

Vargas, V. (2002) 'Feminist contributions and challenges to the World Social Forum'. http://alainet.org/publica/retosfem/en/contrib.html. Accessed 15 September 2011.

Via Campesina (2009a) 'Climate: Time to change our way to consume and produce food'. www.viacampesina.org/en/index.php?option=com_content &view=article&id=793:climate-time-to-change-our-way-to-consume-and-produce-food&catid=48:-climate-change-and-agrofuels&Itemid=75.Accessed 21 July, 2010.

Via Campesina (2009b) *Small Scale Sustainable Farmers Are Cooling Down the Earth*. Jakarta: Via Campesina.

Via Campesina (2009c) 'Press Release: Via Campesina: Traders failed in Copenhagen'. http://indymedia.dk/articles/1977. Accessed 18 May 2010.

Vidal, J. (2009) 'Evo Morales stuns Copenhagen with demand to limit temperature rise to 1C'. *Guardian*, 16 December 2009. www.guardian. co.uk/environment/2009/dec/16/evo-morales-hugo-chavez. Accessed 11 September 2011.

Vinson, R.T. (2006) '"Sea Kaffirs": "American Negroes" and the Gospel of Garveyism in early Twentieth Century Cape Town'. *Journal of African History* 47: 281-303.

Virno, P. (2004) *A Grammar of the Multitude*. Los Angeles: Semiotext(e).

Visram, A. (2002) *Asians in Britain: 400 Years of History*. London: Pluto Press.

Von Eschen, P.M. (1997) *Race against Empire: Black Americans and Anti-Colonialism, 1937-1957*. Ithaca NY: Cornell University Press.

Vulliamy, E. (2011) 'Martin Carthy: "I'm not interested in heritage: this stuff is alive"'. www.guardian.co.uk/music/2011/apr/17/martin-carthy-interview-ed-vulliamy. Accessed 13 September 2011.

Wainwright, H. (2013) 'Place Beyond Place and the Politics of "Empowerment". In D. Featherstone and J. Painter (eds), *Spatial Politics: Essays for Doreen Massey*. Chichester: Wiley-Blackwell.

Wainwright, J., Prudham, S., and Glassman, J. (2000) 'The Battles in Seattle: Microgeographies of Resistance and the Challenge of Building Alternative Futures'. *Environment and Planning D: Society and Space* 18:1, 5-13.

Walker, G., and Bulkeley, H. (2006) 'Editorial – Geographies of Environmental Justice'. *Geoforum* 37:5, 655-9.

Ward, A. (1935) 'England'. *Negro Worker* 2-3:5, 25-6.

Waterman, P. (2003) 'World Social Forum: another forum is possible!' www. opendemocracy.net/debates/article-6-91-1293.jsp. Accessed 16 July 2003.

Waterman, P., and Wills, J. (2001) (eds) *Place, Space and the New Labour Internationalisms*. Oxford: Blackwell.

Wazyk, A. (1957) 'A Critique of the Poem for Adults'. *New Reasoner* 1, 51-4.

Weinberg, B. (2010) 'Cochabamba: dissidents push limits of free speech'. www. ww4report.com/node/8550. Accessed 7 July 2011.

Welsh Committee of the Communist Party (1945) *Report of the First All-Wales Congress of the Communist Party*. Cardiff.

Williams, A.M. (2004) *From the Rhondda to the Ebro*. Pontypool: Warren & Pell.

Williams, C. (2002) *Sugar and Slate*. Aberystwyth: Planet.

Williams, G.A. (1975) *Proletarian Order: Antonio Gramsci, Factory Councils and the Origins of Communism in Italy, 1911–1921*. London: Pluto Press.

Williams, R. (1989) *Resources of Hope*. London: Verso.

Williams, R. (1982) 'The Politics of Nuclear Disarmament'. In E.P. Thompson and others, *Exterminism and Cold War*, 65-86. London: Verso.

Williams, R. (1979) *Modern Tragedy*, 2nd edn, London: New Left Books.

Wilson, E.W. (1974) *Russia and Black Africa*. New York: Holmes & Meier.

Winslow, B. (1996) *Sylvia Pankhurst: Sexual Politics and Political Activism*. London: UCL Press.

Wolford, W. (2010) *This Land Is Ours Now: Social Mobilization and the Meanings of Land in Brazil*. Durham NC: Duke University Press.

Wong, K. (2002) 'The Showdown before Seattle: Race, Class, and the Framing of a Movement'. In E. Yuen, D. Burton Rose and G. Katsiaficas (eds), *The Battle of Seattle: The New Challenge to Capitalist Globalization*, 215-24. New York: Soft Skull Press.

Woods, C. (2007) '"Sittin on Top of the World": The Challenge of Blues and Hip-Hop Geography'. In K. McKittrick and C. Woods, *Black Geographies and the Politics of Place*, 46-81. Cambridge MA: South End Press.

Woods, C. (1998) *Development Arrested: Race, Power and the Blues in the Mississippi Delta*. London: Verso.

World People's Conference on Climate Change and the Rights of Mother Earth (2010) 'People's Agreement'. http://pwccc.wordpress.com/support/. Accessed 19 September 2011.

World March of Women (2004) '2003 WSF: Perspective of Women'. In J. Sen, A. Anand, A. Escobar and P. Waterman (eds), in *World Social Forum: Challenging Empires*, 233-4. New Delhi: Viveka Foundation.

Worrell, R. (2009) 'George Padmore: Pan-Africanist Par Excellence'. In F. Baptiste and R. Lewis (eds), *George Padmore: Pan-African Revolutionary*, 22-36. Kingston: Ian Randle Publishers.

Worsley, P. (1989) 'Non-alignment and the New Left'. In Oxford University Socialist Discussion Group (ed.), *Out of Apathy*, 88-94. London: Verso.

Wright, R. [1937] (1992) 'American Negroes in Key Posts of Spain's Loyalist Forces'. In D.D. Collum (ed.), *African Americans in the Spanish Civil War: 'This Ain't Ethiopia, But It'll Do'*, 119-22. New York: G.K. Hall.

Wright, T.C., and Oñate, R. (2007) 'Chilean Political Exile'. *Latin American Perspectives* 34, 31-49.

Wright, T.C., and Oñate, R. (1998) *Flight from Chile: Voices of Exile*. Albuquerque: University of New Mexico Press.

Yates, J. (1989) *From Mississippi to Madrid: Memoir of a Black American in the Abraham Lincoln Brigade*. Seattle WA: Open Hand Publishing.

Yuen, E., Burton Rose, D., and Katsiaficas, G. (eds) (2002) *The Battle of Seattle: The New Challenge to Capitalist Globalization*. New York: Soft Skull Press.

Zibechi, R. (2010) *Dispersing Power: Social Movements as Anti-State Forces*. Edinburgh: AK Press.

Žižek, S. (2005) 'Against the Populist Temptation'. www.lacan.com/zizpopulism.htm. Accessed 5 July 2007.

Žižek, S. (1999) 'Carl Schmitt in the Age of Post-Politics'. In C. Mouffe (ed.), *The Challenge of Carl Schmitt*, 18-37. London: Verso.

Index

www.ingramcontent.com/pod-product-compliance
Ingram Content Group UK Ltd.
Pitfield, Milton Keynes, MK11 3LW, UK
UKHW040642280225
455688UK00003B/90

9 781848 135956